TURNING POINTS IN HISTORY

General Editor: SIR DENIS BROGAN

1848

The Fall of Metternich and the Year of Revolution

1848

The Fall of Metternich
and the Year of Revolution

BY

DAVID WARD

WEYBRIGHT AND TALLEY

NEW YORK

Published in the United States by
Weybright and Talley, Inc.
750 Third Avenue
New York, New York 10017

Library of Congress Catalog Card Number: 78–125 365

Printed in Great Britain

Contents

PART I

IRRESISTIBLE FORCE: EUROPE IN REVOLUTION

PART II

IMMOVABLE OBJECT

PART III

THE COLLISION COURSE

PART IV

IMPACT—IMMOVABLE MOVED

PART V

IMPACT—IRRESISTIBLE RESISTED

CONTENTS

PART VI

ILLUSTRATIONS

between pages 120 *and* 121

Endpapers

MAPS

by Patrick Leeson

PART ONE

IRRESISTIBLE FORCE:
EUROPE IN REVOLUTION

Chapter I

THE ECONOMIC REVOLUTION

THE PHANTOM of hunger which had stalked the people of Ireland in the early decades of the nineteenth century materialized in tragic form in the famine of 1846. The blight which had visited the vital potato crop in 1845 returned more virulently the following year and in the words of a contemporary traveller, speedily turned the land into 'one wide waste of putrefying vegetation'. This famine and the choice with which it confronted the people of Ireland, starvation and disease, or emigration, are well known. However, the shock of this tragedy, accompanied by its appalling cloud of human suffering and distress, can obscure the real reasons for its sequel: the decline in population. The root cause of the decline in the population of Ireland was that, like populations throughout history, the Irish had outgrown the resources of their land and consequently could only remain at home and die of hunger or journey abroad in search of other lands with fresh resources.

Since the *Völkerwanderung*, the twilight period when the migrant barbarian tribes settled down upon the remains of the fatigued Roman Empire, those lands that today comprise Europe have had an expanding population. The advance has been irregular and for most of the time very gradual, severely circumscribed by the resources man has possessed. On occasion as well, pestilence struck; in the space of a few years the growth of centuries would be lost, as happened during the particularly intense attack of the bubonic plague which scourged Europe in the middle of the fourteenth century. However, after such a calamity numbers again began to rise, the slow advance was resumed—but only to the limits of man's technical mastery of his environment; as that was extended the population could increase, waste would be brought into cultivation, new land opened up. If ever this balance were upset dearth would soon intervene to redress it. Malthus the

3

economist, writing in 1789, saw a 'positive check' intervening in the population growth if a 'preventive check' failed to operate.

The late eighteenth and early nineteenth centuries had seen the balance upset in Ireland; from about three and a half million in 1750 the population had grown by 1840 to eight million. Disaster was obviously predictable. The disaster had been averted so far only by the spread of the potato, whose cultivation enabled many more people to be fed from the same area of land than had been possible hitherto. In fact the staving off of the catastrophe only made it more complete when it came; the collapse in numbers more precipitate and the plight of the people more desperate. Nevertheless the decline in the population of Ireland over the next forty years to four and a half million, however heartrending to those who were compelled to try to live through it, was only different in degree, not different in kind, from the accepted pattern cut by the history of society.

What was different in kind as well as in degree was what was happening across the St. George's Channel in England; here a population of between six and a half million and seven and a half million in 1750 had become one of sixteen million by 1840, but, far from lurching into a ruinous decline as economists had predicted, it continued to rise; by 1870 it had reached twenty-two and a half million and was still climbing. Obviously, this sustained growth was possible not just because the blight which devastated the Irish potato crop did not strike so sternly in England. The population growth in England was possible only because of a complete and unprecedented change in the ordering of society. The form of the traditional society had been destroyed and in its place there had come into being, however crude by comparison with later ones, the first mature industrial society. This phenomenon, even more important in the history of population growth than the transition of man from a nomadic hunter to a primitive farmer, has changed the entire way of life for those areas of the world where it has occurred. Only because of this change is Europe now able to support a population of six hundred million whereas in 1800 it could not always manage to sustain a population of one hundred and eighty million. Of course the circumstances with which the English people had to contend during this transition were appalling, faced as they were by the dissolution of their traditional society, and forced by austere economic demands, unmitigated by any action of the government, to conform to the alien and unsympathetic mould of its successor. However, it should never be forgotten that without such changes only a fraction of the population could have survived at all: conditions in Manchester should be contrasted with those in Mayo.

In the present century many historians have demonstrated that this transformation was not so unheralded as previous writers had suggested. However, there is a danger in laying too much emphasis upon figures of percentage growth of output if other factors, not suited to quantification, are ignored. It is true that when water is being heated the transition from 99 to 100 degrees centigrade is merely a rise in temperature of one degree, but this must never be allowed to obscure the fact that the water has undergone a vital change to steam; in Marxist terms a minimal quantitative change has produced a qualitative change. The changes that overtook the economy of England in the last two decades of the eighteenth century, however far back in time their roots can be traced, mark the 'take-off' from a traditional to an industrial society. If any change in history deserves the name of revolution it is surely that known as the 'Industrial Revolution'.

Over the next century and a half this change was to occur over an increasing area of the world; though not always in quite the same way or at the same speed. The industrial revolution in Britain was to prove a powerful spur in two ways. First as a prototype: British ideas, British experience, British people and British money were all to have a large part in industrializing other economies.* Secondly the new and cheaper British products provided a competitive challenge to continental industries, particularly after the defeat of Napoleon and his Continental System re-opened the ports of Europe to British goods, thus forcing them either to adapt themselves to new conditions or succumb.

By the 1840s some parts of Europe were still virtually untouched by these influences, and nowhere, with the possible exception of Belgium, could an industrial 'take-off', as that in Britain, be said to have occurred. Nevertheless the fabric of the traditional economy of Europe was breaking down and dissolving, and even the early stages of such a process were obviously of fundamental importance

* Deservedly the best known example is the Cockerill family. William, his three sons, particularly John, and his son-in-law James Hodson, played an enormous and varied role in Belgian industrialization.

to society. An appreciation of the process of dissolution is therefore necessary in any attempt to understand events in these years.

The outstanding feature of the traditional society was that it was predominantly rural. The majority of the population derived their livelihood from the land. As late as 1830 in eastern Europe 95 per cent or over of the population was rural. Towns were scattered evenly over the land, in the economically better developed areas rather more densely than elsewhere. The town served as the executive and business nucleus for the plasm of the neighbouring region, the countryside looking to it as the source of most of its manufactured requirements and as a market for any agricultural surplus. There was little trade from one town to another and that was usually in luxury articles for the richer members of society. Shops in the modern sense were unknown in most towns except for capital and other large cities. There were workshops where the local craftsmen made and sold their craft ware; there were markets where the town and its associated rural hinterland traded with one another, but over and above this wants could only be satisfied by the itinerant pedlar and by merchants at the periodic fairs.

The larger the town the more the local countryside came to adapt its economy to the town, growing its food for the townspeople and providing a labour force for the town's merchants to employ in producing their goods, the foundation of the cottage or outwork system of industry. The barrier that checked all attempts at growth in trade between town and town, and hence greater specialization, was the state of transport; in particular its expense. Where goods had to be carried along bad roads by mule and pack-horse transport costs meant that the locally produced article would always undersell goods produced farther afield except where the value of the article in relation to its bulk was very high. Adding to the costs of transport, of course, was the multiplicity of internal customs dues and tolls which articles had to pay travelling in a politically fragmented Europe. Goods in transit along the Po had to pass through five sets of customs barriers and pay a toll each time. Until this problem of transport was solved there was little chance of a large general growth of industry being able to occur.

However, some parts of Europe had progressed much further than the rest and had come to serve many parts of the world with their industries; these were very often luxury industries such as silk and glass manufacture and fine metal work. The processing industries—fish salting, tobacco curing, and corn milling—were expanded; while the greater density of population in such areas stimulated the hinterland to a more advanced state of farming. Much of northern Italy had been developed in this way since the high Middle Ages but Holland, parts of France and, increasingly, Britain had come to play the same role. All these areas had access to the sea and this was the key to their prosperity, for the sea provided cheap and easy transport. Manufacturers were able to sell their wares overseas and the concentration and rationalization, which this expansion of markets allowed, resulted in their under-cutting the producers who supplied only local demands. Distances which were prohibitive if access was possible only overland meant little if localities were joined by the main road of water. England furnishes an example: Londoners from the sixteenth century onwards used coal for domestic heating cut in the north-east rather than from nearer fields because the Tyne and Weir gave north-east coal easy access to the North Sea.

It is not surprising that the breakthrough occurred in one of these more developed areas, nor that it occurred in a textile for mass consumption. Manufactured luxuries by their very nature did not lend themselves to standardization and mass production. However, the sort of scale of growth that 'breakthrough' implies was unlikely for any one area because of the rivalry of the others, unless it was able to capture a dominant share of the world market for some years. There does seem to have been a rising level of incomes in England during the eighteenth century which would increase the size of the home market but this of itself would not have been enough. However, the wars which England had fought during the century had assisted in giving her a dominant share of the world's commerce, and the war against Revolutionary and Napoleonic France, in one sense a continuation of these wars, resulted during the period of Continental blockade in a virtual monopoly for England of oceanic trade.

There can be no doubt that the motor for continental industrialization was Britain. With the collapse of the Napoleonic Empire British penetration of the European mainland began, by no means checked by the ban, not in fact lifted until 1824, on the emigration of skilled workers from Britain. However, the Continent, once again revealed, was by no means economically all of a piece. Broadly speaking the farther east in Europe, the less sign there was of a strong commercial base. Thus the middle classes, symptom and cause of economic advance, were so few as to be of little account east of a line that ran roughly along the Elbe, though there were several areas west of that line, such as southern Italy, where the same could be said. Eastwards the whole structure of society became more feudal. Whereas in France the peasants had been freed by the revolution of their feudal dues and burdens, east of the Rhine the process of emancipation was currently being undergone; in Austria and Bavaria the peasants were not to be given their freedom till 1848, while in Russia they were to chafe under a greater subjection for longer.

As was the case in England, agriculture was most advanced in the vicinity of large towns, stimulated by the markets they provided. Near a large city like Paris, the largest by a long way on the Continent, or in the traditionally urbanized area of the Low Countries and north-eastern France, farming was extremely efficient. Elsewhere, however, in much of northern and eastern France, as throughout western and central Germany, threefield rotation was still the rule with one-third of the land lying fallow all the time; indeed in parts of central France the land was left fallow every other year. At first it may seem to be paradoxical that the most advanced agriculture in Germany lay in the north-east but there the economy was really a colonial one. The land basin of the great Baltic rivers had for centuries been an important exporter of grain but since the end of the fifteenth century this trade had fallen increasingly into the hands of foreign merchants and the profits had gone to the landlords, who were usually German and spoke a different language from the Slavic peoples who tilled their fields. The landowners took the opportunity presented by the peasants' emancipation, usually paid for by the peasants in land, to add to their own holdings and so increase their income.

With the industrialization of Britain as a model, the reasons for the patchwork nature of the economic evolution of the rest of Europe become more apparent; the presence or absence of those factors which had favoured the industrial growth in England being the key. First, eastern, central, and south-eastern Europe, not having shared in the previous economic growth of the more prosperous areas, were at a grave disadvantage in the early nineteenth century. They were very short of capital for the heavy investment that expansion demanded and deficient in technical knowledge and experience, since they lacked the commercial and industrial spring-board from which England had leaped. The power of the guilds in the towns was largely unbroken, reducing the opportunity for innovation and restricting labour mobility. Finally, it is not a coincidence that these areas were mainly ones of poor transport facilities.

Whereas no point in England is further than eighty miles from the sea the lands of central and eastern Europe are by no means so fortunate. It is true that a number of the great European rivers penetrate deep into the land mass but many of them, such as the Danube with its shoals and rapids, or the Rhône, were not really suitable for traditional navigation. Again, many of these rivers flowed through a variety of states, none of which therefore felt responsible for improving navigation and each of which levied its toll; the fourteen sets of dues that a cargo paid to travel from Hamburg to Magdeburg on the Elbe may have been more than the average for similar stretches of river but it was not exceptional before Napoleon's abolition of many of the petty German states. Farther west, in France and the Low Countries, communications were altogether better; France had long since had many canals as well as a fine system of roads. Napoleon, the restored Bourbons and Louis Philippe all sought to improve facilities further so that by 1848 France had 4,000 kilometres of canal, of which nearly three-quarters had been built since 1815. In the Netherlands also the canals were augmented, the Belgian coal mines being joined to Paris in one direction and to Antwerp in the other.

What altered transport conditions was the introduction of steam power which made even swiftly flowing rivers passable. By 1830 steamers were plying up the Rhine, the Elbe and the Weser, among other rivers; the need for constant re-fuelling with coal did not create for river shipping the problems it did for ocean voyages. However, it was the coming of the railways which really transformed the situation. Belgium was the first continental state to build a railway network, the state directing construction, so that by 1845 there were some 350 miles of railroad completed. France and Germany both followed Belgium's example; in Germany, where the greatest changes occurred, the railways shattered the provincial sleepiness and undisturbed economic pattern of the sixteenth century, bringing the chance for real industrial growth and regional specialization by connecting the main towns, and their construction created an enormous demand for the products of heavy industry.

From the example of England, where communications were so important, it is clear why many parts of Europe were slower to advance than others; far from being in a position to compete for world markets they were unlikely to be able to build up a domestic market of any size. With the advent of railways, however, this was no longer the case and other areas, notably Germany, whose transport facilities had hitherto been so much inferior, were increasingly to be in a position to rival the western states.

Even railways could not eliminate the tariff barriers and the multiplicity of small states that so hampered much of European economic growth, though in time they did help to produce the psychological climate necessary for the unification of Germany around Prussia. Perhaps Switzerland, in whose tiny area operated no less than twelve different monetary systems, is the most spectacular example, but Germany, after 1815 still with thirty-nine states, and the politically fragmented Italy, were enormously hampered in moving towards an economic growth based on the rationalization of production. It is not therefore surprising that some form of unification of these lands became the aim of the economically more progressive elements of society, or that real industrialization should wait upon such unification. However, in Germany the emergence of a customs union, the Zollverein, provided many of the benefits before outright unification could take place. Beginning with the Tariff Law of 1818 which attempted to bring together the scattered elements of the Prussian state, an enlarged customs union was formed in 1828 and in 1834 was joined by the south German union of Bavaria and Württemberg to become the Zollverein with a population of over 23 million; it was subsequently enlarged to include nearly all of Germany north of the Habsburg lands.

In Britain, coal was not only available in plenty but conveniently located near to the sea, to the textile producing areas of Lancashire and Yorkshire and to the iron ore deposits. There were parts of the Continent, such as Italy, which did not possess substantial coal deposits and were severely handicapped; but even where there were deposits of coal their location was not always so fortunate as in England. Normandy had, for example, been the centre of French cotton production, favoured with water power, with Rouen as its centre and Le Havre as a great port for world trade, but with no coalfield near by it languished.

The Belgian coalfields were, however, ideally situated and the period of integration with France before 1815 allied to the re-opening of the Scheldt to commerce proved a powerful stimulus to production. By the time of her independence in 1830 Belgium was cutting over six million tons a year. France's break with Belgium cost her more than four-fifths of her annual output; her subsequent shortage checked expansion. Until the 1860s the central highlands provided most of her coal but the deposits tended to be unconnected and therefore expensive to work; an Englishman claimed in 1835 that the cost of coal in Paris was ten times that in Manchester. Holland also suffered from the loss of the Belgian coalfields. A commercial and industrial power in the eighteenth century, she found herself handicapped by the loss of her colonial markets in the Napoleonic period and the lack of coal after 1830.

In Germany there were plentiful supplies of coal from the huge fields of the Ruhr, Upper Silesia and the Saar. But in the pre-railway age they lay inaccessibly at the extremities of the land, so that in 1815 the Ruhr was producing less than three thousand tons a year and the Saar not much over one thousand. With the railways this changed and by 1850 Germany was already producing over six million tons; the Westphalian ironmasters no longer wondered how they could transport coal fifty miles to their ore.

However, German industrialization was still in its infancy. Despite the increase in the number of steam engines employed in Prussian production, from less than five hundred in 1837 to nearly fifteen hundred in 1849, the urban section of the population had risen only from 26½ per cent in 1816 to 28 per cent in 1846. The new industrial towns were smaller than the old cities. In 1850 Essen still only had a population of 9,000 compared to the 97,000 of Cologne. France, even with her start over the rest of the continent, her wealth and the skill of her scientists, was falling further behind Britain; while eastern and south-eastern Europe were barely stirring. Only in Belgium had some sort of economic maturity been reached. An English witness described Belgian textile machines as being 'as good or nearly as good as the best Manchester made machines', and much the same could have been said of her other industries.

The varying speed of industrialization in Europe was matched by the growth of its population, but here the increase, though not uniform, was enormous, from not much over 180 million in 1800 to more than 270 by 1850. In England the unprecedented rise in population was a contributory cause of the Industrial Revolution. In Ireland, where no such revolution occurred, it was a catastrophe. Obviously the fate of the extra millions in Europe was dependent upon the degree of industrialization. Without growth they would not survive. As in Ireland, emigration sometimes provided an escape route and increasing numbers of Germans took it, 97,000 leaving the country in 1847 alone, most of them going to the United States.

The growth in population, occurring at a time of radical change in agriculture and land tenure, saw a migration to the towns of the sort that occurred in England, which was swelled by the vicissitudes of cottage workers losing their livelihood because of the competition of machine-made goods. However, in contrast to England, many of the towns to which the distressed came were not undergoing rapid industrialization. The change from the paternalist, albeit often harsh, life of the peasant to the conditions and discipline of the factory in overcrowded towns might seem cataclysmic to those who were affected, but it was worse still if there was no factory to go to.

In eastern Europe, the migration to the towns differed from that in Britain in another way: the agricultural population frequently had a different culture and language from the people in the towns to which they went. At first this perhaps only served to make them feel more alien but increasingly it changed the entire nature of the towns. These, sometimes for the first time in their history, began to take on the complexion of the districts in which they lay: they ceased to be German islands in Slavic seas.

As the way in which the solvent of economic progress was working becomes clearer, so the results of its action become clearer too. Social change has always produced general unrest, dislocation and suffering. Nor is it surprising that unprecedented social change produced unprecedented unrest, dislocation and suffering. Unrest was rife among those who had been forced out of their traditional mould and had not yet found another in which they could fit; certainly those who canvassed a political solution to problems would be listened to.

In the growing numbers of the middle classes benefiting from these changes there developed an impatience at the slow speed of advance and a desire for acceleration. They were not sure or united about how this might best be achieved but various formulae won support. The desire to unify petty states in Italy and Germany has already been mentioned. A general feeling existed that governments should assist development; in England this might be through the establishment of Free Trade, in France and Belgium after 1815 it was by answering the call of businessmen to raise tariffs. Certainly no ruler should stand against progress as Pope Gregory XVI did by forbidding railways in his lands, or the Emperor Francis by discouraging factories in his empire, especially near Vienna. Faced with rulers who did not share in their aspirations for society, the middle classes, or that section who wished for industrialization, came to demand at least a share in the power of government. Once again economic and social ends were seen as best pursued by political means.

Chapter II

THE POLITICAL REVOLUTION

TO THE historian writing today what transformed Europe can be seen to have been industrialization, but to most people living at the end of the eighteenth century the political revolution in France seemed a much more significant and recognizable change. Nevertheless, whereas it is now comparatively simple to recognize the Industrial Revolution, it is extremely difficult to grasp what the French Revolution was; indeed to know if it was the French revolution with the geographical exclusiveness which that title implies. The people were in no doubt that they were living through a revolution, but what was that revolution, when did it start, when did it finish, and what did it achieve? Research, far from answering these questions, serves rather to complicate them. The clear lines of old textbook certainties dissolve under the pressure of inquiry. Even the wrong sign-posts have an attraction for the lost and as yet we have no other comforting guide-lines to take their place.

Variations on a Marxist theme of class warfare, occasioned by the struggles of the middle class to overthrow the aristocracy, by exploiting an alliance with the lower orders, are not adequate as explanations. Generalizations about the 'aristocracy', 'the middle classes', 'the working class' and 'feudalism' have been shown on examination to be almost meaningless because of the great variation inside these categories, if indeed they are valid as categories in the first place. This is not to say, however, that clashes of economic and social interest were not of paramount importance at various stages in the revolution. It is simply that no convenient formula can be drawn up which expresses the revolutionary events.

The revolution was, above all, an overthrow of the existing government and various attempts to replace it. The breakdown in the administration and the executive that confronted France in the late 1780s was real. Whether historians are right to link this crisis with one throughout the whole of the 'West' at the time is open to question, but the fact of crisis in France is not. First of all, of course, the crisis was financial. The Crown, for some time in financial difficulties, was, after the War of American Independence, faced by imminent bankruptcy. It was the Crown's attempts to avoid this which changed a situation of chronic difficulty into one of immediate crisis.

It had become obvious to successive ministers that the time was past for temporary expediencies and shifts. If more money was required it could only be obtained by a re-casting of the framework of taxation. New wells must be drilled since the rate of flow from the existing ones could not be increased. There was no difficulty in seeing where the sites for such wells were. The nobility, among whom were some of the richest people in France, the Church and many of the townspeople were grossly under-taxed.

However, it was not only in fiscal matters that these groups were privileged. They were also entrenched politically, administratively and judicially. Any attempt to tax the under-taxed would therefore have first to overcome their very real powers of obstruction. In fact many of the privileged were quite prepared to pay more tax, but they were determined that the price of such a concession should be a constitution for France which would give them political control of the country.

This was certainly not the view of the underprivileged, who supported them, nevertheless, in their struggles with the ministers of Louis over tax reforms. The opposition which confronted Calonne when he tried to get his tax proposals accepted was essentially divided. But as yet it was monarchical absolutism rather than aristocratic ambition that was seen by the politically interested members of the Third Estate as inimical to their interests. The opposition combined long enough for the power of the government to begin to crumble away. By this time a united front was no longer possible, the collapse of governmental power allied to the political inadequacy of the king had allowed the Third Estate to take control of the situation and make their bid for political power in the name of the people of France.

The initiative of the Third Estate was to be of enormous consequence. A principle on which to base a claim to authority was needed; it was not enough that traditional authority had faltered. To step in and shoulder aside the wraiths of hereditary sovereignty and Divine Right required unassailable justification. It was to be found in the assembly's role as the gathering of the representatives of the people of France. The clearest statement of this is perhaps the assembly's own, in the 'Rights of Man' which it drew up. 'The principle of all sovereignty rests essentially in the nation. No body and no individual may exercise authority which does not emanate from the nation expressly.'

This belief that government sprang from the governed, a belief which translated the King of France into the King of the French, was not the one which had guided affairs over the past centuries.

What were the aims of those delegates of the Third Estate, who soon were to become the core of the National Constituent Assembly? Having made their bid for power, what did they try to achieve? The chief danger in trying to answer this question is one of over-simplification. Like any large body of men, the majority of whom are unknown to one another, the representatives of the Third Estate differed in their wishes and aspirations. Nevertheless some sort of unity of purpose can be distinguished among them. The wish to regenerate and revive their country was common to these men, as was the desire to sweep away an entrenched, office-holding aristocracy who seemed to sit obstructively athwart so many roads to reform. It was felt, particularly by the talented, that the fields of political and social life should lie open to talent and that the barriers to promotion, erected by privilege, should be pulled down. There should be civil freedom and equality before the law, and such symptoms of despotism as arbitrary arrest and prolonged im-prisonment without trial must disappear. The process of regenera-tion demanded a greater tidiness and uniformity in French life, thus anomalies of region just as much as those of class should perish. Trade within France should be freed from the shackles of internal duty and regulation. All this achieved, the victories of reform would be displayed and, at the same time, guaranteed in a new constitution. The essentials of this constitution were to be an elected legislature separated from the executive which would be invested in a con-stitutional monarchy.

This was to be a new France, and, no doubt, pains at its birth were to be expected. However, the upheaval which occurred was to bring distress on a totally disproportionate scale. The old France, with all its divisions and anomalies, was to die and a new France was to be born, but not one wrapped in the swaddling clothes of con-

stitutional monarchy. Instead of the emergence of a settled government, enjoying the support of the majority of Frenchmen, there
followed a series of governments and, indeed, constitutions, born
and dying in violence until, with the centre ground of French
politics blasted away by bombardment from both sides, democratic
government based on consensus became impossible. At this stage
the revolution was transposed into the Napoleonic dictatorship; the
preservation of some, involving the sacrifice of other, of the ideals
and achievements of the previous decade. The large plebiscite
victories which he won might suggest that Napoleon did indeed
satisfy the governmental wishes of the majority of Frenchmen. But
this would be a misleading impression, for Napoleon was never
able to rest his authority upon a base of firm and wholehearted
support. If he was successful he was accepted, but failure exposed
the paucity of his credit balance and was unredeemed by reserves
of loyalty. This was clearly demonstrated in his fall.

Despite the efforts of Napoleon and his agreement with the Pope,
the revolution was never sanctified by the Church. The collision
between the revolution and the Church had been the result of the
National Assembly's attempt to solve France's financial problems
by seizing the Church's property while taking the chance to carry
out a wholesale reform of Church organization and government.
With the outbreak of war those who took the side of the Pope and
the Church found themselves proclaimed and treated as traitors,
and the schism became deeper. However, the revolutionary tradition
after 1792 was republican as well as anti-clerical. Probably it was
futile to expect a king reared in absolutionist notions, even so well-
intentioned a king as Louis XVI, to be willing, or even able, to
co-operate in the experiment of constitutional monarchy. In fact
Louis never co-operated sincerely: at best he temporized and
sought to win delay, at worst he intrigued with foreign governments.
Once again with war this behaviour was seen as treasonable, and his
dethronement, trial and execution were always likely.

The period which was to be the most potent in the formation of
the revolutionary tradition, both for believers and non-believers,
was that of the Jacobin dictatorship and the Terror. Of course the
Terror cannot be entirely explained by the war, but had there been
no war it is impossible to believe that the Jacobins would have been
able to get into a position of power from which they were able to
attempt to practise their principles.

The majority of deputies to the Convention in 1792 were men of the centre, more or less moderate, who found themselves responsible for a country where the official executive was powerless, the dethroned king a prisoner of the Commune of Paris, and the enemy at the gates which a suspected host of potential traitors within the walls might at any time throw open. It is not surprising that over the next year and a half, urged on by the people of Paris, the deputies would consent to see the most determined group in the Convention, the Montagnards, speak for the French nation. Moderate men were to organize the victory during the period of fiercest terror, alongside fanatics, because they saw this as the only way to save their country. But it was not just as the party of wholesale war that the Jacobins won their support; their willingness to temper their economic policies was also of enormous importance.

The economic situation in France in 1789, and after, was heavy with danger. A growing rural population and the beginnings of industrial change were producing a situation which famine, or the fear of famine following a bad harvest, could render explosive. The dislocation of the economy, with emigration and consequent unemployment among those directly and indirectly concerned with providing the wants of the *émigrés*, the inflation caused by the increasing issue of paper currency and the general pressure of demand, created among the poorer classes in towns a growing insistence for government intervention to hold down prices and attack profiteers. It also produced an organized and articulate movement among these poorer townspeople which became increasingly influential until, by August of 1792, through the media of the Insurrectionary Commune and the sectional assemblies of Paris, it seemed to control the whole course of the revolution. The Sans Culottes, claiming the *droit à l'existence*, were never a political party, but anyone wishing to dominate France in 1792 could only do so with their support. This support the Jacobins secured with their obvious revolutionary fervour and their acceptance of the principles, in 1793, of the maximum in prices of basic commodities.

Though the popular movement in the towns became most organized and most powerful in 1792 it had existed much longer and had been instrumental in the success of the assembly's struggle with the king in 1789. However it was only in 1792 that the demands of the Sans Culottes began to distort the policies of the deputies.

But in the countryside the great agrarian uprising of July and August 1789, the Great Fear, had forced a change in the policies of the assembly. Faced with the choice, as the only ways of restoring peace, of either supporting and strengthening the executive (in other words, the king), or acceding to the demands of the peasantry, the assembly chose the latter. Hence the 'abolition of Feudalism' which had not been, in its entirety, in the programme of the deputies.

Invasion, civil war, treason on all sides; this, set against a background of economic distress, can fairly be termed a 'national emergency'. National emergency thus explains the fact, even if not altogether the manner, of Jacobin rule. The Terror, a weapon forged in heat generated by war and famine and bearing recognizable marks of its forging, was obviously concerned with the ruthless prosecution of the war both at home and abroad and committed to the elimination of all those who stood in its path. 'The state must be saved. Nothing is unconstitutional, save what ruins it.' That is how Robespierre put it. At the same time, standing firmly on the side of the poorer people of the towns, *le menu peuple*, who provided the revolutionary armies of the frontier and the shock troops in Paris, the Terror waged war on the extremes of economic inequality. This was expressed in the revolutionary song, 'We must shorten the giants and make the small folk taller'. These traits of the Terror were to be expected from the circumstances of its creation, but what of the Jacobin aspirations embedded in it?

The Jacobins, more than 50 per cent of whom were middle class, cherished a France of small landowners, small property owners and the smaller industrialists and commercial men. They did not object to the right to own property, merely to those who owned too much of it. From the Club in Paris through the many affiliated clubs and popular societies, the Jacobins saw themselves as the only true guardians of the revolution, 'the open eye fixed on the repositories of power'. But they saw their role in affairs as extending beyond being a reservoir of revolutionary talent and an organized scourge of reaction. They, or rather many of them, came to see themselves as bound up in the need to regenerate the French people, just as much as the institutions of state. 'The transition from evil to good, from corruption to probity' was how Saint-Just described the part of the Terror; to Robespierre it was the 'despotism of liberty against tyranny'. The preoccupation with virtue and the attack on luxury and vice were essential ingredients in the make-up of the Jacobin. 'A gambler, a drunkard, a bad father cannot be a republican' was firmly stated by the Jacobin club at Nancy.

In the mind of a Robespierre or a Saint-Just, revolutionary dictatorship was concerned to 'compel men to be good'. Such a state was seen as the necessary preliminary for the proper functioning of democracy. It was only when this was achieved that the 'General Will' described by Rousseau would be freely and correctly ascertainable by the people. Until then the people would be misled and perverted to such an extent that the 'will of all' would not be the 'General Will' and therefore the genuine sovereign. This provided the true justification for the Terror in the eyes of many of the Jacobin leaders and one that overrode all other considerations. This ruthlessness against evil in pursuit of virtue is above all epitomized by Robespierre, the 'incorruptible'. Perhaps the most important legacy of Robespierre and the rule of the Jacobins was the belief in a revolutionary minority, the repository of 'knowledge' and 'virtue' who would be concerned to seize power and, by dictatorial means, implement their policies, in this way 'forcing men to be free'.

The circumstances of the revolution were such, that the Jacobins, in order to secure the defeat of the counter-revolutionaries, pursued policies which seemed to verge upon hostility to the middle class, from which the majority of their members came. However, at this time in France the middle-class master still worked alongside his workers, many of them hoping to become masters themselves, so that the class-split did not yet exist in its nineteenth-century form. Also the revolution was primarily political rather than economic, and the middle classes had not yet come to see the dangers for them in the translation of demands for popular sovereignty from political into economic terms, with the implications for private property and wealth which that state of affairs was to have. In fact, it was Robespierre and the Jacobins who curtailed the almost direct democracy of the Paris sections and attacked the leaders of the Sans Culottes. Nevertheless, the tradition of the Jacobins was that of the party of the people. 'Under Robespierre blood flowed and we had bread. Now the blood has ceased to flow and we have no bread.'

It is not surprising that the army which, in the period after the fall of the Jacobins, was increasingly used to maintain the government in power, come to demand a share in that power in the person of Napoleon. However, it is not just as the guardian of the revolution in France that the army was to become increasingly important in the 1790s, it was also as the disseminator of the revolution abroad. In the war which France fought after 1792 there was a basic contradiction. It was both a war between states and a war of the revolution against counter-revolution. Thus the war was partly an export of the revolution, a crusade for the freedom of other Europeans. 'The French nation renounces the undertaking of any war with a view to making conquests, and it will never use its forces against the liberty of any people,' the assembly had decreed in May 1790, and the deputies voted for war in 1792 still with this view. However, *'guerre aux châteaux, paix au chaumières'* soon breaks down if the cottagers rally to defend their king, their church and their lord. In the main, what sympathizers the French soldiers found were from the middle class rather than the cottagers.

The war was also a war of the French nation against other states and hence was always liable to become one against other 'nations'.

Although the revolution was avowedly international in its aims, from the start it had very strong nationalist features. The concept of national sovereignty vested in the people rather than in some traditional ruler concentrated loyalty on the people as the basis of the state. In this way regional anomalies, as well as perhaps being unjust, were seen as harmful to the nation. 'There should be no tongue in the Republic other than French, which would have the effect of bringing equality nearer,' was a resolution passed in a Provençal Jacobin club. The tradition of the 'Nation in arms', a spontaneous upsurge of the people, which by its zeal and ardour inspired France's victory over her enemies, personified by Danton in 1792, with all attendant patriotism, added force to the growth of nationalism in France.*

As the war progressed, the annexation and exploitation of the victorious revolution became more overt and the expropriations of

* The legend of French victory because of superior determination rather than technique was still potent in 1870 when repeated demands were made in Paris for a *sortie torrentiale* of the National Guard to hurl back the Prussians besieging the city.

French armies heavier, until under the later empire of Napoleon personal aggrandisement sometimes seemed to dictate policy rather than national interest, let alone a belief in internationalism. However, France, seeing herself as the incarnation of the revolution, obviously would find it difficult to distinguish her own interests from those of the cause which she served.

Under Napoleon, the influence of France and the revolution spread throughout Europe; to the borders of Russia and Turkey, no country emerged unchanged. Conservative Prussia under Stein and then Hardenberg adopted some of the French reforms, in her attempts to overcome the humiliations after Jena; personal serfdom was abolished and entry into the officer corps was widened to include sons of burghers as well as the sons of nobles. 'The state which refuses to acknowledge them [the principles behind the French Revolution] will be condemned to submit or to perish,' wrote Hardenberg. Whereas in those lands directly governed by France or by her satellites, many of the fruits of the revolution were received; from the legal, in the Civil Code of Napoleon, to the social, in the abolition of feudalism or the opening of many careers to talent.

Napoleon's rationalization of boundaries and territorial adjustments in peace treaties drastically reduced the number of dwarf states in Europe. In the old Holy Roman Empire, itself abolished as a result of the changes, the number of states was cut nearly ten times. Internal customs were often abolished and standard systems of weights and measures introduced. All this gave people a taste for the benefits of efficient government and of belonging to a larger territorial unit, which did much to foster nationalism in Germany and Italy among some sections of society. At the same time, the rapacity of French exactions and the high-handedness of her ruler stirred up an anti-French feeling which often resulted in a growth of national consciousness.*

However, the importance of Napoleon's conquests went much further. The Japanese victories over the colonial powers in Asia in 1942–3 have had an effect which the ultimate defeat of 1945 did not nullify. The impression of the superiority of the white man on which so much of colonial rule had rested was gone. Hence it proved impossible to revert to a pre-war situation. The sweeping away of

---

* Napoleon's kingdom of Westphalia, under the rule of his brother Joseph, lost 38,000 either dead or taken prisoner out of a population of two million.

old boundaries and traditional rulers by Napoleon meant that the mystique of the governors would never be the same again to the governed. After the changes of the revolutionary and Napoleonic period, further change would always seem possible and revolution the way to achieve it.

Chapter III

REVOLUTIONARY HERITAGE—FORCES FOR CHANGE

THE INDUSTRIAL REVOLUTION was a phenomenon which only began to penetrate the Continent after 1815, and so obviously its effects on the social and political life of people were only starting to be felt in Restoration Europe. However, the French Revolution, although proclaimed by Napoleon to have ended, was still very much an organic force and Europe after 1815 continued to be greatly affected by it. First, in the straightforward sense that those who believed in change and movement looked to France, and used French models, for their inspiration and hope. Opposition to the governments of the time, in the politically absolutist climate, had no hope of achieving its wishes by working through constitutional means, and therefore saw revolution as the only possible vehicle. It was generally believed that the revolution would first begin in France and then spread through other European lands. Thus with the overthrow of the Bourbons in 1830 and the establishment of the bourgeois monarchy in France under Louis Philippe many revolutionaries thought that their moment had arrived; only after becoming increasingly disappointed with the French king did they again turn to waiting for another revolution in France as their signal.

It is legitimate to talk of 'the revolution', anyhow until 1830. First, because the revolutionaries saw their cause as common. 'A victory for republicanism in France would mean the end of tyranny in the world' was how the Chartist leader George Harney expressed this feeling. This sense of solidarity arose partly, as will be seen later, because of the way in which governments came together across Europe to preserve the system and scotch revolution. It was also the result of the French Revolution, when the message had been carried across Europe by the French armies. Secondly, although the opposition comprised extremely diverse, and potentially mutually antagonistic, groups, their first concern was to change the status quo. As in France prior to 1789, when the middle classes supported the aristocrats in their fight against royal 'absolutist' encroachments, the diversities and antagonisms remained latent. Thus the barricades in Paris in 1830 were constructed and manned by the poorer sections of society, rather than by the richer middle class whom they brought to power. It is true that in the 1830s when constitutional monarchies were established in France, Britain and Belgium, many of the *haute bourgeoisie* were satisfied and they ceased to belong to the opposition, moving across to the government side. However, even with the fear of Jacobinism which had existed since 1794, it was only in Britain that the number of middle-class recruits to the politically satisfied was very large. In France the majority of the middle classes still found themselves ranged on the side of the opposition.

On the whole, the distinctions within the opposition to the political establishment, which the events of 1848 were to bring so sharply into focus, corresponded to the various stages of the French Revolution. First, the phase of the opening years which culminated in the setting up of the constitutional monarchy in 1791. The liberal aristocrats and the richer bourgeois had been the chief beneficiaries of this reform and these sections of society were to be the main exponents of the liberal tradition of the early nineteenth century. The France of Louis Philippe saw the setting-up of a constitution more or less in accord with their views. Secondly, there was a much more democratic and radical tradition; one more akin to the beliefs of the Jacobins, though eschewing some of the principles of Robespierre and Saint-Just, which seemed too extreme. In France the followers of this group extended much further to the Right than in England after 1832. In other words, whereas in England the Reform Bill managed to appease many more of the middle class than it enfranchised, in France, many of Louis Philippe's opponents who found themselves supporters of the Jacobin tradition were really much closer to the Girondins in their aims. The third tradition, growing out of industrial advance, looked back to the Sans Culottes and was to become the socialist opposition. Finally, arising out of the revolution at different stages, both joined to and cutting across the other divisions of the opposition, came nationalism. It was perhaps the last which was to determine the outcome of the events of 1848 in central and eastern Europe.

B

Although, as we have seen, the Jacobins dealt with economic matters primarily as a means to a political end, some of the policies of Saint-Just and Robespierre did appear socially egalitarian. The pressure for such policies came mainly from various leaders, or aspirants to leadership, among the Sans Culottes. These men, such as Jacques Roux, who asked, 'what is liberty when one class of men starve another?', as well as feeding the Sans Culotte hatred for the rich middle class, came to see that political freedom and equality meant little without economic equality. After the fall of Robespierre and the Jacobins the condition of the poor in Paris sharply deteriorated and it was this, together with anguish at the betrayal of the principles of the revolution, that led to the conspiracy of Gracchus Babeuf.

In his paper *Tribune of the People*, Babeuf attacked the new constitution of the Directory and clamoured for the adoption of the 1793 Jacobin constitution. He castigated a government which tolerated such povery and distress; his own seven-year-old daughter was to die of hunger while he was in prison following the closure of his paper, and he demanded economic equality as the only basis for political equality. On his release from prison he started a 'Society of Equals' and published a manifesto. 'We proclaim that no longer can we endure, with the great majority of mankind, toil and sweat in the service and for the benefit of a small minority.' The society opposed the Directory and worked for 'A Republic of Equals'. On the club being closed down by order of the Directory, Babeuf and his society were forced underground. In the form of an insurrectionary committee, they planned a coup by which they would seize power and prepare the way for elections to a new national assembly. The constitution they drafted was socialist in attitude. Among other measures, there was to be a national community of goods and invidious but socially necessary jobs were to be shared out among all citizens. The conspiracy was planned with some precision, various strategic buildings, such as bakeries, were to be seized, and attempts were made to capture the loyalty of the army. However, the conspiracy was sprung by police agents infiltrating into the committee, and Babeuf and other leaders were arrested and subsequently executed. The Babeuf insurrection was both an attempt to conclude the 'unfinished business' of the revolution and a forerunner of the socialist schemes to grasp power through revolt, of the future.

The tradition of a group of professional revolutionaries who would seize political power and hold it in the name of the people as a popular dictatorship, attempting to destroy the power of the wealthy and the bourgeois, lived on. It was greatly fostered in 1828 by the publication of *La Conspiration pour l'égalité dite de Babeuf*. This, purporting to be a digest of 'Babouvism', was written by the Italian exile Buonarrotti, who had been a follower and fellow conspirator of Babeuf. One of Buonarrotti's disciples, Blanqui, was to carry on and develop these ideas. He took part in the rising of 1830 in Paris which brought Louis Philippe to the throne (for which he received a medallion), but soon he was plotting again. Seeing capitalism as the chief enemy of the people he sought to stage a revolution against the established order. He planned his revolt through the secret society he led, which ultimately became the *Société des Saisons*. The coup was staged in May 1839; the Palais de Justice was seized and the Prefecture of Police was attacked. However, meeting with a repulse the conspirators were forced to retire to the barricades which they had constructed and await the popular rising in their favour which they expected. This totally failing to materialize, the revolt was soon suppressed and the leaders arrested.

The conspirators had looked to the newly developing working class for their support and it was the emergence of this class, as a consequence of the industrial revolution that was now beginning to affect Europe, which was to transform the early 'socialist' ideas into one of the dominating forces of the nineteenth century. However, this change was to require not just the emergence of a working class but the realization by that working class that socialist ideas presented it with the opportunity for progress and betterment.

It was natural that, with the recognition of the human suffering and distress attendant upon industrialization, various plans would be presented for their mitigation. These schemes, often bracketed together as 'Utopian Socialist', had one factor in common: the belief that unbridled, undirected capitalism must not be allowed to continue to grow unchecked and further exploit the workers. The plans varied enormously and were sometimes contradictory. Saint-Simon, welcoming industrialization, wished to set up a new 'technocratic' state, which would control the machinery of production and the distribution of wealth. Fourier, on the other hand, desired a society on a pre-industrial level of economy, with craft industry and farming. He envisaged communities of some sixteen hundred people which would occupy five thousand acres.* Proudhon dreamed of federated autonomous communes, whereas Cabot and Owen both at various times tried to set up ideal societies in the New World.

Some of these men made no attempt to win popular support for their ideas, and even in Blanqui's rising, which certainly expected to obtain it, there was no support forthcoming. Despite their discontent and suffering the people failed to rally to these reformers. Their importance lay in the fact that when revolution did break out in 1848, there were individuals and organizations demanding that the opportunity of furthering economic and social equality be taken. One such was Louis Blanc, the French journalist, who wrote *L'organisation du travail* in 1839 advocating state socialism. The government must recognize the right of all men to work, and as a step towards this must open social workshops, eventually to be run by the workers themselves, who would be guaranteed a wage. He was later to find himself a member of the provisional government in Paris in 1848. The existence of these socialist leaders was to add power to the revolution by stirring up popular feeling, but at the same time their emphasis on the class rivalry of worker and capitalist was almost certainly to lead to the revolutionaries falling apart more rapidly than they would have done otherwise. This even before they had achieved their common aim: the destruction of the ruling power. In this sense the opening paragraph of Marx's *Communist Manifesto*, published in 1848, was accurate. 'A spectre is haunting Europe—the spectre of communism; . . . where [is] the opposition that has not handed back the branding reproach of communism against the more advanced opposition parties?'

Although it was only to have a minimal effect on events in 1848 it would be misleading to conclude this survey of socialism in Europe without some mention of Karl Marx's *Communist Manifesto*. This was not some blueprint for a Utopia but claimed to be the description of man's future based upon a reasoned analysis of the past; hence 'scientific socialism'. It might seem strange that it was from a German that this work came rather than from an Englishman, for England had a much larger working class than any other country

* It might be of interest to point out that if the scheme had been adopted there would not now be enough land in France to accommodate the population, while in Italy rather less than half the present population would be supported.

at this time, and it was the working class in England that gave birth to Chartism, the principles of consumer co-operation and trade unionism. However, the Manifesto did owe much to the development of the working class in England for Marx deduced his principles largely from his knowledge of conditions in England coming from the description of his friend Friedrich Engels, particularly in the latter's book, *The Condition of the Working-classes in England*, published in 1845.

Marx's most original contribution to socialism, and his most important, was the view that the overthrow of capitalism was not merely socially desirable but inevitable. Taking Hegel's doctrine of the dialectic—thesis being met by antithesis and the clash producing synthesis—Marx applied it to the material world. 'The ideal is nothing else than the material world reported by the human mind and translated into terms of thought.' He saw history as the story of a series of struggles between classes, the dominant class at any time representing that group of people which owned the forces of production. When, because of invention and the growth of new techniques, these forces changed, so new classes struggled to overthrow the old. Thus capitalism, as represented by the bourgeois, carried the seeds of its own destruction: 'not only has the bourgeoisie forged the weapons that bring death to itself; it has also called into existence the men who are to wield those weapons—the modern working class—the proletarians'.

Forced by competition into recurrent economic crises of over-production and slump, Marx saw the bourgeois turning to ever greater exploitation of the workers. (Later he was to rationalize this process, using the labour theory of value, as the Law of Increasing Misery.) This would result in increasing numbers of the bourgeois being 'precipitated into the proletariat'; often to lead it in the vital struggle against the bourgeois. The proletariat might have to become the ruling class to ensure the defeat of its enemies but with its victory 'it will have swept away the conditions for the existence of . . . classes generally and a new classless society will emerge'. Believing this, Marx was not interested in attempts to improve the lot of the working class or to win a share of power by widening the franchise. Revolution must follow the prescribed pattern, other aims were futile and sometimes might even be harmful if they prolonged the birth-pangs of the new society.

Although Marx did not attach much importance to the question of the franchise and electoral reform, most opposition groups in the Restoration period did. Though opposition groups were almost united in demanding free elections to a legislature they were often divided as to the extent of the franchise. From the demands of the Chartists in England (for equal representation, universal suffrage, annual parliaments, no property qualification necessary for election, voting by ballot, payment of members of parliament) to Guizot's confidence in a very limited franchise in France, where he felt that political power should 'be vested in the highest element of society, the element that is independent, enlightened and capable', there was much room for disagreement. However, a broad distinction can be made between the varying opinions about the form free elections should take. On the one side were men who believed that sovereignty rested inalienably in the people and that it could be exercised only by them. On the other side, there were those who saw sovereignty emanating from the people but being exercised in their name by a limited number; although they might disagree about how large this number should be and who it should consist of. This division was sometimes obscured; as in France in 1848 when many who believed in a delegated sovereignty found themselves on the same side as those who believed in the full sovereignty of the people. Nevertheless the division was still there and led finally to the bitter fighting which broke out between the former revolutionary allies in the 'June Days'. Those who believed in the sovereignty of the people and therefore demanded universal suffrage, or something very close to it, can be termed the 'democrats' or 'radicals'. Like the liberals, for such the others were, the democrats believed in civil liberties like equality before the law, freedom of the press and freedom from arbitrary arrest. They differed in seeing liberty as only possible if the 'General Will' was allowed to rule, expressed through frequent elections in which all men would participate. The problem that was later to present itself to the democrats was that of a population, particularly in the rural areas, which was so backward and politically uneducated as to support reaction with their votes. However, this paradox, of a democracy rejecting the democrats, was only to arise in 1848 when the democrats became strong enough to demand the implementation of their wishes. In fact the people of Paris in 1792 and 1793, in demanding the right to speak for France as a whole, had shown their realization of the counter-revolutionary nature of a mass vote.

'Liberal' as a political label was a nineteenth-century creation. It was first coined in Spain when the party wishing to institute a constitutional government, who rebelled in 1820, were known as *liberales*. The label was used to classify a great variety of opinion but liberals did all share a belief in free institutions. This was not a belief in free institutions for their own sake but because they thought through them alone man was capable of progress, and progress towards perfection. The liberals were attached to free institutions, passionately upholding the rights of the individual, and opposed to arbitrary government whether the government was of an hereditary despot or a popular democracy. Benjamin Constant, a liberal opponent of reaction under the restored Bourbons in France, explained this position clearly. He saw liberty as 'the triumph of the individual, as much over a government which seeks to rule by despotic methods as over the masses who seek to render the minority a slave of the majority'. For 'an arbitrary act remains an arbitrary act even when committed by the whole nation against a single individual'.

In economic matters the liberals believed in the minimum of state interference, seeing the government's role to be guardian of the free market, a ring-master of *laissez-faire*. There might be the need to abolish restrictions and impediments inherited from the past in the form of protection, local barriers to free trade, guild power and legal monopoly, but on no account should the state intervene to try to influence the workings of the free market. Whether the liberal was an optimist after the pattern of Adam Smith, who saw an unrestricted market naturally working for the betterment and good of all, or whether he was more pessimistic, like Malthus, he still believed initiative to be doomed to failure. 'The poverty of the incapable, the distresses that come upon the imprudent, the starvation of the idle, and these shoulderings aside of the weak by the strong, which leave so many "in shallows and in miseries", are the decrees of a large, far-seeing benevolence', wrote Herbert Spencer in 1851. While even the institution of free libraries was criticized in England as 'founded upon theft and upon the violation of the most sacred thing in the world, the liberty of your fellow-man'.

It is easy to see in liberalism, as did Karl Marx and other contemporaries, a creed motivated solely by self-interest; to see the growing middle class adopting it as a means to their own political power and naked economic exploitation of society. Guizot and other French liberals fought the government under the restored Bourbons in the name of liberty and freedom, but, in power themselves, during the reign of Louis Philippe, they acted differently. They maintained a narrow franchise, refused to pass any measure for social amelioration (even declining to pass a poor law), and finally went so far as to restrict the freedom of the press and the right of association. However, the title of Louis Philippe, 'King of the French by the grace of God and the will of the nation', was not just a meaningless phrase. Guizot, speaking in the French assembly in 1837, claimed, 'the very perfection of our system of government consists in the fact that political rights, limited by nature itself to those capable of exercising them, are made subject to expansion as political capacity is acquired by more people'. He genuinely did believe that the franchise would widen at a satisfactory pace with the growth of prosperity.

The liberals were always very aware of what had happened in the French Revolution and feared 'the tempestuous tyranny of popular sovereignty' as Constant describes it. Instead, they sought to place political power in the hands of property-owners and the wealthiest class of society. To this end they preferred rather to retain the hereditary sovereign, though of course firmly shackled in a constitution, than to plunge into republicanism.

It is quite possible to attack them justly for their over-caution, but not so easy to arraign them for hypocrisy. Perhaps it is profitable to compare this distrust of popular sovereignty with the refusal of the Paris sections, already referred to, to accept the democratic will of the majority of French people, since they believed that large numbers of the peasants were so much in the power of the local priest or lord and sunk in ignorance as not to know what was in their own interest.

There was of course a hint of 'jobs for the boys' in the liberals' demands for a constitution; a search for a place in the sun of political patronage. But this was nothing peculiar to nineteenth-century liberalism. Even Fouquier-Tinville, the Public Prosecutor of the Revolutionary Tribunal at the height of the Terror, obtained his position not through revolutionary zeal and hatred of reactionaries but because of patronage. He had written to his distant cousin Camille Desmoulins, newly at the Ministry of Justice, portraying his large family and small fortune and appealing for some preferment. Above all, the rather smug-seeming belief in self-help, allied to reluctance to assist the less fortunate in climbing the 'greasy pole' of success, can sometimes be explained by the natural feeling in a man that the way he has succeeded is the best recipe for the success of others.

It would perhaps be fairest, then, to allow for some sincerity and idealism as well as desire for self-advancement in the platform and wishes of the liberals. But, however motivated, there was a continuing pressure among the middle classes and students of Europe, after 1815, for liberal constitutions and free institutions. Where the middle class was numerically weak and lacking in self-confidence, as in much of southern and eastern Europe, the pressure was less and fairly easily contained. Where the middle class was large and powerful, as in France, failure to regard the pressure resulted in the overthrow of the Bourbons and the creation of the constitutional monarchy of Louis Philippe. At the same time, of course, the growth of the economy of Europe increased the middle class even in those areas where it had hitherto been at its weakest.

Various references have been made to factors favouring the growth of national consciousness in Europe. The important influence of this force in future events demands an attempt to draw these references together so as to present the whole in some coherent form.

The word 'nationalism' is of nineteenth-century origin but of course this does not mean that the concept which it describes had no previous existence; certainly the word 'nation' was used in the Middle Ages. There has been, perhaps as long as man has existed, a human dislike and distrust of strangers—a dislike and distrust which could lead to hostility and violence. There is a legend concerning the inhabitants of the small Durham port of Hartlepool who, on discovering an abandoned boatload of monkeys stranded on some rocks, brought the unfortunate creatures ashore and hanged them in the town square. They did this because they had been told that Frenchmen had tails and England was at war with France at the time. The story may well be apocryphal but its currency does illustrate the sort of primitive xenophobia which is the ancestor of some of the less pleasant traits of modern nationalism. Sir John Fortescue, writing his *The Governance of England* towards the close of the fifteenth century, seeks an explanation for the French peasantry's lack of rebellion in the face of intolerable oppression and poverty. 'It is cowardice and lack of heart and courage, which

B*

no Frenchman hath like unto an Englishman,' he affirms. When confronted by foreigners, particularly as invaders, this sort of feeling could, combined with a love of homeland and loyalty to locality and local institutions, create a sense of unity among men which would render their defence more determined and spirited. This phenomenon, obviously akin to the modern concept of patriotism, is clearly discernible in the desperation with which many of the Netherlanders defended themselves against the Spain of Philip II, or the determination of the French (notwithstanding Fortescue) to cast out the English invader in the latter part of the Hundred Years War.

Perhaps what best distinguishes this patriotism from nineteenth- and twentieth-century nationalism is that the latter is based upon the belief in the existence of separate groups of people, 'nationalities', irrespective of the political or ecclesiastical units in which they at present live. Furthermore, it has the explicit programme of trying to embody these peoples in the form of territorial units, nation states. On the one hand this can lead to an attempt to expel people from a state, on the other to a break-away from an alien state and the merging with another; an exodus or an in-gathering. This was to develop with time, sometimes by a sort of over-spill of the energy required to achieve such an objective, into a competitive urge between one nation state and another. These attempts became to certain peoples of overriding importance, their realization more desirable than the alleviation of poverty or even the preservation of self. Why was it that a simple love of fatherland could develop in this way and why should it do so in the nineteenth century?

In the eighteenth century there had been a growth of what is sometimes described as cultural nationalism. This was for the most part confined to scholars, or at any rate the educated, and had little popular, even less political appeal. It consisted of the re-discovery of submerged and divergent cultures among the peoples of Europe, most often through folk arts, folk tales and old legends. It had a strong historical bias and soon came to be concerned with the study of language. Frequently, as in the case of the Grimm brothers with their *Fairy Stories for Children and Home* or the Lutheran pastor Herder, it was associated with the early stages of that rejection of the rational known as pre-romanticism.

Herder, who became court chaplain at Weimar largely because of the efforts of Goethe, saw cultures as the products of different nationalities; a realization he first came to at Riga when living among the Latvians. Since men thought in language, Herder saw it as representing more than a medium of communication; it affected what men had to communicate. Man's relations with his fellows, his environment, his self-knowledge—thus even himself—were to some extent the result of language. Herder termed those sharing a similar culture in this way a *Volk* or people. He believed these *Völker* were created by God and saw their eventual metamorphosis into nation states as part of the divine 'Grand Design'. In fact he believed that if humanity was to reach the extent of its potential it was first necessary that each *Volk* must be responsible for, and govern, itself. Herder himself was not concerned with politics and certainly did not foresee aggression between nations. Like many people of his time he saw war as the outcome of the selfishness and ambitions of kings, not the antagonisms of peoples. 'Fatherlands do not move against each other,' he proclaimed.

At first this movement was purely one of scholars. Even so it had one important result in central and eastern Europe in reviving local cultures. For whereas the German or Italian scholar had always been aware of German or Italian culture a different situation existed among many of the peoples of central Europe. Even an historic people like the Czechs of Bohemia had come to lose their own culture. Whereas the peasants spoke the vernacular, the son of the peasant who was fortunate enough to gain an education, and thus make a career away from the land, would come to speak German and therefore acquire German culture. Hence any revival of his native culture would be likely to have important consequences. The production of dictionaries and grammars began to create a language where there had merely been a variety of local dialects. Symbolic of this was the foundation of the National Museum in Prague in 1818.

Although it was likely enough that cultural nationalism would have a vogue at the universities, as indeed it did, it does not follow that it would necessarily have grown into the force of political nationalism which the nineteenth century was to know.

The spread of the Industrial Revolution making many of the middle class wish to belong to larger units played a part; as did the effects of the conquests and territorial adjustments carried out under the French Revolution and Napoleon. Perhaps most important, however, was the increasing recognition of the principle of sovereignty of the people, spelled out by the French Revolution. Stressing the governed rather than the governor as the basis of the state, this concept attacked the view of the state as being a territorial aggregation, founded upon the proprietary rights of the ruler without respect to the people who lived there; seeing it instead as the embodiment of the people.

Together or singly, these factors lay behind the nationalist view of scholars becoming the opinions of a great number of other people as well. The amazing popular success of the lectures of Fichte, delivered in Berlin in 1807–8 and subsequently published, serve as an example of this departure.

However, until 1815, the position was extremely confused. The French occupation of Spain triggered off a bitter war fought by Spanish patriots and partisans resisting the invader, but these men were certainly not fighting for the principle of sovereignty of the people. In many other countries the so-called 'patriots' found that by pursuing the liberal ideals of the revolution they were opposing the loyalties and 'national' interest of their own people. It is difficult to see how nationalism would have emerged as one of the forces of 'revolution' if this situation had continued, allied as it often was to reaction. However, with the defeat and downfall of Napoleon all was changed. Now with the settlement of the Congress of Vienna, the peoples of Europe found that the forces preserving the order of the *ancien régime*, the forces opposing popular sovereignty and liberalism, changes in territory or constitutions, were the same. Italians who wished to realize their aim of a united Italy and Italians who wanted a constitution saw the Austrian Emperor and his Chancellor Metternich standing in their way. 'Austria spells despotism in Europe—remove Austria and it is over—Down with Austria has to be the European cry!' is the message of Mazzini, one of the most influential of Italian nationalists. The rulers of Europe seemed to be united in their fear of change and looked to the great centres of reaction at Vienna and St. Petersburg for guidance. It is not surprising that, seeing these common enemies, the liberals and nationalists after 1815 were misled into the belief that they had common ends and common means to achieving them.

An example of the conjunction of the nationalist and revolutionary efforts of society can be seen in the Carbonari in Naples after 1815. The Carbonari probably originated among the charcoal burners of Franche Comté and came into southern Italy with the French troops. There they became a secret society dedicated to freedom against tyranny, although even so they were used by the hardly liberal King Ferdinand in his attempts to regain his throne from the French. However, with the restoration of Ferdinand in 1815 the Carbonari were able to oppose his government, confident that at the same time they were forwarding liberty and nationalism. The weakness of the Carbonari in Naples and of their allied societies throughout Italy was that they were totally disunited and lacked a proper programme. 'Just war against the government, no more', was how Mazzini described their aims. A rising in Naples in 1820, led by General Pepe, was followed rather than accompanied by a rising in Genoa and Turin, in the north, in the following year. It is easy to laugh at the disunity, the complicated rituals, the cloak and dagger aspects of the Carbonari, and to see their failure as farce. They did, however, provide the only channel for opposition to the existing governments in states ruled by despots without constitutions, and they did succeed, as in Naples in 1820-1 or in central Italy in 1831, in securing temporary control of various Italian states.

One member of the Carbonari, who became impatient and felt that no further progress towards Italian unity and freedom was possible through the society, was Giuseppe Mazzini, the son of a doctor and professor of Genoa. Mazzini had become disillusioned with the Carbonari and their failure to act in 1830 when revolution in Paris brought Louis Philippe to the French throne. His betrayal, by the leader of his own Carbonari lodge in Genoa, and the collapse of the central Italian conspiracy, when it eventually came in 1831, caused his disillusion to grow and were behind his determination to found in 1831 his own society from exile: Young Italy.

Mazzini was determined that his society would be in the open, with a clearly formulated and coherent programme. Nevertheless he was forced into the same sort of conspiratorial role as played by the Carbonari: the invisible ink, the false-bottomed trunk containing letters, the passwords and the dramatic oath-takings. In fact as a conspirator his record was very much worse than that of the Carbonari; far from seizing power anywhere, his best laid plan, involving invasion of Savoy from Switzerland coinciding with a general insurrection in Italy led from Piedmont, was a total failure. The Piedmontese rising was sprung by the police in the summer of 1833, the anticipated revolt in Naples failed to occur. Meanwhile

the invasion of Savoy (though led by Ramorino, an experienced
revolutionary soldier who had seen service with Napoleon) got no
further than the customs posts on the frontier and managed to
achieve little in Savoyard territory beyond planting a tree of liberty.

However, in his aim of formulating a clear plan for Italian unity
Mazzini was very much more successful. He believed that 'a
Country is not a mere territory; the particular territory is only its
foundation. The Country is the idea which rises upon that foundation; it is the sentiment of love, the sense of fellowship which
binds together all the sons of that territory'. With these beliefs,
Mazzini poured forth in his writing, from exile in France, Switzerland and England, his hopes and desires for Italy. These writings,
though confined in their appeal to the educated and very often the
young, did spread the belief in a united Italy.

He sought to replace the selfishness he saw in the French and
subsequent revolutions with something finer. He wished to super-
sede the 'Rights of Man' by the 'Duties of Man'. 'The theory of
rights enables us to rise and overthrow obstacles, but not to found
a strong and lasting accord between all the elements which compose
the nation.' Mazzini believed that the individual could only advance
in step with mankind but he saw that a single man's capacity to
influence humanity was minimal. There was a need for some
association through which the individual would be able to work for
human progress; Mazzini saw this in the nation. Thus the creation
of an Italian state was essential. 'Do not be led away by the idea of
improving your material conditions without first solving the
national question. You cannot do it,' he was to write. He saw the
task of a united Italy as being to take the lead in the formation of a
community of nations.

Mazzini believed that the only satisfactory form of national unity
for Italy was a republic. 'How can you call yourselves free in the
presence of men who possess the power to command you without
your consent? The Republic is the only legitimate and logical
form of government,' he was to claim in his *Duties of Man*. However, all Italian nationalists were by no means united in this view;
in the early sixteenth century Machiavelli, lamenting the lack of
unity of Italy in the face of foreign invaders, had seen the position
of the Pope, both an Italian prince and the head of a universal
Church, as the root cause of Italy's woes. Nationalists of the
nineteenth century were still faced with the same problem: the

need to reconcile the conflicting interests of the Papacy if Italy was to be able to coalesce. Schemes were put forward to unite the country around the Pope. Gioberti in his *Il Primato*, published in 1843, recommended that Italy should federate with the Pope as its president. The executive power would be in the hands of a College, composed of the various other Italian princes. Others, such as D'Azeglio, looked to the kings of Sardinia-Piedmont to act as a base for the unification of Italy. As well as disagreement over what should serve as the nucleus there was division, over what form of constitution would best suit the new state, between the popular democratic ideal of Mazzini and the more moderate, liberal hopes of D'Azeglio and Balbo.

Germany shared with Italy the historic role of having been the home of one of the two heads of western Christendom. The Holy Roman Emperor, although reduced by the end of the Middle Ages to a meagre authority inside Germany, was still far too powerful to allow any other claimant to take the lead in unifying the area into a realistic nation state. 1806 had seen the end of the Holy Roman Empire, but the Habsburgs, recast in the form of the Austrian Emperors, were still the predominant German power at the time of the collapse of Napoleon. German unification had three possible forward routes at this time: unity based on Austria, unity based on Prussia or unity in which no single state predominated but all subscribed to a central authority above the individual states. The last for a time seemed the most likely, though the power of Austria could obviously not be ignored. The war of liberation of 1813 saw an upsurge of national feeling which forced princes to comply in order to preserve their positions. Frederick William III of Prussia was forced to abandon the French alliance and turn against Napoleon or risk civil war in his lands. Stein, the former Prussian minister, now in the service of the Tsar of Russia, was working for the creation of a German national state. He was the inspiration of the Council of Administration, a body designed to take over the administration of territories as they were reconquered from the French. However, the speedy recognition of many of the returning princes and other former rulers by the Allied powers soon broke the scheme. The idea of a Germany united by the German people lived on, but with no German institution or sovereign to act as a skeleton or focus of loyalty the idea remained an idea, empty of reality.

The wreck of Stein's hopes was, above all, the work of Metternich. This was not because he wished for the alternative, German unity under Austria; although there were those who did. They could claim the support of the philosophy of Novalis, which hoped for the regeneration of society through the traditional institutions and the recovery by rulers of their old authority: Germany reborn would advance clothed in legitimacy.

Though the ruler of Prussia had found himself briefly and reluctantly at the head of a national crusade in 1813, there were few Germans who looked to him to take the lead in the pursuit of their nationalist aspirations. However, with the gains made in the resettlement which followed Napoleon's fall, of German territory in place of lost Polish territory, with her increasing share of the burden of German defence, but above all with the growth of the Zollverein, Prussia did begin to play a more dominant role in the German Confederation. This was increasingly to enhance her claims to German leadership.

It is indicative of the essential unity of 'the revolution' in Europe after 1815 that, not only in Italy but elsewhere, the fall of the restored Bourbons in France and the accession of Louis Philippe should ignite the gunpowder of revolt. Two uprisings, one successful one unsuccessful, occurred in the Low Countries and in Poland respectively. Since 1815 Belgium, once the Austrian Netherlands, had been incorporated into the new kingdom of the Netherlands under the House of Orange. Mounting dissatisfaction with Dutch rule did not seem to threaten the position of the king until the revolution in France. The rising which occurred in August spread farther than many wished and ended in the complete separation of the two states, each under a separate king.

The acquiescence of the great powers in Belgian independence was of vital significance in the successful outcome of the revolt, just as the failure of the other powers to intervene was crucial in the Russian subjugation of the Polish uprising. The Polish state, after centuries of existence, had disappeared from the map of Europe in three partitions between 1772 and 1795, carried out by Prussia, Russia and Austria; Russia gaining the largest share. Some historians have seen in this nation, henceforth in search of a state, the first emergence of modern nationalism. The creation by Napoleon of the Grand Duchy of Warsaw, carved from much of the land previously seized by Austria and Prussia in the partitions, involved a partial resurrection. This state became the basis of 'Congress Poland' set up at the Congress of Vienna with the Russian Tsar as its king.

Disillusion increased among the Poles at this arrangement and in 1830 there was a nationalist rising against Russia. However in the absence of anything more positive than moral support from the rest of Europe, the Poles were unable to resist the Russian armies, who recaptured Warsaw and ended the revolt in 1831. Recognition of nationalism as a growing force for change and its manifold nature should not lead one to exaggerate its effectiveness. The Polish revolt had not involved the great mass of the peasantry, and reflection on the fate of Mazzini's insurrections, or the torpor of Germany, supports the impression of the, as yet, undeveloped character of nationalism as a force for change.

At first glance it might seem that the heritage of revolution, working through European society in the early nineteenth century, found another of its manifestations in romanticism, the protean movement which so fundamentally affected all branches of culture of this period. It is true that the belief in reform according to reason and empiricism, which was an important force in early stages of the French Revolution, was one of the beliefs against which romanticism was in revolt. Nevertheless, the belief in the primacy of the individual, the parentage of Rousseau, the breaking away from 'a system' and rigid form, together with the overriding need felt for self-expression,* were all shared by romanticism and the mood of revolution. Many of the romantics heralded the coming of the revolution in France with joy.

> France standing on the top of golden hours,
> And human nature seeming born again.

This was the opinion of Wordsworth, who was in France at the time. And despite Wordsworth's subsequent conversion to reaction, other, later, romantics proclaimed the ideals of the revolution and attacked the succeeding period of conservatism. They were by no means confined to one country; Mickiewicz in Poland, Hugo and Lamartine in France, Heine in Germany and Shelley and Byron in England being a few of the more obvious examples. 'You have

---

* Lamartine was the first French poet for some time to write in the first person.

repaired legitimacy's crutch,' says Byron of Wellington in 'Don Juan' and he asks,

> And I shall be delighted to learn who,
> Save you and yours, have gained by Waterloo?

Above all, however, romanticism seems allied to that aspect of the revolution which became incarnate in nationalism. The importance of romanticism in the discovery of 'cultural patriotism' was immense. But unlike Herder, perhaps best described as a pre-romantic, romantics took an interest in politics as well, and behind most of the nationalist causes in Europe there were romantic writers. In Italy they played a major part, and included Manzoni 'the avowed chief of the romantic school in literature', his son-in-law the painter and writer D'Azeglio, the playwright Guerrazzi, the poet Silvio Pellico and Mazzini himself. Perhaps it is in the life and writing of Byron, however, that the causes of romanticism and nationalism finally seem to fuse. His attachments to Italy and Greece and his longing for their freedom were, through the medium of his poetry, to reach a wide audience and undoubtedly helped to create a body of opinion favourable to them, that was materially to assist in the winning of Greek independence.

> Fair Greece! Sad relic of departed worth!
> Immortal, though no more; though fallen, great!
> Who now shall lead thy scatter'd children forth,
> And long accustom'd bondage uncreate?

This was Byron's question in 'Childe Harold' (published in 1812) and his own death at Missolonghi in 1824, during the Greek revolt against the Turks, might be construed as his attempt to find the answer.

Byron did much to fire Delacroix, the French romantic painter, and some of the latter's subjects, such as 'The Massacre of Chios', clearly show his influence. In his well-known 'Liberty on the Barricades' Delacroix typifies the conjunction of the romantic artist and the commitment to political liberties. 'We work till our last gasp, what else is there to do except get drunk when reality no longer corresponds with one's dreams,' he wrote.

Yet in Byron himself, closer scrutiny shows this picture of romanticism to be too facile. Hater of despotism he was, but sometimes rather in the tradition of an eighteenth-century English Tory squire than that of the conventional romantic in love with his fellow men.

'. . . I think them [the Austrians] damned scoundrels and barbarians, their emperor a fool, and themselves more fools than he; all which they may send to Vienna, for anything I care. They have got themselves masters of the Papal police, and are bullying away; but some day or other they will pay for it all. It may not be very soon, because these unhappy Italians have no union or consistency among themselves; but I suppose Providence will get tired of them at last, and show that God is not Austrian.' So Byron wrote in 1820, and in another letter his list of the requirements of the Greeks fighting for their freedom against the Turks—'first, a park of field artillery—light and fit for mountain service; secondly, gunpowder' —demonstrates a realism perhaps not usually associated with a romantic poet. On the other hand the attempt, in 1832, by the Duchess of Berry, to raise France for her son and initiate a Bourbon restoration, was just as romantic in its conception as any escapade of the time.

In fact many of the romantics were to turn in horror against the revolution in France and tie themselves in the future firmly to reaction, fearing the tyranny of the mass which they saw emerging as the direct effect of revolution. Others were to feed upon the historical revival, so often a part of romanticism, and thus be drawn back by their diet to a belief in traditional authority, both civil and ecclesiastical. They looked backwards to Arcadia rather than forwards to Utopia. In this context can be seen the conversion to Catholicism of such men as Friedrich Schlegel and the romantic dramatist Wermer. Wermer, indeed, was ordained a priest and in the Vienna of 1814 preached reaction from the pulpit before vast congregations, among them the assembled diplomats of Europe.

The closer the study of the romantics and their writings, the more woebegone the generalizations become. Walter Scott, often seen as one who helped to scatter the seeds of romanticism, really had little of the romantic about him. Of course he shared the fascination with the past felt by many of the romantics. His popularization of the Border ballads and his revival of the Middle Ages in his novels were seminal. However, his cast of mind was hostile to the true romantic; 'of all sorts of parade I think the parade of feeling and sentiment most disgusting,' he wrote.

Romanticism, as manifested in the culture of the period, was affected by social and political changes, and it, in turn, helped to direct these changes. 'I do not know what we must believe, but I believe that we must believe,' said Madame de Staël.

Part of the difficulty in classifying romanticism stems from the essential paradox at its core. The striving, the pitting of self against fate or against nature must be set alongside the search for peace and tranquillity, the longing for equilibrium, again expressed in the relationship of man to nature.

At any rate, a movement which, described by some as the parent of the Oxford Movement and by others as the originator of revolutionary republicanism, is far too complex to be seen merely as one of the streams of revolutionary heritage—a force for change.

PART TWO

IMMOVABLE OBJECT

Chapter IV

CONSERVATISM AND PRINCE METTERNICH

S O MUCH for the forces of change; what of the opposition which they had to encounter? Not surprisingly, voices were soon raised in alarm at events in France. Some of these were the voices of people who were physically suffering from the results of the revolution. Monarchs and aristocrats, who had lost their thrones and their lands, were certain to extend their hatred of the revolution which had uprooted them into a hatred of revolution in general. Their opinions were shared by those who, although not affected directly, nevertheless recognized the revolution as a threat to their way of life and interests. The Jacobin period of the French Revolution, with the execution of the king and the Terror, added many to the number of those who were shocked and terrified by what they saw as a breakdown of law and order. 'We have a great and awful example before our eyes of the effects of wild theory and speculation which by attempting to reform real abuses, has produced a system and scene of horror unequalled in the history of the World. . . . In short if the Governments of Europe do not destroy Jacobinism, Jacobinism will eventually succeed in destroying them.' In describing events in this way Lord Darnley was not untypical of what even the more liberal of his class thought.

However, all opposition was not in the form of empiric reaction to the effects of the revolution. There was also a general philosophic attack on the principles of Enlightenment which were seen as having produced the revolution. The belief that the individual and society could advance towards perfection through the use of reason was ridiculed by writers. Perhaps the best known of such attacks was that of Edmund Burke who, in his *Reflections on the French Revolution* and other writings, scorned the vanity of men who imagined that they could impose doctrinaire abstractions on society against the historic background. He believed in history, 'the known march of the ordinary providence of God', and human experience, as the only real basis for society and its constitutions. He attacked the whole attempt at abstract judgment and explained his distrust by asking the question, 'am I to congratulate a highwayman and a murderer who has broken prison, upon the recovery of his Natural Rights?' 'The circumstances are what render every civil and political scheme beneficial or noxious to mankind,' he argued. In Burke and many who followed him, the principles of conservatism, the justification of the authority of a king, an aristocracy or a church, were found in history. And sometimes this appeal to tradition even became a harking back to a supposed golden era in the past, often rejecting as well the advance of the Industrial Revolution.

In some cases, notably the French *émigrés* de Bonald and de Maistre, the attacks on Man's attempts to build his own Utopia had a religious basis. De Maistre saw authority as theocratic, resting upon the power of the Pope and hence he preached Ultramontanism. He went so far as to see the revolution as a punishment for unbelief. Lammenais, a French priest, who was eventually to move through a liberal Catholic stage before emerging as a near socialist, was an ardent ultramontane who saw the Church as the only fountain of authority.

However, in addition to this philosophical explanation of the alliance of Throne and Altar being the backbone of the Restoration, there was another, more practical, reason for the Church's support of the restored monarchs. The Church had suffered at the hands of revolution, both in France and wherever the French armies went. Lands and endowments were confiscated; priests imprisoned, tortured and killed. Two Popes, Pius VI and Pius VII, had both been seized by the agents of the revolution and subjected to acute physical discomfort. Popular movements against the revolution such as that in La Vendée, and the Sanfedisti in Italy in 1799, had derived their inspiration, and sometimes their leaders, from the Church. However, beyond all this, the Pope had a further reason for his opposition to popular sovereignty and the principles of revolution. No Pope since the Council of Trent had doubted that the spiritual government of the Church should be autocratic, both by apostolic tradition and practical necessity. This fixed belief led to the inability of successive Popes to conceive of the secular government of the Papal States as not being autocratic. So long, therefore, as Popes were committed to being absolute rulers in their own states, they were really committed to the support of absolutism elsewhere.

More than any other individual of the time Prince Clemens von Metternich, foreign minister and, after 1821, Chancellor of the Austrian Empire, seemed to symbolize opposition to change. 'Metternich was a principle; a banner which one part of the century followed while another stood up against it,' wrote one contemporary; another pictured him as 'the Don Quixote of legitimacy'. Those who wished for change, a policy of movement, saw in the Austrian Chancellor their enemy; just as he saw all conspiracies as part of one universal conspiracy, so they discerned in all obstruction and opposition the hand of Metternich.

Subsequently, as well as during his lifetime, he has been seen as a man who sought to dam up the flood of history and finally, in the absence of any constructive and statesmanlike plan, was submerged and swept away when the dam broke. He is blamed for merely seeking to dam rather than divert or harness, and castigated for not realizing the inevitability of the deluge nor seeing that the extent of the catastrophe might well only be increased by its postponement. Metternich himself once employed the metaphor of the dam when describing the situation which confronted him. 'If you had on your estate, on that high ground which overlooks the Elbe, a vast reservoir threatening at any moment to flood your rich fields and which must one day overflow, would you straightway breach the dam and let the torrent ravage your lands? Would you not rather pierce it carefully and let the water flow out slowly and safely in order to irrigate your fields instead of devastating them?' However, it is difficult to detect any sign of such an attempt in his own policies.

There is a passage in his memoirs where Metternich, describing his momentous interview with Napoleon at Dresden in 1813 when he was seeking to mediate between France and the Prussian-Russian Alliance, says: 'I felt myself, at this crisis, the representative of all European Society.' If this was so it was the European Society of the eighteenth century and, though he may have emerged victorious in 1814 from his confrontation with Napoleon, Metternich and the European society of the eighteenth century were eventually to collapse before the new forces which challenged them. Thus Metternich has been attacked both as the man who fought to prevent the new world being born and as the man who failed to prevent the old world dying. He may have spent his life 'in propping up mouldering edifices' as he claimed, but he never tried to pull them down and rebuild, incorporating new materials and new techniques.

Even so, a closer look at Metternich and his policies today, from the vantage point of the hundred years from which he always asked to be judged, reveals a much more complicated type of conservative than the blind reactionary as whom he has so often been portrayed. An examination of the symbol will help to show just what manner of conservatism confronted the revolution.

The Metternichs came from the Rhineland, where their estates consisting of some seventy-five square miles and containing six and a half thousand people, straddled the Mosel between Trier and Coblenz. It was in Coblenz in 1773 that Clemens Metternich was born. His father, Franz Georg, was a Reichsgraf, one of the Imperial nobility, owing allegiance to no one but the Emperor, in whose service he worked. It was only after 1791, when Franz Georg became Minister Resident for the Austrian Netherlands, that he began to serve the Habsburgs in their capacity as hereditary rulers rather than as Emperors of the old Holy Roman Empire. Because of this background, which education at the Universities of Strasbourg and Mainz did nothing to counteract, Clemens Metternich was never provincial in his habits or tastes and always demonstrated a Europeanism in his outlook. (His father wrote to him at the university, advising the need to improve his German and intimating that they would correspond in German to this end although he might continue to write to his mother in French.)

Metternich first encountered the French Revolution while a student at Strasbourg, when he witnessed the plundering of the Stadthaus, 'perpetrated by a drunken mob which considered itself the people'. Because of the collapse of Austrian rule in the Netherlands before the French invasion, which his tenure of office had done little to prevent, Franz Georg left the Low Countries and moved to Vienna in search of future employment. A new source of income was particularly important because the French armies had also overrun the Rhineland and with it the Metternichs' own lands. Perhaps the most important result of the Metternichs' removal to Vienna was the marriage in 1795 of Clemens to the Princess Eleanor, granddaughter of the old Austrian Chancellor Kaunitz. Although an arranged match, the marriage would have been unlikely to have occurred had not the Princess fallen in love with Metternich; certainly he was not a very important capture. This connection was to help the young Metternich in his career, as was the Emperor's appointment of Coblenzl as his Foreign Minister in 1801. Coblenzl was a friend of the Metternich family and was behind the young Metternich's posting as ambassador to the Saxon Court at Dresden in the same year. From Dresden Metternich was moved to Berlin in 1803 and then, in 1806 at the request of Napoleon, became ambassador in Paris. This swift rise was completed in 1809 when, in the aftermath of the Austrian defeat at Wagram, Francis made Metternich his Foreign Minister. This was notwithstanding the fact that the war policy, the failure of which Wagram had signified, had been undertaken partly because of Metternich's advocacy from Paris.

The critical year which followed, culminating in the defeat of Napoleon, fully justified the speed of his promotion and, in 1813, earned him the reward of being raised to the dignity of an Austrian prince. The ascendancy which Metternich built up among the politicians serving Francis received its full recognition when, in 1821, he became Court Chancellor and Chancellor of State. These then, in brief outline, were the circumstances of the rise to power of the great conservative Chancellor.

To move from Metternich's rise to his personality and character is, at once, to find reasons why he has been so much disliked. Perhaps the first impression which strikes the historian who goes to Metternich's writing is one of his conceit and vanity; the assurance that he alone knew what was right. Certainly many of his contemporaries saw him as arrogant. He writes in his memoirs, 'I cannot help telling myself twenty times a day: "O Lord! how right I am and how wrong they are!" '; of his reflections upon himself compared with other statesmen. The manner in which he writes of other people has the effect of raising him above his fellows and conveys that this position, in the writer's eyes, is the one he is accustomed to in society. His remark to Guizot, his fellow exile after the 1848 revolutions, '*L'erreur ne s'est jamais approché de mon esprit*', may have been ironic but certainly his account of his reactions to reading a newly published book on his part in the events of 1814 is not. Feeling called upon to try and judge himself after three hours reading, he finds it impossible to accuse himself of any mistake or negligence. Metternich's conceit extended to his fastidiousness in dress and manner and he always seems to have been supremely conscious of the impression he was making on others. But not only in political and social intercourse is his vanity apparent; even when musing on the improvements to the garden of his estate he considers 'my own skill does the undertaking no harm'.

This belief in his infallibility naturally led Metternich to talk constantly of himself, a trait which, with the years, became garrulousness. His ceaseless propounding of the principles on which he acted and his self-justification and praise were increasingly boring to his listeners. Bores are seldom popular and the later Metternich certainly wearied his acquaintances. This loquacity was perhaps sometimes merely a symptom of his prevarication. 'Sir, I have sat in Council with Prince Metternich for twenty-five years and it has always been his habit to speak there without coming to the point;' claimed one colleague. His indecisiveness has been put down to a lack of courage; 'Metternich is a man who shrinks from every vigorous measure,' was the view of Stein. Perhaps it was the result of his enjoyment of the practice, rather than the end-product, of intrigue. Wellington saw Metternich as considering 'all policy as consisting in finesse and trick'.

Conceited, sententious, opinionated, indecisive and a bore; the mixture is hardly one to attract. But what perhaps damned Metternich more in the judgment of the latter half of the nineteenth century was his air of frivolity; viewed by itself, despicable, but in obstructing progress, unsupportable. This lightweight quality was demonstrated in the manner of his love affairs; the almost feminine curiosity which he passed off as a genuine scientific enthusiasm; and his dilettantism towards the arts. Revealing here is his account of how he read novels, always turning to the last page first so that he might see which characters were killed and which married. The comment of Mme de Lieven on his second marriage in 1827, '*le chevalier de la Sainte Alliance a maintenant fini par une mésalliance*', captures this aura of flippancy and irresponsibility which surrounded him.

Yet, of course, Metternich was far more than this. His vanity was also his style, his fastidiousness was his elegance and his prevarication often the result of his awareness and the product of his intelligence. For one who rose so far and so fast on charm, good fortune and intelligence it is not surprising that the younger Metternich gives the impression of the lightweight and the lucky.

After 1815, with time and failure, he became less brittle, more serious and his personality deepened. To read his letters on personal matters, such as the death of his daughter Clemantine, at once reveals a man of sensitivity and feeling. After her death he describes how those sitting at conference with him, hour by hour, during the days of his fears and grief, have detected nothing. 'I have, happily, the gift of keeping my feelings to myself, even when my heart is half-broken.'

The butterfly, with which Metternich is sometimes equated, does not know that its life is to be so short. It does not consciously flutter in defiance of its imminent extinction. Metternich once wrote, 'I am a child of light and need brilliant light to be able to live.' But he knew that the sun which shone was going to set. At Clemantine's death he explains, 'I soon return to business, which makes a barrier between me and myself.' In the course of his long career Metternich must often have needed to 'return to business'; to clothe himself in his vanity and omniscience.

But the unpopularity of Prince Metternich was above all due to the policies he pursued, and thus to the principles upon which his policies were based. Metternich himself would never acknowledge that he had a 'system' but claimed that basic principles, underlying history, could be ascertained and serve the statesman as guideposts. Historians have argued as to just how much Metternich did base his actions upon 'principles' or to what extent he was merely an opportunist who cynically rationalized his behaviour after the event. Much of this controversy is artificial, however, since Metternich never claimed to have discovered before he became a practising politican a coherent political philosophy which he proceeded to apply. Obviously, some of the philosophy he met at university rubbed off on the not over-industrious student, and as he began to experience events at first hand his experiences fused with his cast of thought to produce an amalgam. To seek to disentangle the two parts, though of interest, becomes a sterile exercise when taken to extremes. He was far too flexible and realistic to believe that the statesman should not change his mind. 'The most enlightened and unyielding of governments must come to terms with the best established usurpation,' he conceded over the Greek Revolt. His principles were the result of his experiences and impressions, yes; but this is not to say that they were cynical and insincere.

First among Metternich's beliefs was his attachment to repose;

repose between states, repose within states. This repose, or order, could only exist in a state of equilibrium and it was the prime object of statesmen to preserve this equilibrium. Hence the antipathy shown by Metternich to the revolution which was affecting Europe throughout his adult life, his theoretical attachment to the preservation of the balance being completely confirmed by his own experiences. From the time of his own first meeting with the French Revolution at Strasbourg, 'the doctrines of the Jacobins and their appeal to the passions of the people, excited in me an aversion which age and experience have only strengthened'. 'I considered,' he wrote, 'the Revolution, as it burst forth in France in 1789, as the starting point of all the misfortunes of Europe.' He could still write in 1832, 'there is only one serious matter in Europe and that is revolution', and he sought until his fall in 1848 to preserve Europe from once again suffering its ravages.

Metternich saw the cause of revolution as based on Man's presumption. He thought that the rapid progress of human knowledge had outstripped the growth of wisdom with the result that man had come to believe that he was able to find answers to all problems which faced him. 'Presumption . . . makes him, in short, the sole judge of his own faith, his own actions, and the principles according to which he guides them.'

Metternich detected this presumption as present mainly in members of the middle class. 'It is principally the middle classes of society which this moral gangrene has affected, and it is only among them that the real heads of the party are found'. Though members of the upper classes may occasionally join with them the agitated class is 'principally composed of wealthy men . . . paid state officials, men of letters, lawyers, and the individuals charged with the public education.' The restless classes were, to Metternich, motivated by personal greed and ambition and were seeking to produce disorder which they would then exploit for their own ends. 'They resemble those opportunists who break into the house which they have set on fire, not to save the valuables, but to make off with them.' He feared their ability to exploit others particularly because of the liberty which the press enjoyed, 'a scourge unknown to the world before the latter half of the seventeenth century and restrained until the end of the eighteenth century'. Metternich believed that his age possessed 'more than any preceding age the means of contact, seduction, and attraction whereby to act on these different classes of men'. Among the middle class he did not particularly fear the students, he referred to their societies as unpractical puppet-shows; nor the professors, who he believed to be most unsuited to conspiracy. The danger he dreaded from the universities was that they might produce a whole generation steeped in revolutionary attitudes. Sometimes these fears of Metternich and his search for plots and revolts even created the evidence he was looking for. In the words of the British diplomat Sir Robert Gordon, 'Nothing can surpass Prince Metternich's activities in collecting facts and information upon the inward feeling of the people.' But Gordon goes on to hazard that 'phantoms are conjured up and magnified in the dark, which probably if exposed to light, would sink into insignificance; and his informers naturally exaggerate their reports, aware that their profit is to be commensurate with the display of their phantasmagoria'.

Faced with this restlessness the government, above all, must govern. The disruption and disorder which threatened Europe should be checked, allowing a period of quiet in which there might be some chance of equilibrium re-emerging. In the meantime, governments must fight to preserve everything that was legal because the malcontents were seeking to destroy legality. Believing that 'if monarchies disappear, it is because they give up', Metternich saw the people, as a whole, finding no appeal in this 'presumption' and in abstract theories of progress and improvement. 'The wishes of the immense majority of the people are to maintain a repose which exists no longer.' 'The first principle to be followed by the monarchs . . . should be that of maintaining the stability of political institutions against the disorganized excitement which has taken possession of men's minds; . . . and respect for the laws actually in force against a desire for their destruction.' If changes were to be made they should be made voluntarily by the governments and never wrung from them as the price of compromise.

However, the danger of revolution was more than just a threat to the state where it existed. Besides there being the danger of a successful revolution spreading, disorder in a state was likely to lead to war between states, since it upset the equilibrium of their inter-relationship.* 'When anarchy reaches a climax in any great

* A modern counterpart to this belief might be seen in the 'Domino Theory' of the U.S.A. in South-East Asia.

state it always leads to a civil or foreign war and often both tribula-
tions at once.' It was this reason as well as his natural 'European'
attitude that induced Metternich to see the problem of revolution
in a wider context than that of any one country. 'Since, however,
an isolated state no longer exists . . . we must always view the
society of nations as the essential condition of the present world.'
This was why governments must hold together to resist revolution.
Just as the individual must have the right to put out a fire in a
neighbour's house which threatens his own; a state should intervene
if events elsewhere threaten its security. However, Metternich
never believed in intervention as a matter of principle; there were
occasions after 1815, for instance French intervention in Spain,
when he disapproved of one state meddling in another's affairs.

This conviction partly followed from the Chancellor's belief that
relations between states were dependent upon those states' permanent interests, something deeper than their constitutions or
religious and governmental ideologies. 'States which are subjected
to the representative system are not for that reason either the
natural allies of each other or the implacable enemies of states under
a different system.' Metternich felt that the permanent interests
were determined by geographical and environmental characteristics
and obviously the statesman who wished to be successful in his
handling of foreign affairs must base his policies upon their correct
appraisal.*

When considering the principles and beliefs from which Metternich formulated his policies, it should be stressed that he saw
the same need for repose between states as inside them. The
equilibrium which he strove to preserve might be challenged by one
state, forgetting the fundamental requirement of reciprocity in its
dealing with other states, seeking to dominate its fellows. This
challenge could be met by the other states coming together to
resist it—the classical balance of power.

At the age of twenty-eight, in his first state paper, Metternich
laid down what he thought to be the main object of the new alliances
which Austria should seek as 'the invigorating of our political
forces, the preservation of internal peace, and the attainment of a

---

* This assurance is the cause of some of the resentment felt by Metternich
for Canning when the latter pursued policies over the Greek Revolt which
Metternich was sure were against the permanent interests of Great Britain.

position which, as far as unforeseen circumstances allow, will enable us to act a part corresponding to the extent and power of the first rank'. These aims of the young diplomat were to remain the aims of the mature statesman, and not just in regard to choosing alliances, but fundamental to all his policies.

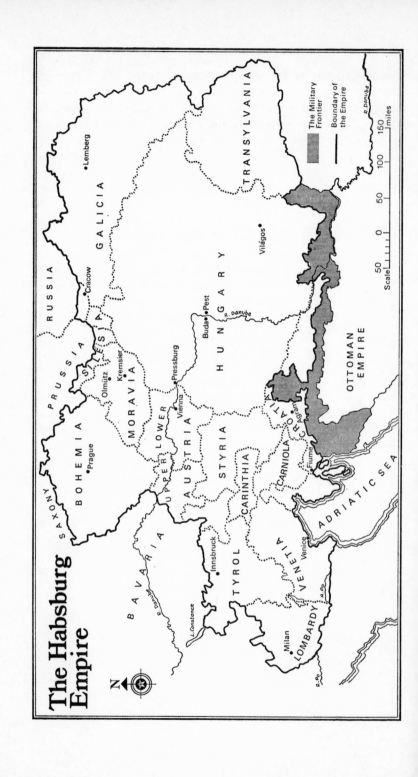

The Habsburg Empire

N

The Military Frontier

Boundary of the Empire

Scale

50   0   50   100   150
miles

RUSSIA

PRUSSIA

SAXONY

BOHEMIA
•Prague

SILESIA

GALICIA
•Lemberg

•Cracow

MORAVIA
Olmütz•
•Kremsier

LOWER
UPPER
AUSTRIA

Vienna•
•Pressburg

HUNGARY

Buda•
•Pest
R. Danube

•Világos

TRANSYLVANIA

BAVARIA

R. Danube

L. Constance

Innsbruck•

TYROL

STYRIA

CARINTHIA

CARNIOLA

CROATIA

Fiume•

•Zagreb

OTTOMAN
EMPIRE

VENETIA

Venice•

LOMBARDY

Milan•

R. Po

R. Po

ADRIATIC SEA

R. Danube

Chapter V

THE HABSBURG EMPIRE

THE AUSTRIAN EMPIRE, which Metternich served for his entire working life, was, as such, created in 1804. Before then the Habsburg rulers were only Emperors in so far as they were the Holy Roman Emperors. Thus Maria Theresa had for a time not been Empress, and had merely held a series of titles, rather than one common unifying one, to depict her sovereignty over her hereditary lands. The Austrian Empire, although supplying a single title, is a misleading description, in that it implies the hegemony of a particular power over a larger area, as with the British and Roman Empires. Other empires in history such as the Napoleonic Empire or the Empire of Alexander have been named after an individual, implying the crucial role in their construction played by that individual. But the Austrian Empire did not represent the political or military supremacy of one state or people, nor did it form the conquests of one man. It was, fundamentally, a territorial aggregation built up by marriage and inheritance in one family.

Probably, the most accurate description of the Empire is the one by which it is often referred to, albeit incorrectly, the Habsburg Empire. Though becoming the Austrian Empire in 1804 and the Austro-Hungarian Empire in 1867, the Habsburg lands were united only in the reigning dynasty, and of course the collapse of the Empire coincided with the collapse of the dynasty.

The Monarchy has been aptly described by one historian as 'a kind of vast holding company, under which a great many subsidiary corporate structures remained very much alive'. Geographically it was, in fact, to change its composition during the years of its existence; the revolutionary and Napoleonic wars together with the peace that followed were to see contraction and expansion as well as alteration. However, the heartlands remained the same: the historic kingdoms of Bohemia and Hungary with their

59

tributary provinces and the hereditary duchies of south-east Germany centred on the 'East Mark' of the old German monarchy, Austria.

Because of the way in which the territories had been acquired the union remained purely personal, in the actual person of the ruler, in defiance of the Pragmatic Sanction of 1713 which had sought to make the Habsburg lands a legal unit. Thus the Hungarian lands owed their allegiance to the king of Hungary and not to the Austrian monarch. It is not possible to discern any logical reason why these parts should have constituted a whole. There was no fundamental economic or geographical unity, despite, with the exception of the Netherlands, their physical proximity. The Empire had no common nationality or language and it did not even share the same religion (besides Catholics and Protestants many of its subjects were of the Orthodox Church). Some of the Habsburg lands were part of the old Holy Roman Empire and were to be part of the German Confederation, whereas others, such as the kingdom of Hungary, were not.

Any attempt to comprehend the history of the lands governed by the Habsburgs demands some understanding of the people who inhabited them. The pattern of the differing peoples which comprised the Habsburg Empire was the product of migration: its particularly complicated nature arose not only from several migrations but because they came from different directions. First, there had been, in the early Middle Ages, the movement of Slav peoples westwards, pressing up against and mixing with German peoples who themselves had come from the east. Then another people from the east, a fierce, nomadic, warrior race, the Magyars, spread across the surface of the Slav peoples. They moved farther west, terrorizing and plundering as far as the Atlantic coast, before finally being penned back into the Danube valley by the efforts of the German monarchs. A proud and warlike people, they continued to control the lands alongside those in which they settled, inhabited by other peoples.

Later, in the period of the Middle Ages which saw the Crusades in the Holy Land and the Reconquista in Spain, German Christians, also in search of booty, lands and salvation, carried the Cross eastwards against the Slav peoples. In the far north a Crusading Order, the Teutonic Knights, created what was to be the ancestor of Prussia, but, farther south also, Germans conquered and converted the people they found in their path, appropriating their lands. Thus, the Slavs who were washed over by this German tide found themselves being ruled by German landlords and German bishops and owing allegiance to the Church of Rome. Although the German military advance was halted and even, in places, thrown back, German merchants and traders continued the eastward migration. They followed the rivers and the sea, often settling in the midst of Slavic peoples at some important river-crossing or natural harbour. In the south, along the Mediterranean coast, a similar advance occurred but here the traders were Italians.

Farther south and east, Christianization was also proceeding, but stemming from the Eastern Roman Empire, Orthodox rather than Roman. However, the close of the Middle Ages witnessed yet another movement westwards, of a non-Christian people: the Ottoman Turks. They destroyed the states in their path until they came up against the Habsburg states in south-east Germany. The Ottoman advance was also checked and the Germans resumed their drive eastwards. Bohemia, defeated at the Battle of the White Mountain in the early stages of the Thirty Years War, was settled by Germans and others who were loyal to the Habsburgs. However the kingdom of Hungary (the old Magyar-dominated lands) although added to the Habsburg possessions was never conquered and resettled as Bohemia had been. Likewise when Italian lands were acquired by the dynasty, or Polish territory during the partitions of that kingdom, no colonization occurred which might drive out the landowners and plant a new class of alien colonists.

Therefore, omitting the Netherlands which were lost in the wars with revolutionary France and not regained, the people of the Empire can be placed in two categories. First, those sometimes described as the 'dominant nations', the Germans, the Magyars, the Italians and the Poles. These peoples were represented at all social levels, from that of the peasant to that of the landlord, and it was they in the main who provided the landlord class: the local dignitaries, the urban middle class and the Imperial bureaucracy. The second category embraced the 'subject nations': the Czechs, the Slovaks, the Croats, the Ruthenes, the Serbs and the Slovenes as well as the non-Slavic Rumanians from Transylvania. They were primarily peasant nations and had few representatives among the socially dominant classes; the representatives they did have usually adopted the culture of the rest of their class. However, even this broad classification is not strictly accurate, as the Croatian gentry, for example, cut across it.

The great nobles, with the exception of the Poles and the Italians, did see themselves as belonging to the whole rather than to the part where their lands lay. This was largely because they owed their lands and positions in the first place to the Habsburgs and they never really came to identify with their localities and the people who lived there; instead they looked to Vienna and the Habsburgs' Court as their kernel. In 1815, this state of affairs still applied to the Hungarian magnates, who to some extent continued to take the part of Vienna against the people of Hungary, but very soon their attitude was to change as they came to identify more with their fellow Magyars. The only other factors for unity in the Habsburg Empire were the army and the bureaucracy, the latter being German in culture if not always in origin.

The error of seeing the Habsburg Empire as representing a colonial power riveted on top of a number of distinct nations, each one seeking the destruction of the state and the opportunity to express itself independently, should now be manifest. Certainly it is an error which precludes any understanding of the history of the state and certainly it was the reason why so many European liberals of the time completely failed to comprehend the situation.

The eighteenth century faced governments all over Europe with the need to raise more money to finance increasing expenditure, particularly expenditure on war. Existing taxes could be increased but this remedy always proved unpopular and often decreasingly productive. The two most obvious ways for governments to enlarge their revenue were to extend taxation to the untaxed, or anyhow the under-taxed, and to increase the yield of the current taxes. The latter approach could be accomplished by cutting down on inefficiency and corruption in tax collection, and by encouraging a growth in national income, the wealth on which taxes were raised. It is this solution rather than abstract theory, which really affords the explanation for the actions of those monarchs described as the 'Enlightened Despots'.

Among the eighteenth-century governments, none perhaps was faced with more need for change and reform than that of the Habsburg Empire. The Seven Years War had demonstrated quite clearly that the existing revenue was quite inadequate, despite earlier attempts to increase it. Thus it was that under Maria

Theresa, Joseph II and Leopold II the Habsburgs took the lead as the great reforming monarchy of Europe. The reforms gathered pace with the death of Maria Theresa, so much so that their author, her son Joseph, has been termed the 'revolutionary Emperor' and the 'crowned Jacobin'. He sought to initiate a uniform tax throughout his lands which, based on income derived from land, would be much more equitable than the existing taxes. The new tax would apply to the nobility who had previously been grossly undertaxed and in many areas untaxed. To this end Joseph instituted a new land registration. And to accompany his tax reforms the Emperor set about emancipating the serfs. He aimed at a general commutation of their forced labour services, generally termed the Robot. He decreed their personal freedom and tried to remove them from the jurisdiction of their landlords in criminal matters, seeking to extend the state's criminal jurisdiction to include them. In order to further the economic expansion of his lands Joseph encouraged competition by restricting the powers of the guilds, by granting religious toleration to foster immigration, and by allowing the freedom to pursue any occupation. 'I am prepared to grant the right of citizenship to anyone who is qualified, who can be of use to us, and who can further industrial activity in our country,' wrote Joseph. At the same time he tried to expand home production by pursuing a fiercely protectionist policy with regard to his territories as a whole. Partly because of his introduction of toleration, partly because of its role as an obstructionist vested interest, Joseph found himself proceeding against the Church. Attacks on the contemplative Orders brought him money from the sale of monastic lands, which he used in his general reorganization of the Church as the religious organ of the body politic.

It is not surprising, especially when the lack of real political unity in the Habsburg lands is taken into account, that Joseph's policy encountered bitter opposition from those who were privileged. In Hungary for instance, to ensure that the land was properly surveyed as a preliminary to being registered, troops were required. Joseph, although enormously industrious and almost entirely politically directed, lacked patience and tact. When faced with opposition his usual tactic was merely to apply more pressure and certainly not to compromise.

However, it was Joseph's over-optimistic foreign policy which finally precipitated the collapse of his plans. An unpopular and expensive war with Turkey led to open disaffection; the Habsburg government in the Netherlands broke down and the Hungarian nobility, backed by a wide section of the people, stood in outright defiance of their sovereign. Joseph was forced to withdraw at least some of his reforms if he wished to preserve the integrity of the monarchy. But it was not merely the partial surrender to the entrenched section of privilege that lay behind the reversal of the reforming and enlightened policies of the Habsburgs, ushering in the age of conservatism and reaction. By itself, this merely might have led to delay, not a change in direction.

Encouraged by the policies of reform, there were emerging in the Fourth Estate (in the Habsburg Empire the nobility and knights were two separate estates) a growing number of people who demanded root and branch change. The restriction of aristocratic privilege led to a questioning of privilege as such. Reforms of the Church were followed by a growth of scepticism and the fashion for irreligion among the educated middle classes; and not solely the educated middle class either, for the loss of faith was reported to extend to 'cobblers and scythe makers'. The Hungarian Public Prosecutor said of the students that 'one generation was ruined'. Peasant agitation was caused by frustration and delays in reforms being carried out and the lack of a significant amelioration of their lot. The Turkish war, with its ensuing increase in taxation, the rise in prices and food shortages fused together the mood of intransigence and opposition. 'One looks in vain now for these . . . loyal and contented people,' was the comment of one police official.

It was this opposition and dissent which first alarmed Joseph into a reconsideration of his policies; he became anxious about the spread of attitudes which, in his own words, seemed 'to undermine all religion, morality and social stability'. In 1786 he established the police as a separate government department under its own minister, the reactionary Count Pergen. They ceased to be primarily concerned with law enforcement and instead sought to control public opinion and search out popular disaffection. 'To discover any discontent arising among the people, all dangerous thought and especially any incipient rebellion, and to nip them in the bud where possible,' was how Count Pergen saw his department's duties. He did not scruple to go outside the normal and prescribed processes of the law in order to secure the arrest and punishment of those he considered dangerous. At the same time, education was brought under strict supervision and censorship was tightened up, considerably restricting the press. Thus Joseph's retreat from 'enlightenment' was carried out on two levels. Firstly, he introduced measures of restriction and repression to deal with dissatisfaction primarily among the Fourth Estate. Secondly, on his deathbed in 1790, he partially surrendered to the privileged classes.

His successor, Leopold II, perhaps the most astute of eighteenth-century monarchs, had learned his statecraft as Grand Duke of Tuscany. He immediately set about pacifying Prussia and disentangling himself from foreign embroilment as the only way of strengthening his position at home; subsequently strenuously resisting any premature military involvement against the revolution in France to help his sister Marie Antoinette. He appeared to give way to many of the demands of the nobles by withdrawing Joseph's patent on the land tax and the commutation of forced labour services of the peasants. Also, he summoned all the Provincial Estates to provide further opportunity for the voicing of discontent.

However, some of this apparent appeasement was merely finesse, for at the same time he smiled on peasant resistance to the re-introduction of the Robot. He allowed the cities to petition for representation in the Diets, in the case of the province of Styria with success. He even sponsored the publication of works attacking aristocratic pretensions in Hungary. In this manner Leopold, by playing off resentments in the Fourth Estate, was able to moderate the feudal reaction. He reversed some of Joseph's decisions on the police, insisting that they remain under the authority of the law and ending their separate existence as an autonomous body of state, with the result that Count Pergen resigned and was not replaced. So long as Leopold lived, with his bold and imaginative policy, it would be incorrect to talk of reaction from the Habsburg throne. However, even Leopold, despite his consummate diplomacy, might in the end have found himself in the position, which his son more readily accepted, of war with revolutionary France, and this assuredly would have enforced modifications. As it was he unexpectedly died in March of 1792 and was succeeded by his inexperienced, twenty-four-year-old son, Francis.

Francis II, entirely lacking his father's delicacy of touch and imagination, was of a conservative and autocratic cast.* He had

* He became Francis I with the dissolution of the Holy Roman Empire in 1806.

C*

neither the wish nor the ability to pursue Leopold's policies. Although not a brutal man he had no belief in constitutionalism and enlightenment, thus the secret police re-emerged and in 1793 Pergen resumed control as autonomous Minister of Police. Similarly, censorship became stricter and a tighter watch was kept on dissent. It was the war which really shaped Francis's attitude, however, for the need for financial assistance from the provincial Estates demanded that he should win the support of the privileged orders who controlled them. At the same time the war with its attendant economic burdens was extremely unpopular among the Fourth Estate and led to increased opposition. War also meant that this opposition gained added significance, particularly in the light of events in Paris and in the context of the Empire's military failure. Such was the background of the so-called Jacobin Conspiracies, one of which occurred in Austria and one in Hungary.

Although, in reality, the conspiracies posed little threat to Francis, the trials and punishments which followed in 1795 nevertheless led to a much more repressive policy. In a series of edicts, among other measures, capital punishment was restored for civilians (it had in fact never been abolished in Hungary) and to stir up discontent in print was made a punishable offence. The power of the police was enormously increased; in 1801 they gained control of the censorship and they became much more rigorous in their supervision of government officials, many of whom, because of their past connections, were suspected of dragging their feet in the new reactionary policies. Soon, applications for teaching posts had to be submitted to the Ministry of Police and education was much more closely controlled; Francis saw education as being concerned with the production of 'well-behaved religious and patriotic citizens'. Industrial growth was retarded since its results were seen as potentially disruptive. Towns were restricted in size, as were individual firms, so as to minimize the numbers of the proletariat. Finally, doubts as to whether the Robot should be compulsorily commuted were resolved, the peasants remaining subject to it until 1848.

Joseph II had said of his nephew Francis, 'he hates reflection'. Certainly the events of the 'Jacobin Conspiracies', following the young Emperor's experiences of the results of his uncle's reforms, combined with events in France to give him a hatred of all change and reform. From this early point in his reign until his death in

1835, preservation became Francis's first objective, strengthening its hold over his mind with the buffeting that the Empire took at the hands of Napoleon and the French. The Emperor's enormous capacity for hard work (he usually started his working day at seven in the morning) did nothing to compensate for the essential triviality of his mind. The effort and enthusiasm he put into reading the reports of his police spies, besides being indicative of this triviality, was typical of the uselessness of his misdirected interests and energy.

For the Emperor in the Austrian Empire was not merely the source of authority and sovereignty. He was the motor of policy and even administration. The government of the Empire was carried out by departments of the Emperor's Court, which were responsible to him. There was in no sense an Imperial 'government', composed of advisers and ministers with some corporate responsibility and policy. The Emperor was, in effect, his own prime minister with permanent secretaries in charge of each department to serve him. Thus the whole administration of the Empire took on the cautious and immobile pattern cut for it by its master. The bureaucracy, which under Joseph had been designed to preside over and effect a transformation of the Empire, became frozen and static, rigid in its allegiance to maintaining the status quo. 'Believe me, he who has to serve for any time in the immediate entourage of the Emperor, must become either a philosopher or an intriguer or an ox, in order to endure it', was the comment of Count Kolowrat, an Imperial minister of the time.

Despite his frequently expressed admiration for Francis—'few sovereigns have brought more honour to their crown than the Emperor Francis,' he wrote in his memoirs—Metternich was alive to the failings of his master. 'He deals with affairs in the manner of a drill which cuts ever deeper, until suddenly to his surprise he emerges somewhere without having done more than make a hole in a memorandum,' Metternich explains. Later he criticized Francis's preoccupation with watching over the educated classes of society, in which the police became one of the chief instruments of government and in upholding a censorship 'more irritating than efficacious'.

It is thus manifestly incorrect to portray the structure and philosophy of Habsburg government in the Restoration era as part of the reactionary policies of the Chancellor, Prince Metternich.

At times he may have been the pilot, seeking to steer the vessel between shoals and rapids, but his general course, the attempted destination of the voyage, just as it is not the decision of the pilot of the ship, so it was not the decision of Metternich. By 1821, when his appointment as Chancellor gave Metternich some share in the responsibility for domestic matters, the course of the Habsburg Empire was already clear.

However, Metternich did have a policy for Austria and one that he urged upon the Emperor, even if he never did so to the point of threatening resignation unless it were adopted. It developed from his ideas of nationality and the state. He saw nothing false or outdated in a state being based on land owned by a family; something fundamentally opposed to those ideas of nationalism which, developing in the early nineteenth century, saw the state as the expression of a people. Nevertheless Metternich recognized basic differences between the various peoples of the Austrian Empire and never strove to eliminate them. The provincial Diets which, with the exception of the Hungarian, had little power and were purely advisory, representing an extremely narrow section of society, should be patronized; as should the current drive to resuscitate dying native tongues and patois. Metternich was far too hostile and frightened of constitutionalism to allow the formation of the sort of representative institutions which might have led to a true federative structure, but at the same time he did seek to preserve the traditions of the different peoples.

'The Austrian monarchy is a composite whole, formed of separate districts which are historically or legally, from reason of necessity or consideration of prudence, held together by having one common head,' he wrote. This head was the monarchy and no other institution or system of government could unite these lands. 'There is one reason for this, the non-existence of the Austrian people.' He claimed that 'it is impossible to imagine . . . a popular sovereignty superimposed on other sovereignties of the same kind and origin'.

Thus, Metternich was concerned to preserve and extend the various historical provinces and their traditions, but at the same time to strengthen and improve the working of the central, monarchical government: 'the careful regulation of the reasonable long-existing differences sanctioned by speech, climate, manners and customs in the various districts of the monarchy, under a strong, well-organized central government.'

The strengthening and improvement of the central government was to be achieved by various reforms. At the centre of these were to be a newly created Council of Ministers to act as an executive and a larger body, an Imperial Council (Reichsrat), which would be concerned with advice on general policy. In this way, Metternich hoped to overcome the problem of a hopelessly harassed executive, made up of rival departments, totally failing either to co-ordinate their work or to consider the policies behind their actions. Something like the Council of Ministers was created but the Emperor never really sought to develop it and continued to execute his policies by dealing with the different departments separately. The Reichsrat, despite repeated promises by Francis, including one within three months of his death, was never formed. Metternich planned it to consist partly of men nominated by the Emperor and partly of men chosen by the Provincial Diets.

These schemes of Metternich's remained, for the most part, as schemes and were not put into practice. To what extent can the Chancellor be blamed for this; was he not serious enough or was it, as one historian has claimed, because he was merely a sycophant of the Emperor Francis? Certainly he was unable to go against the Emperor's wishes without the danger of dismissal, and this would have achieved little. However, perhaps the most important factor in the Chancellor's lack of determination in the pursuit of his reforms was that, in his heart, he knew the 'Austrian Problem', in the long run, to be insoluble. A dynastically based state such as Austria could not come to terms with the notion of popular sovereignty without dissolution; concession to the forces of change could only result in destruction.

Chapter VI

METTERNICH AND GERMANY

AT FIRST sight, the German Confederation which followed the
Napoleonic period, a travesty of all that the nationalists and
liberals had come to hope for during the final months of the
war against the French Emperor, was a deliberate attempt by
Metternich to thwart the nationalist principle. Certainly the leaders
of the German Vormärz saw Metternich as their arch-enemy whose
fall was necessary before their cause might advance. So, too,
historians have seen him as a man who at best failed to take a great
opportunity because of his craven conservatism, and at worst,
betrayed the German people to the anachronistic structure and the
outdated way of life of his own class. It is true that Metternich was
more responsible than any other man for the creation of the Confederation, and true that it was neither a nationalist nor a liberal
institution. Also it was used by Metternich as a weapon against
change among the German states. It was not, however, the work of
a blind reactionary but largely the outcome of circumstances.

Until 1806, the Holy Roman Empire continued to exist, although
during the final decade it was much concerned with its obsequies.
Described recently as 'an aggregate of authorities with rights', the
Empire had given some expression to the multiplicity of states in
Germany and tried to act as guarantor of their mutual relations.
The Habsburg monarch had, save for a brief period between 1740
and 1745, filled the office of Holy Roman Emperor since the
fifteenth century but the dynasty had gained small profit from the
position. The central problem, which had faced the Habsburgs
since the early sixteenth century, had been that if there was to be
some form of territorial grouping in Germany, although they might
derive little from being its titular head, they could not allow another
prince to hold such an office. For a rival prince as Emperor might
always have been able to manipulate the machinery of the Empire
to the discomfort of the Habsburgs, particularly if allied to one of

the enemies of the dynasty outside Germany. The only other reason in favour of the continued tenure of the Imperial title was that it gave some sort of unity to the Habsburg sovereignty over its scattered lands. During the hegemony of Napoleon, the possibility arose of a reconstruction of the Reich by the French Emperor, either with himself or some vassal at its head. It was the fear of such an eventuality that led Francis to dissolve the Reich in 1806. So, lacking in confidence as to the future of his Empire, it was better for the Emperor that it cease to exist.

The Holy Roman Empire had consisted of over three hundred states, whereas the Confederation which followed the downfall of Napoleon was reduced to thirty-eight (subsequently thirty-nine). Thus obviously the Napoleonic period was of tremendous importance to the history of Germany. Without entering into a detailed narrative the main pattern of these changes can be portrayed quite shortly. First, by a series of steps, the result of military success against German and Habsburg armies, a portion of Germany was incorporated directly into France. In 1797 the left bank of the Rhine was lost but the area was later considerably extended; notably in 1810 when the north German coast from Oldenburg in the west to Danzig in the east was annexed to France, largely because of Napoleon's need to control the seaboard for the success of his trade embargo on England.

Secondly, beginning as part of a process of finding compensation for those rulers who were deprived of land because of the French annexation of the west bank of the Rhine but continuing with separate treaties between various German states and Napoleon, there came about large-scale secularization and mediatization. These are the terms which describe the absorption by the larger states of the lands of the ecclesiastical princes, the imperial Free Cities and the many tiny principalities (among them that of the Metternich family) which lay inside or on their borders. 1803 saw virtually the end of the ecclesiastical territories and by 1806 the process was largely completed; the lands of the old Imperial Knights were incorporated and the Holy Roman Empire dissolved. As a corollary of this went the rise of the states which had devoured the others, as the clients or friends of France. In 1806 these states became part of Napoleon's newly created Confederation of the Rhine (the Rheinbund) with himself as Protector. They foreswore all alliances with foreign powers and closely bound themselves to

France. Bavaria and Württemberg both became kingdoms in 1806, Hesse-Darmstadt and Baden became Grand Duchies and farther north Saxony was raised to the status of a kingdom and had its territory enlarged.

Thirdly, there came the creation of new states: the Grand Duchy of Berg, the Duchy of Frankfurt and the Kingdom of Wesphalia, carved out of lands that were free for resettlement and handed over to men Napoleon wished to reward. Finally there occurred the spoliation of Austria and Prussia as a result of their defeats. Austria, escaping the more lightly in loss of territory, was forced to cede land to Bavaria. Prussia was enormously reduced; her population of over nine and a half million in 1806 had dropped to under five million a year later.

Besides the consolidation of states within Germany during the Napoleonic period, considerable changes took place inside many of the states themselves. In Prussia, for example, in the aftermath and humiliation of crushing military defeat, a thorough-going reformation was pushed through in the administration of the state, its social laws and the army, by Stein, Hardenberg and the soldiers Scharnhorst and Gneisenau. In Bavaria, Napoleon's urgings for greater efficiency from a member of his Rheinbund combined with the desire for reform of the more liberal elements of the middle class and the need for consolidation in a time of extensive territorial change. A constitution of 1808 abolished the old Estates and created a uni-cameral legislature with a degree of election. Sweeping administrative reform was accompanied by social changes, abolishing serfdom and introducing a measure of equality before the law. Similar changes occurred, without the social reforms, in Hesse-Darmstadt. The new states of the Rheinbund, to a greater or lesser extent, synchronized their local and administrative structure with those of France.

At first sight it might seem that all these changes were purely the outcome of the French Revolution. But, when examined in the light of what had been happening in the late eighteenth century in various states, the inescapable conclusion is that the Revolution was merely accelerating a process already at work—as a reagent rather than a catalyst perhaps. When Louis X of Hesse-Darmstadt dissolved his Estates and refused to re-convene them, demanding the end of freedom from taxation that had hitherto been the privilege of some of his subjects, the actions of Joseph II at Vienna are brought to mind; although, of course, Louis could be confident that Napoleon and the French armies would ensure compliance if obstruction threatened supply and hence the promised subsidies to France.

Thus, the Germany which lay exposed as the Napoleonic tide began to ebb was a much-changed one. Quite obviously many rulers had gained from the immersion and would clearly resent any attempt to restore the old situation. Others had equally obviously lost and would demand redress and plead for restoration. Some monarchs would look to their new constitutions as aids to their power; not just rosettes signifying their support of the revolution, now to be tossed away having served their purpose.

To understand Metternich's policy in this situation it is not enough to consider it in a purely German context; it is necessary to examine it in the context of the European situation as a whole.

The danger from France, of the total dismemberment of the state, was obviously the most serious threat confronting Austria in 1809. Nothing less than extinction as a great power faced the Habsburgs when Metternich became foreign minister. It was this situation which led Metternich to tell his Emperor in that year, 'We can seek our security only in adapting ourselves to the triumphant French system.' It was this situation again, rather than unprincipled opportunism, which forced Metternich to delay until the last minute before declaring for the Russo-Prussian alliance against Napoleon in 1813. He well knew that premature involvement in a Franco-Russian conflict would merely mean that the conflict would take place on Austrian territory, with no guarantee that Russia would not make peace with France at Austria's expense and withdraw on herself; a possibility which Austria could not face after 1809. Russia's previous alliance with Austria in the Austerlitz campaign, and the history of her alliance with Prussia in 1806–7, did nothing to alter the Austrian conviction of Russia being prepared to fight to the last—German. But, however great the danger facing Austria from France, Metternich was wise not to concentrate upon it to the exclusion of all else. The twentieth century has finally proved that apparent victory can bring disaster in its train. 'To win the war but lose the peace' has become a cliché, so aware are we of it as a contingency. Metternich thus, during the Napoleonic wars— and after, was concerned with much more than the defeat of France and the emasculation of revolution. His achievement was not just to preside over the defeat of Napoleon, but to preside over the defeat of Napoleon without bringing disaster to Austria. Nowhere was disaster more likely to occur than in Germany.

The most important power in the old Holy Roman Empire after the Habsburgs was the Prussian state. This, like Austria, included lands that were not inside the Empire, notably ex-Polish lands in the east. The eighteenth century had seen the aggression of Frederick II successfully wrest the important province of Silesia from the Habsburgs, and its subsequent incorporation in the Prussian state.*

Thereafter Austria's attempts to regain Silesia had been a major preoccupation of her foreign policy. Despite participating with Prussia in two of the partitions of Poland, and periods of co-operation and alliance with her against revolutionary and Napoleonic France, Austria continued to distrust Prussia. The rivalry between the two powers was never very far from the surface. Prussia's further ambitions were a constant concern to Austria. Even if the Prussian monarch seemed to be amenable to Habsburg influence, as for much of the time Frederick William III indeed did—'although below mediocrity in intellect and judgment, [he] is yet at bottom a good sort of man' was how Metternich's secretary Gentz described him—there was always a party in the Prussian state which wished to pursue a much more forward, expansionist policy. A particular fear, based on events in the eighteenth century and Napoleonic wars, was that Prussia might be assisted in her policy by Russia.

It was the eighteenth century that saw the emergence of Russia to the status of a major European power. Under Catherine the Great she had taken the lead in the partitioning and rape of Poland and had fought a series of successful wars against Turkey. The peace of Kutchak-Kainardji in 1774 had signalled the arrival of Russia on the Black Sea and had given her freedom of navigation there, besides the right to send her merchant ships through the straits into the Mediterranean. The peace also allowed Russia to establish an Orthodox Church in Constantinople and to make representations on behalf of it 'and those who serve it'. 1774 thus

* The transfer of Silesia, an old province of the kingdom of Bohemia but mainly occupied by Germans, had been particularly significant because it not only increased the power of the Prussian monarch at the expense of the Austrian but brought about a change in the proportion of Germans to non-Germans living in the two states.

saw the beginning of the Eastern Question in its nineteenth-century form; the situation of a decaying Turkish Empire which seemed on the verge of final collapse, confronted by expansionist Russia. This development presented the problem of what was to be done after the collapse, or alternatively how to prevent such an event. Russia advanced farther during the Napoleonic wars, which brought her to the mouth of the Danube. Her increasing influence in the Balkans, fostered by her community of race with the Slavs and her community of religion with the Orthodox Christians of the area, faced Austria with a serious threat. Britain also resented the Russian advance, fearing her emergence as a Mediterranean naval power. Napoleon's invasion of Egypt brought France into active participation in the affairs of the Middle East and added another ingredient to the problem. However, this was by no means the full extent of Russian expansion. With the defeat of Napoleon in 1812 and the decision of the Tsar Alexander to follow the retreating Grande Armée westwards into Germany, the possibility arose of the Napoleonic hegemony over central Europe being replaced by a Russian one. It was not just in Poland where Napoleon's creation of the Grand Duchy of Warsaw out of Prussia and Austrian Polish possessions meant, on his defeat, that a new settlement must be made. In Germany and western Europe generally Russian pre-dominance became a possibility.

The Tsar Alexander has always been a baffling figure, to historians as well as contemporaries; although, it is true, Metternich claimed to have understood him, leaving a brilliant character sketch in his memoirs. The paradox of Alexander is illustrated by his very accession. His complicity in the plot to overthrow his father, the mad Paul, seems quite clear yet so too does the sincerity in his disavowal of responsibility for the murder, and his obviously genuine grief at its occurrence. 'There is no cure, I have to suffer, it cannot be altered,' he was to say. Like Napoleon, towards whom his attitude was so ambivalent, he subordinated the interests of his country to his own, but unlike Napoleon, no clear pattern of his own wishes can be traced. 'Too weak for ambition, but too strong for pure vanity,' Metternich described him. The only consistent theme which emerges from his shifts of policy, from the friend of reform to the agent of reaction via religious mysticism, seems to be a basic wish to discover the solutions to Europe's problems and impose them himself, at the same time receiving universal gratitude for so doing. It is not surprising that it was fear of Russian aims which conditioned Metternich's German policy.

It may now be apparent that Russia did not have the society or institutions to serve as the base for German hegemony: that to see 1813 in the light of 1945, with no United States to intervene, is to misunderstand the times. Nevertheless Metternich and other European leaders did fear Russian ability to dominate Europe. Alexander's talk of replacing Napoleon with Bernadotte (the ex-French marshal, by then King of Sweden), his sponsoring of Stein's schemes for the reorganization of Germany, his involvement by family tie with the rulers of Baden, Württemberg and Oldenburg, together with the extent of Russian military victory over the Grande Armée, added up to a serious threat. It was thus of primary importance that, once Russian victory became possible in 1813, Austria should do all she could to influence events: either to mediate an accommodation with a chastened Napoleon, or this being refused by the French Emperor, at least to control the pace and form of the invasion of France, and to prevent her total emasculation. (In this context the appointment of Schwarzenberg a diplomat rather than a soldier, as commander-in-chief of the allied troops becomes immediately explicable.)

Metternich's task was to break the power of France in Germany, at any rate east of the Rhine, without in any way building up Russian influence west of the Vistula. To this latter end the Tsar might seek to work through the German kings and grand dukes of the Rheinbund or through the sort of 'German' body which Stein was seeking to create. Either way, it was crucial for Austria that the existing rulers of German states were not driven into Russia's arms or back into the French embrace, which attempts to restore the situation of 1789 or to build a new German Empire under Austrian leadership would assuredly achieve.

The magnitude of Metternich's task thus becomes clear and his German policy can be seen as far more than pointless reaction or rigid conservatism, what Stein called 'a contemptible patchwork'. This is not to say that Metternich wished for German unity but was frustrated from working towards it in 1813–14 by the complexities of the situation; on the contrary he did not believe that historically or culturally Germany was suited to unification. Rather, the German policy of Metternich was a brilliant series of contrivances in an attempt to preserve the Austrian monarchy in a period of almost unprecedented turmoil in Europe. He was determined that the Germany that was left after Napoleon's defeat, its future already partly decided by previous treaties and agreements of the Allies with former members of the Rheinbund—the first of which was that of Ried in 1812 with Bavaria—should not again fall under foreign hegemony. This was why he strove for some constitutional and territorial grouping in Germany, because he feared that, in default of it, the various states would all treat separately with foreign powers. 'So many princes of varying size set down in the centre of Europe haphazard and without any guarantees, indulging in isolated political opinions, could only give rise to a state of restlessness and turmoil for themselves and for their neighbours.' The situation described thus by Metternich was one which he saw as opening the door to foreign influence which could only be to Austria's disadvantage.

The actual form of the new Germany, laid down in principle in the First Peace of Paris of 1814, was embodied in the Federative Act of 1815. The Confederation was really a diplomatic alliance of sovereign states. The lands lost to France were regained and Napoleon's new creations, such as Westphalia, were abolished, but the mediatization and the rationalization both stood. The member states agreed to two principles: first that they would not engage in war with one another and second that there would be a permanent alliance to ensure the internal and external security of Germany.

The Confederation had its capital in Frankfurt, where the Federal Diet met. In no sense was this an elected legislature of the sort liberals demanded. It was really a conference of ambassadors, men chosen by, and under instruction from, the various member governments. Whether the Diet met in full assembly or, more usually, in the restricted small council, the voting was so arranged that neither one of the large states nor all the small ones together could override the remainder. For example Austria, as president of the Diet, was never able to implement her wishes without the concurrence of the majority of the other states. There were articles in the Act of Federation which seemed to favour development towards unity. One sought to provide a legal unity with the setting up of a German court. Another attempted to secure the granting of constitutions in all states of a similar nature, featuring some sort of parliament. However, partly because of the deliberately differing interpretations of these, Germany remained fragmented, in her

laws, her coinage and her commercial life. Thus each state controlled its own foreign policy and defence; although a military
constitution was produced in 1821 projecting a common army of
ten corps, three to be provided by Austria and three by Prussia.

The absence of a federal legislature or even any federal executive
meant that there was no focus for German patriotic feeling, of the
kind born in the War of Liberation against Napoleon. It is in this
sense that Metternich and his emperor can be seen as deliberately
opposing and inhibiting the fulfilment of German aspirations and
standing against the tide of history. To go further, as some historians
and propagandists have, and see Metternich as responsible for
preventing the creation of a unified Germany in 1814, is totally
unrealistic. States, unlike stars, are not created by a process of
explosion and instantaneous fusion.

Metternich saw the Confederation as the best answer in the
circumstances to Austria's problems and its creation therefore
rested upon Austria's interests. However, the Confederation as it
was constituted in 1815 was not entirely to Metternich's liking.
In the first place the evolutionary and liberal spirit was able to
survive in many German states and in some was even given the
official blessing of the ruler, in the form of the constitutions that
had been granted. Very often, the reason why the rulers of such
states as Bavaria, Baden or Württemberg granted some sort of
representative assembly or legislature was the wish to strengthen
their power. An elective assembly implied the loss of power or the
abolition of the old feudal Estates, long a check on the central
ruler. Also, it was a way of bringing newly acquired territory
together with some sense of common purpose—a very important
consideration to many German rulers after 1815, facing as they did
the need to absorb new lands. Thus it was self-interest as much as
belief in liberalism which led rulers to grant constitutions.

Nevertheless, Metternich saw that the lack of an adequate
censorship of the press, the failure to control students and their
teachers in the universities and even the existence of constitutions,
were factors making for revolution in Germany and as such hostile
to the interests of Austria; first, most obviously, because he feared
that the agitation would spread to the hereditary lands of the
Habsburgs. Clearly Metternich and more particularly his master, the
Emperor Francis, had no love for the sort of liberal and national
sentiments which were so in vogue at many German universities.

Secondly, Metternich distrusted Prussia's intentions in Germany and thought that she might take advantage of any opportunity, such as one presented by a political breakdown, to gain predominance. 'A daughter of the Reformation [Prussia], she is seeking to strengthen her influence in the conflicts of the present age by following the path of the Revolution.' Or again, writing in 1818, 'We think we can see, and every day confirms us in this opinion, that the seat of German Jacobinism is in Prussia.' However, too hectoring an attempt to quosh the constitutions and institute press censorship would merely arouse the hostility of many rulers, a hostility which the Tsar might be expected to exploit. Metternich therefore had to be cautious.

The opportunity to reduce the Confederation more to his own liking was given to Metternich by the German students. The Burchenshaften, or societies of students, arose out of the hopes and desires felt by many educated Germans in the aftermath of the Wars of Liberation, times when it was felt that to fight against the foreigner was also to fight for liberty. The despair felt by students at the failure of their hopes to bear fruit, aided not a little by the irritation and frustration inescapable from the small-town, provincial existence they led, created political argument and dissent. In 1817 a large number of Protestant students gathered at Eisenach, in the lands of the Grand Duke of Saxe-Weimar, to celebrate the tercentenary of the Reformation and the fourth anniversary of the battle of Leipzig. On October 18 they marched to the Wartburg, the place of Luther's sojourn after being put under ban of the Empire by the Diet of Worms. Here, they took part in what was really a very harmless demonstration, despite being reported to Metternich as 'a terrifyingly scandalous scene' and a 'Jacobin orgy'. The eight hundred or so students, together with about thirty dons, burnt various works by authors felt to be reactionary and the acts of the Congress of Vienna, throwing them on to the fire with forks normally used for shifting manure, to the accompaniment of patriotic speeches and cries of 'Long Live Liberty!' and 'Down with tyrants and their perfidious ministers'. The next day, after taking communion from a local Lutheran pastor and swearing on the sacraments their hatred of tyranny and their determination to struggle for German liberty, the students returned to their universities.

Metternich used reports of the incident to alert the Tsar of Russia and others to the dangers of revolution in Germany. It was,

however, the murder in 1819 of Kotzebue the author of some of
the works burned at the Wartburg and now in the employ of the
Tsar, by Karl Sand a theological student and member of the
Burchenshaften, which really gave Metternich the opportunity he
wanted. 'All my efforts are directed towards giving the affair the
best possible sequel and to taking as much advantage of it as possible.
I shall act vigorously to this end' was how Metternich described the
opening he saw.

The result, after a meeting between Austria and Prussia at
Teplitz, was a gathering of the ministers of the nine most important
states of the Confederation at Karlsbad. The substance of their
decisions, known as the Karlsbad Decrees, was then pushed
through the Federal Diet at Frankfurt in September 1819. These,
together with the conclusions of the conferences between the
German states at Vienna which followed, had the effect of repairing
what, to Metternich, were the deficiencies of the original constitution.

All periodicals and books of less than twenty pages were made
subject to censorship, for the execution of which the various states
were held responsible to the Confederation. Extended laws were
passed against student societies, 'since at the basis of this association
lies the completely unpermissible premise of a continuing community and correspondence between the various universities'.
Officials at each university were charged with the task of supervising
teachers and students in such a way as to give their attitude 'a
wholesome direction' and of debarring any student or teacher who
did not comply. A commission was set up in Mainz to investigate
and direct proceedings against 'the demagogues' who were believed
to be behind the agitation, although the proceedings were to take
place in the individual states. Finally, attempts were made to
discourage representative assemblies in the various states which
were not conducive 'to the maintainance of the monarchical
principle and in complete conformity with the character of the
Confederation'.

The success of Metternich's German policy can be judged after
1830 when revolution in France and the fall of the Bourbon Charles
X triggered off a series of disturbances and revolts in Germany.
Liberal constitutions were granted in Saxony, Hesse-Cassel and
Hanover but nationalist demonstrations failed to develop into
anything more serious, and 1832–3 saw reaction again in control,

Metternich using very much the same tactics that he had employed after 1819. When, in 1834, the newly freed press in Baden was declared to be inconsistent with the Press Law of 1819 and returned to its former state, and four years later the constitution in Hanover was rescinded, the forces of change in Germany were once more reduced to impotence.

Chapter VII

METTERNICH AND EUROPE

'WE MUST always view the society of nations as the essential condition of the present world,' declared Metternich. Certainly he never failed to struggle for European equilibrium, believing that a stable Austria could only exist in a stable Europe. He was in the position of one who tries to defend a castle inside two concentric circles of fortifications. The outer circle guards the equilibrium and the peace of the Continent, the inner bastion shields the German lands, and the actual castle is the Habsburg territories. The castle can, in emergency, be held by itself, even with parts of the wall destroyed or in enemy hands, but its long-term security depends upon the lines of fortifications which surround it being successfully defended. The end of the Napoleonic wars saw the enemy expelled from the fortifications and the walls being repaired.

The Congress of Vienna and the Congresses which followed were attacked by progressives throughout the nineteenth century as being an attempt to restore a world which would have been better left for dead, the world of the *ancien régime*. The statesmen who re-drew the frontiers of Europe in the First and Second Peaces of Paris and at Vienna were castigated for having totally disregarded the principle of national sovereignty, the principle enunciated by revolutionary France. The Italian Massimo D'Azeglio wrote: 'We believe that all the ill will and the revolutions of those thirty-two years, the unrest, the moral disquiet which has agitated society . . . that all these have been caused by the enforced and unnatural order given to Europe by the Congress of Vienna.' Instead, the delegates tried to construct a Europe to their own liking, one which favoured the major powers and dynasties, ignoring nationalist and liberal aspirations. The spirit of the reaction was seen as most clearly expressed in the Holy Alliance, and the High Priest of the policy was identified as Metternich.

However, since the signing of the Peace of Versailles at the conclusion of the First World War and increasingly with regard to subsequent events, historians have come to praise the diplomats who drew up the peace after the Revolutionary and Napoleonic Wars. Their cynicism is seen as understanding, their selfishness as realism and their disregard of nationalism and liberalism as a statesmanlike refusal to pander to popular emotions. Above all they have been congratulated upon preserving Europe from a 'general . . . conflagration for a whole century of time'. In fact, no peace can be held responsible for events of the future, least of all for a whole 'century of time'; it can only seek to avoid leaving too explosive a legacy.

What perhaps is most striking about the Peace of Vienna is the leniency which the allies showed in their dealings with France. She was 'treated with a moderation of which no perusal of history furnishes examples in similar circumstances' was the comment of Talleyrand to his king Louis XVIII, although he was admittedly seeking to claim credit for his own part in this outcome. Nevertheless the generosity is apparent. It was chiefly the policy of Castlereagh and Wellington, with Alexander and Metternich both in broad agreement. Prussia, particularly after the return of Napoleon from Elba and the Waterloo campaign, sought to secure a punitive peace. 'Alsace and Lorraine must be surrendered to us' was the Prussian general Blücher's demand and many of his compatriots went further.* This moderation, although seen in France as a national humiliation which must be expunged in a new drive for the 'natural' frontiers, was nevertheless not such a disgrace that the future régimes of Louis Philippe, or even of the Second Republic, were compelled to seek its redress. This policy, the determination not to overload the restored French monarchy with too onerous a burden, certainly deserves praise and perhaps can fairly be attributed to that very isolation from popular feeling for which the statesmen have so often been censured.

The peace was primarily an attempt to prevent the re-entry of revolution, dressed in a French garb, on to the stage of Europe; and secondly, an opportunity for reciprocal compensation among the major powers for all that had passed. In this way it sought to create a balance in affairs which had some chance of survival.

---

* A strange ancestor of Marshal Hindenburg's demand for room to manœuvre his left wing from the negotiators going to talk peace with Russia in early 1918.

England made gains overseas, but her greatest gain was that the wars, as the last round of a century of colonial war with France, had given her undisputed, and indisputable, mastery of the seas. The Austrian Netherlands were joined to the United Provinces and the new state elevated to a monarchy under the Stadtholder of Holland, Prince William of Orange. It was hoped that this would provide enough stability so as not to invite, and enough strength to deter, future French aggression. Similarly the monarchy of Sardinia-Piedmont, on France's south-eastern frontier, was strengthened by the acquisition of Genoa. Austria, in compensation for the loss of the Netherlands and some of her Polish territory, received Venetia (the old Republic of Venice), thus, with the re-acquisition of Lombardy, gaining a very firm control of northern Italy.

Farther south, members of the Habsburg family ruled over Modena, Parma and Tuscany; the Papal States and Naples also found themselves subject to Austrian influence. To Metternich, the only alternative to an Italy under French influence was an Italy under Austrian influence. Metternich saw an unstable Italy as a constant invitation to French involvement and had no confidence in the Italian States' ability to look after themselves. In the light of previous French descents into Italy (and the subsequent one of Napoleon III), Metternich's determination to maintain Austrian hegemony as essential to Habsburg security is hard to fault. To attack him for not assisting in the creation of an Italian national state is ludicrous. The Italians themselves did not wish such a state, and to look no further, the Papacy in 1814 was pressing for the complete restoration of its lands, so far was it from being prepared to take part in a general merging into a new unitary state. With the large credit balance the Papacy had built up because of the heroic resistance of Pope Pius VII to Napoleon, the other negotiators were in no position to refuse the Papacy's request; Metternich had to accept that the Legations should be returned to Rome, though in terms of their political, social and economic life they were more fitted to remain joined to Lombardy, on the opposite bank of the Po. To complete the defence of Italy Metternich would have liked to create something of the same sort of Confederation as was to exist in Germany, under Austrian patronage. This would have made it more difficult for outside powers to involve themselves in the affairs of Italian states. However, this proposal failed, both the king of Sardinia-Piedmont and the Pope, terrified of the Habsburg embrace, refusing to accept it.

Where the victorious allies found their attempt at reciprocal compensation most difficult to apply was in Poland and the connected state of Saxony. Napoleon had made King Frederick Augustus of Saxony Grand Duke of Warsaw, and the defeat of the French left the Grand Duchy as an obvious target for the victors' claims. It had been built up out of Prussian and, to a lesser extent, Austrian Poland. The most likely answer might seem to have been its reversion to these powers. However, here was the area where Russia looked for gain. The Tsar Alexander, whose armies were in occupation, saw Poland as an important acquisition for Russia in her western advance. However, Alexander had another motive for his interest. He had a sincere attachment to making the grand gesture and found the idea of re-creating a constitutional Polish state just such a gesture. As he cast himself in the role of the king of such a state his plan had the added advantage of promising to further Russian interest at the same time. If Prussia were to lose her Polish lands she would obviously require compensation elsewhere and Alexander looked to Saxony to provide this; a proposal which met with the approval of Prussia.

However, the other powers, Britain and Austria, disliked both the expansion of Prussia into Saxony, and more particularly, the extension of Russian power into Poland, an extension which threatened the equilibrium of Europe.* The clash was eventually resolved in a compromise which saw Alexander the king of a reduced Poland, created from the Grand Duchy of Warsaw but with Posen reverting to Prussia and Galicia to Austria. Prussia was compensated with some two-fifths of Saxony and gains elsewhere, notably in the Rhineland; Frederick remaining king of the remainder of Saxony. The significance of the argument which preceded the compromise was twofold. First France, in the person of Talleyrand, was able to take advantage of the dispute in order to win a position in the inner councils of the great powers, even to the

---

* In resisting the Prussian annexation of Saxony Talleyrand opposed the suggestion that the king of Saxony might be compensated with lands on the west bank of the Rhine which, in the event, passed to Prussia. 'As a result, instead of a weak, Catholic, Francophile dynasty on the French border, Louis XVIII had the King of Prussia.' (D. W. Brogan, *The French Nation*, p. 12.)

extent of taking part in a secret defensive alliance with Austria and Britain in case of attack by Russia or Prussia; thus carrying further the process of France's rehabilitation among her former enemies, which the return of Napoleon from Elba and the renewal of war which this provoked were unable to reverse. Secondly, the row over Poland showed the danger posed to European balance by a victorious Russia and the recognition of this threat by Metternich and the other statesmen.

Such was the territorial shape of Europe at the conclusion of the Napoleonic wars, but of themselves, the new frontiers could not be expected to prevent a recurrence of French aggression; the instrument for this was sought in the Quadruple Alliance. This pact, a renewal of the alliance which had defeated Napoleon and had been forged since 1813, was signed by Russia, Austria, Great Britain and Prussia in November 1815 at the same time as the Second Peace of Paris. It sought to maintain the frontiers of France, as laid down in that peace, from any attempt at revision for the following twenty years and to preserve Europe from any French aggression. A return of the Bonaparte dynasty to power would be taken as such an aggression.

Also stemming from the Quadruple Alliance, under Article Six, was the agreement by the powers to reconvene 'for the purpose of consulting upon their common interests, and for the consideration of the measures . . . The most salutory for the repose and prosperity of Nations and for the maintenance of the peace of Europe'. It was this which was to be the basis for the future meetings of the powers described as the 'Congress System'.

That the settlement constituted a barrier to revolution originating in France and spreading from there, is clear enough. However, those who pressed for change in Europe after 1815 thought they discerned something more far-reaching, an alliance of reaction pledged to defend the status quo against all attacks. Having tried to re-create pre-revolutionary Europe, the victorious powers were now to join to preserve it. It was this preservation along with the policies of the German Confederation and the absolutism practised in the Habsburg lands that together were seen as the 'system' of Metternich, however much its supposed author might deny the existence of any such thing. At the time and subsequently, this determination to resist change internationally became identified by many with the Holy Alliance, which was suggested by the Tsar and later signed by the monarchs of Europe, with the exception of the Pope and the Prince Regent. The Holy Alliance wished to ensure that rulers would henceforth regulate their actions in both domestic and foreign affairs 'according to the benign principles and precepts of the Christian religion'. Certainly to liberals the Holy Alliance came to be the hated symbol of reaction in Europe and in the guise of the Alliance between Russia, Austria and Prussia it was seen as seeking to guarantee all thrones against attack. In fact the Holy Alliance had little practical influence on events. 'The Holy Alliance has never played a part in anything and it is precluded from doing so by the simple fact that what is in effect nothing can only produce nothing,' commented Metternich. It was seen by other statesmen as unreal, to be signed to humour the Tsar. 'This document has no more sense or value than that of a philanthropic aspiration disguised beneath the cloak of religion' was Metternich's judgment. Although Metternich might from time to time have encouraged the Tsar to confuse the Quadruple Alliance with his own brain-child, in order to secure for the former some parental affection, the Holy Alliance as such was never the basis for conservative power in central Europe.

At first, the basis of such a force for Europe as a whole was the Quadruple Alliance. Through it the restored Bourbons were assisted and the peace treaty guaranteed. At the same time Metternich, by preserving the solidarity of the Alliance, strove to minimize the potential dangers of a maverick Russia pursuing her own policy in Europe. This was something which Metternich feared almost as much as a renewed outbreak of revolution in France. Particularly was this so as long as the Tsar Alexander, advised by a motley group of non-Russians, persisted in flirting with ideas of imposing constitutional governments on various European lands. The more Russia, through the alliance, was won to a policy of immobility in the face of the threat of revolution from France, the easier it would be to prevent her from pursuing a policy of mobility in her foreign affairs generally.

With the rehabilitation of France, signified by her admission to the new Quintuple Alliance at the Congress of Aix-la-Chapelle in 1818, it became impossible to retain the notion of an alliance directed against France, despite the simultaneous secret renewal of the Quadruple Alliance. It is here that the significance of the dispute over Poland at the Vienna Congress becomes apparent. For after 1818 opportunity for discord among the powers grew; with the expansion of the Quadruple Alliance into a pentarchy there was no longer a single, unifying enemy. At the same time Metternich's suspicions of Russian policy grew, increased by his findings of the evidence for Russian intrigue on his Italian tour in 1819.*

It was this desire for unity rather than an over-exaggerated fear of revolution that led Metternich to expand the alliance against revolutionary France into an alliance against revolution generally. But Metternich did not become an 'interventionist' against revolution solely for this reason. On the contrary he had always upheld the legitimacy of putting out a fire in a neighbour's house, even if to do so required a forced entry. It was, however, the reason for Metternich becoming an interventionist against every revolution. In this he found the force necesssary to restrain Russian independence by magnifying the danger to the Tsar of a general European revolution.

When a revolt occurred in Naples in 1820, Metternich at once saw that this directly threatened the security of Italy and therefore the Habsburg Empire. At the same time he did not wish to act unilaterally, fearing that this would present Russia with the opportunity to intrigue in Naples at Austria's expense. Before Austria moved to try and restore the situation she must have Russia's support or approval. Failing to gain such approval directly, Metternich was forced to acquire it through the medium of a congress. This congress, called at Troppau in 1820 and continued at Laibach in 1821, put forward the concept of intervention by the powers against revolution. 'States which have undergone a change of government, due to revolution, the results of which threaten other states, ipso facto cease to be members of the European Alliance. . . . If, owing to such alteration, immediate danger threatens other states the powers bind themselves, by peaceful means, or if need by arms, to bring back the guilty state into the bosom of the Great Alliance.' So reads the Troppau protocol. It was in the role of agent for the Alliance that Austria was empowered to act in Naples and in Piedmont. However, this victory for Metternich was an expensive one, for Castlereagh, although having no objection to Austria putting down revolution in Naples or elsewhere in Italy on her own account, did object very strongly to her doing so in the

---

* Reports, for instance, of La Harpe, the Russian Tsar's former tutor and now an adviser, having presided over a meeting of Carbonari.

name of an alliance of which Britain was a member. 'The extreme right of interference between nation and nation can never be properly made a matter of stipulation or be assumed as the attribute of any alliance,' he wrote firmly. It was suspicion of this possibility which had led Castlereagh merely to send an observer to Troppau and was to make him dissociate himself from the 'moral responsibility of administering a general European police'.

However, Metternich had managed to win Alexander to a policy of immobility and the extent of his success was demonstrated by the Greek revolt. The rising of the Greeks in the Morea and the Aegean Islands against the Turks in 1821 presented an enormous temptation for Russia to intervene on the side of the Greeks, her co-religionists: a likelihood that was strengthened by the traditional hostility felt by Russia for Turkey and the possibility of territorial gain at the latter's expense. Finally, but by no means least, Alexander's love of the role of patron, which a successful intervention would have allowed him to play, must have pulled strongly in the direction of Russian involvement. Even so Metternich was able to convince Alexander that the Greek revolt was merely another manifestation of the general revolt against established order; therefore any such involvement on the side of the revels would be against his real interests. But the result of Metternich's success in convincing the Tsar of the reality of the danger of revolution was that he was no longer able to pursue a policy of *laissez-faire* over the revolution in Spain and had to consent, at the Congress of Verona in 1822, to the decision in favour of French intervention in the name of the Alliance: this, although Metternich saw no particular danger in the Spanish revolution and knew that Britain would not be able to continue a member of the Alliance if such intervention occurred.

Henceforward Britain was lost to the Alliance, an event made the more complete by the death of Castlereagh and Canning's assumption of power at the Foreign Office. With the death of Alexander and the accession of his brother Nicholas in 1825, it seemed that Russia might also be lost. Nicholas proceeded to pursue a much more independent policy, moving via an alliance with England and France, of which Austria had no part, into a declaration of war with Turkey in 1828. Nevertheless, despite the setting-up of an independent Greek kingdom, a minor triumph for the revolution in Europe, the Russians had not really thrown over the conservative alliance. In 1833, when the Tsar and the Austrian Emperor met at

D

Münchengrätz, the alliance was renewed and solidarity proclaimed. The rash of revolutions in 1830, particularly those in France and Poland, had helped to convince Nicholas of the essential community of interest of the Eastern Courts and the real dangers of revolution. Also, in other respects, Nicholas seemed to be less threatening to Metternich than had been his brother Alexander, since he had less interest in pursuing the sort of grandiose, personally motivated foreign policy which had upset European equilibrium at the time of the defeat of Napoleon.

In conclusion, the forces of change in Europe were still confronted by an alliance of the conservative monarchs, even if Britain and France were no longer part of it. Also, governments continued to see revolution in neighbouring states as a shared danger to be resisted, rather than the embarrassment of a rival, inviting exploitation. Finally, although Britain and France showed themselves capable of working together against the wishes of the Eastern Powers by assisting Belgium to gain her independence and neutrality in 1830, perhaps more significantly France made no move to annex Belgium. In this the rulers of Europe still saw the dangers posed by a European war and the necessity, in order to preserve Europe from revolution, of preserving European peace.

Even in the upheavals of 1848 Britain and Russia, the only major powers which did not experience revolution, realized the need to stop the revolts leading to European wars which would merely increase the dangers of revolution. As Lord Palmerston said at the time: 'We are at present the only two powers in Europe that remain standing upright, and we ought to look with confidence to each other.'

PART THREE

COLLISION COURSE

Chapter VIII

THE CHALLENGE OF THE NEW

'... MY WINDOW, which looks west over the gardens of the Missions, is open; it is six o'clock in the morning; I can see the pale and swollen moon; it is sinking over the spire of the Invalides, scarcely touched by the first golden ray from the east: one might imagine that the old world was ending and the new beginning; I behold the light of a dawn whose sunrise I shall never see.' So wrote Chateaubriand in November 1841, virtually at the close of his memoirs. The Europe of the Restoration which had taken shape in 1815 was much altered by the 1840s, and on all sides it was felt that greater changes lay ahead. The map itself had altered, with new states, such as Greece and Belgium, having come into existence. Moreover with the great rise in population, the growth of towns and the spread of industrialism, it was a different continent. But Europe had also altered politically; the revolt of the Greeks, the revolt of the Belgians, and above all the 1830 Revolution in France, had clearly demonstrated that the aims of the victorious allies of 1814–15 could be successfully thwarted. A nationalist revolt resulted in the creation of a new state in Greece; a liberal, constitutional Belgium was born; and the restored Bourbons were dismissed and a constitutional king given to France in the name of the Sovereign People. In Britain the Reform Bill became law. Well might Chateaubriand feel that the new world was beginning. Well might those seeking to preserve the old world feel their task to be impossible.

It is tempting to see the Europe of the Restoration as gradually metamorphosing, the superstructure, in Marxist terms, having finally to adapt itself to these changes in the substructure. The 1840s thus become a time when the substructure has already changed to such an extent that the existing superstructure is obviously about to collapse.

However, this temptation to seek for a neat, causal explanation

93

of the past is usually one best avoided. The series of separate explosions of an internal combustion engine can become, at a distance, the smooth purr of a Rolls Royce. So, viewed through the reversed telescope of history, events can sometimes recede into a pattern, lending an appearance of gradualism and inevitability which, at the time, just did not exist. Evolution is the result of irregular and chance mutations and is therefore an erratic process. Very often history is the result of similar chance mutations and the historian, like the gambler, must not confuse an odds-on favourite with an inevitable winner. In this period, in which the forces of change were about to collide with the powers of conservatism, chance was to play its part on both sides.

Despite the increasing confidence felt by the supporters of movement and change in the 1840s, the election of a liberal Pope was not anticipated; indeed, by most it was regarded as an impossibility. Nevertheless, in 1846 Cardinal Mastai-Ferretti, Bishop of Imola, was, on the third ballot, elected to the Pontificate as Pius IX, at the age of fifty-four.

Although Pius was soon to be regarded by all as a 'liberal Pope' he was not the obvious candidate of the less reactionary cardinals. Their choice was Gizzi and the election had seemed at first to lie between him and the favourite, Cardinal Lambruschini, who had been the previous Pope's Secretary of State.

The consequences of Pius's election were so great that historians have been surprised that nothing was done by Metternich to prevent it. However just as for other powers, so for the Papacy, Metternich believed that there were permanent, underlying interests which would always dictate the policies of the ruler, whatever his own attitudes prior to his accession had been. Metternich had written to his ambassador in Rome: 'We are persuaded that any good Pope, any really enlightened Pope, will at the same time be an "Austrian Pope", since he could never fail to be aware that in Austria he has a neighbour who is as loyal as she is powerful and who is the most zealous guardian of the interests of the Church and of social order.'

What Metternich feared was the election as Pope of a zealot who might pursue bigoted policies, because 'a Pope has only to provide an example and a rallying-point for extremists in all countries to pave the way for and start a conflagration the effects and repercussions of which would be incalculable'. For these reasons the election

ITALY

N

Scale
50   0   50   100
miles

Inset map (upper):

Scale
50   0   50
miles

LOMBARDY

VENETIA

Novara

R. Ticino

Milan

Pastrengo

Vicenza

Verona

Venice

Peschiera

Goito   Custoza

Mantua

R. Po

R. Adige

R. Po

PIEDMONT   PARMA   MODENA

Main map:

H A B S B U R G

E M P I R E

S A R D I N I A

LOMBARDY

VENETIA

R. Ticino

Milan

R. Po

Verona

R. Mincio

R. Adige

R. Po

PIEDMONT

PARMA

MODENA

THE

LUCCA

TUSCANY

PAPAL

STATES

A D R I A T I C   S E A

F R A N C E

Corsica

Rome

Gaeta

Naples

THE

SARDINIA

TWO

SICILIES

Palermo   Messina

of Pius did not seem of enormous consequence to Metternich. However, perhaps Metternich had not paid enough attention to the character of Pius and the character of the times. Pius was totally inexperienced in diplomatic and political matters and knew next to nothing of Europe outside the Papal States. Therefore he might find it hard to discern where the 'permanent interests' of the Papacy lay and by the time he had discovered it might be too late to follow them. Also Metternich erred in his conception of 'permanent interests'. Long-term interests there might be but they could change, and Metternich was not able to see that the interests of the Papacy in the nineteenth might not always be the same as the interests of the Papacy in the eighteenth century.

To appreciate the importance of the election of Pius it is necessary to understand something of both the situation in the Papal States and the condition of the movement for reform in Italy at the time. Under Gregory XVI the government of the Papal States had certainly been inefficient and repressive but whether it was particularly cruel or corrupt by the standards of other Italian states is open to question; despite D'Azeglio's description of it as 'nothing but a great society of thieves'.

What perhaps angered and horrified progressive opinion most were the activities of the Centurions. The answer to the need for a security force which would not be too expensive, the Centurions had been created on the basis of an auxiliary, volunteer police, to maintain order in the Papal States. However they were in fact legalized gangs of bully-boys pursuing private grudges and their own ends. Pius himself while Bishop of Imola had frequently conflicted with these irregulars whose operations he thoroughly disliked and sought to curb. (On one occasion while Pius was at prayer they pursued their quarry into Imola Cathedral and there set about him.)

However, the inadequacies of government in the Papal States had a much wider audience than the inhabitants of the territory. In 1831 a conference of ambassadors had met in Rome to draw up a memorandum of suggested reforms for the administration, and public opinion continued to be fired by writings attacking Papal misrule. Therefore in a situation of this sort, if the death of an old and, in terms of his government, immobile Pope was followed by the accession of a man who attempted to reform and modernize, the change was certain to make a great impact.

By 1840 the nationalist movement in Italy, although on the whole still restricted to the more enlightened among the ruling class and the young of the professional and middle classes, was becoming more powerful. However, Mazzini with his belief in the creation of a single Italian Republic and advocacy of conspiracy and violence to forward his aims alienated most of the more influential classes in Italy.* His anti-clericalism and anti-Papalism offended the religious, his republicanism and democratic teachings frightened the aristocratic and middle classes.

Thus, many in the 1840s were concerned to find another form for their nationalism, one which would not be so repugnant to the majority and hence divisive to Italians. The popularity of the writings of Gioberti, which preached a federation around the Pope, was the particular result of their constituting a doctrine of nationalism that offered hope to the non-revolutionary and pro-clerical.

However, so long as the Papal States were governed by a reactionary Pope and plunged in a mire of misrule and economic backwardness, it was difficult to see much future for Gioberti's teachings. It was this that helped persuade men such as D'Azeglio and Balbo to look to Piedmont to take the lead in unifying Italy, as well as strengthen their belief that the Piedmontese army would be vital to the success of the enterprise. But all this would change with a reformist Pope; so again the election of Pius can be seen to have been catalytic.

Although at first unknown to those to whom his election was announced in June 1846, Pius very soon came to earn an enormous popularity with the Italian people. This charismatic quality which he seemed to possess in the first year of his Pontificate, compared to the later revulsion epitomized by the pelting of his coffin with mud at his funeral, has led to excessive judgments of the man which make it difficult to form a reasonable impression of him or his ideas. 'Overflattered and over-censored, ill understood and ill judged, by every party' was the estimate of Farini who worked alongside him in Rome after 1846.

Perhaps recently he has been portrayed too much as a kindly innocent, the unworldly parish priest lost in the power politics of high office, pushed into extravagant actions by his 'liking to be

* The Italian states were Lombardy-Venetia (under Austria), Sardinia-Piedmont, Tuscany, Parma, Modena and Lucca, the Papal States and the Kingdom of the Two Sicilies.

D*

liked' by the people. Certainly he was swept away by the tide of events and certainly he failed to see the consequences of his actions, but 1848 saw many, much more seasoned politicians equally at a loss; after all Louis Philippe grossly misinterpreted the political portents and no one has accused him of political innocence and inexperience.

Pius was most at home in a pastoral role where the qualities which Cardinal Newman accorded him, 'his uncompromising faith, his courage, the graceful mingling in him of the human and the divine', combined to make him a most successful bishop; so much so that on his translation to Imola from Spoleto the people of Spoleto petitioned Rome that he might continue as their archbishop. At Imola he continued to attach primary importance to the welfare of his flock as one story told of him bears out. A parish priest sent a particularly delicious fish to the bishop only to have it returned untouched with the comment 'that he ought to employ his spare money in helping the poor instead of offering dainties to his bishop'.

However his simplicity can be overdrawn. Newman goes on to refer to 'the humour, the wit', and his wit was more than the gentle humour of a simple man of God. Perhaps two anecdotes will serve to illustrate this wit and hence illumine his character. When he was still at Imola the gonfalonier's wife wanted him to become the godfather of her baby but the gonfalonier objected, disapproving of the bishop's liberalism. On being elected Pope a few weeks later Pius wrote to the gonfalonier, asking: 'You refused as godfather the Bishop of Imola, would you accept the Bishop of Rome?' Then, much later in his pontificate, the story was told of Pio Nono in conversation with his Secretary of State, Antonelli, lighting a cigarette and handing the case to the cardinal, who said:

'You know, Holiness, that I have not that vice.'

'You know, Eminence,' replied the Pope, 'that if it were a vice you would have it.'*

However politically inexperienced, Pius was genuinely a progressive. He came of a family considered liberal and he had liberal acquaintances at Imola: the delay in his becoming a cardinal is usually claimed to have been due to his progressive tendencies. His period as Archbishop of Spoleto had not pleased everyone at

* The first anecdote can be found in Hales' *Pio Nono*, p. 33. The second is recounted in Ingram Bywater's *The Memoirs of an Oxford Scholar*, Oxford, 1917.

Rome, nor did some of his actions at Imola. He had read books usually thought of as advanced, such as Gioberti's *Il Primato*, and certainly he embarked upon his Pontificate with a view to reform.

But the impetus Pius gave to the forces of change in Europe came through his early actions as Pope rather than by his intentions.

His amnesty to political prisoners and exiles (over 1,200 were affected) was the first of the actions that helped to persuade Europe that the new Pope was a reformer; 'God never accords amnesties,' remarked Metternich. This was followed by a series of economic and social reforms.

What, however, heartened progressives the most was the Pope's concession to the principle of lay participation in government; particularly in the creation of the Consulta, an elected body to advise the Pope of which only the President need be a cleric.

Diplomatically, Pius clashed with the Austrians over the occupation of Ferrara. Allowed to garrison the citadel, the Austrian commander decided to reinforce his troops. Meeting with obvious signs of hostility he decided to occupy various key points in the city as well. Pius protested vehemently at this action and was rewarded in December 1847 when the troops retired within the citadel. 'Each day the Pope shows himself more lacking in any practical sense,' observed Metternich at this time. It might seem that this *démarche* was the result of the Pope's wish to appear as an Italian patriot but it more probably was the outcome of his very strong feeling for the essential integrity of the Papal States and his anger at any transgression of this. The same feelings were to motivate his actions when confronted with the altogether more serious disregard for his territory in 1860 although in this case the aggressor was the new Italian state itself.

Whatever the reasons that lay behind his actions their result was to convince Italians that they had a genuinely liberal and nationalist Pope, one who wished to implement the ideas of Gioberti. From the moderates to Mazzini, those who wished for change took heart and gained in confidence.

'The Revolution has taken hold of the person of Pius IX and of public opinion by raising again the old banner of the Guelphs in the name of the Holy See,' was Metternich's reading of the situation.* The story is told that Ferdinand, King of the Two Sicilies, sent his

* The Guelphs were the medieval Papal party in the struggles with the German Emperors.

children to bed at night to pray for the Pope who 'did not know what he was doing', and Metternich foresaw disaster: 'he has allowed himself to be taken and ensnared, since assuming the tiara, in a net from which he no longer knows how to disentangle himself, and if matters follow their natural course, he will be driven out of Rome.'

The excitement caused on all sides by the feeling that, as expressed at the time by Robert Wilberforce, there was 'a Radical Pope teaching all Europe rebellion', was enough to force other Italian rulers to give way and make concessions to demands for reform. The British Minister in Florence at the time wrote to Lord Palmerston: 'The spiritual power of the Pope is an element of the utmost consequence in this universal movement in Italy.'

Among the other Italian rulers roused by the election and subsequent actions of Pius IX was Charles Albert, King of Sardinia-Piedmont. No Italian state in the immediately post-Napoleonic period was more reactionary than Piedmont and in no sense could it be seen as the leader in social and political reform in the years which followed. Charles Albert had become king in 1831, still greatly agitated by his part in the Carbonari rising of 1821 when for a time he had filled the role of regent and seemed to work with the conspirators. He had had to expiate his revolutionary sins, taking an oath to Metternich never again to introduce or sanction a constitution.

His aims are difficult to discern; he has been portrayed as the great patriot leader and as an incompetent and traitorous bungler. He does appear to have followed the traditional policy of the House of Savoy, which was one of balance between France and the Habsburgs, seeking to play one off against the other in order to expand or at any rate to exist.

The reforms of Pio Nono and the projects of the Pope to secure customs unions and military alliances, not to mention the idea of a confederation, forced Charles Albert to act more decisively and made it more difficult to maintain his political absolutism. His fear grew that unless he made gestures towards reform and Italian feeling he might find himself outflanked and his hopes for an enlarged Piedmont gone for ever.

At the same time as this swell of agitation for reform in Italy which extended to those Italian states which were part of the Austrian Empire, Metternich had to face increasingly confident manifestations of revolution elsewhere. One such example occurred in Switzerland. As a Radical Swiss leader of the time said, 'Switzerland is the microcosm of Europe. Those involved in this conflict are well aware that the crisis in Switzerland is merely part of the developing crisis in Europe.'

Switzerland was a sovereign republic, composed of separate cantons which had been given full independence and a guarantee of perpetual neutrality at Vienna. It was especially important to Europe because it served during the Restoration period as a launching-pad for revolutionary propaganda, a refuge for political exiles and a place where conspiracy and revolt could be plotted.* So long as political refugees sought sanctuary in the Cantons Metternich felt the need to interfere in and watch over events; for instance, his agents harried Mazzini when he was an exile there.

Ever since the revolutions of 1830, which had influenced Switzerland, an increasing number of the Cantons had become more liberal and reformist in their attitudes. The growing reformist element in the Cantons was partly democratic, partly more moderately liberal, but it was united in wanting a greater degree of centralization for the Republic and an extension of power for the Federal as distinct from the Cantonal. The conservatives wished to preserve Cantonal powers as they were. Crisis in fact came to a head over a religious dispute and led to a league being formed by the more conservative and Catholic Cantons to protect themselves. The formation of this league, the Sonderbund, in December 1845, was eyed with favour by Metternich who, although no Catholic zealot, saw the rising power of the democrats and centralists as a threat to European order.

Increasing support for the reformers gave them control of a majority of the Cantons and they used this majority to declare the Sonderbund incompatible with the Federal Pact and demanded its dissolution.† As this demand was not complied with war broke out in November 1847, resulting in a complete defeat for the Sonderbund. This was followed in 1848 by the introduction of a new, more centralized and democratic structure for the Republic, with adult male suffrage.

* Interesting in this context is the attempt in 1830 of the German Diet to bar German students from the universities of Zurich and Berne.

† Although only having a small majority in terms of Cantons the reformers represented over 80 per cent of the population of the Republic.

Metternich had sought to prevent this outcome and had approached the other leaders of the great powers to try to arrange intervention. However, in this he was thwarted by Palmerston who prevaricated until the Sonderbund was defeated. 'Today the powers are faced with Radicalism in control,' claimed Metternich, seeing, the Swiss war as 'a harbinger of revolt in Germany.' The failure to intervene further strengthened the confidence of the party of revolution.

In Germany also, the forces for change were gathering in the 1840s. These can be examined from two closely related aspects: first, the growing pressure for constitutions in those German states which did not have them and the extension of the constitutional right where such did exist; and secondly, the increase in nationalism, partly exhibited in relations with non-Germans, partly in the desire by Germans for more unity than the Confederation allowed them.

The 1840s saw a revival of liberalism despite Metternich's apparent success in stifling revolutionary tendencies after 1830. In Baden for example after 1843 the liberal members of the assembly agitated for the return of a free press, and were finally successful in 1847. In Bavaria, liberalism was given an opportunity to grow because of the involvement of King Ludwig with his 'Spanish' dancer, Lola Montez. She supported the liberals at first when she arrived in Bavaria in 1846 but opposition to the king mounted over the whole affair. His mistress was disliked as a foreigner, her meddling in political matters was resented, but most of all she encountered hostility because the infatuation of the fairly elderly king seemed unsuitable and ridiculous.* And, in addition to the liberal advance in Germany, the south German constitutional states witnessed the development of a democratic opposition led by such figures as Hecker and Struve. These men were behind a great popular gathering of democrats from the south-west and the Rhineland at Offenburg in the autumn of 1847.

However, more significant for Germany, was the change of king in Prussia. In 1840 Frederick William IV had succeeded his father and Prussia modified her political course. Prussia was so much larger and more powerful than any other member of the Confedera-

---

* Lola was really a Scot, and she had once been the reigning belle of Simla. Later she was to be prosecuted for bigamy in England, to horse-whip a newspaper editor in Austrialia, and to visit reformed prostitutes in the U.S.A., before dying at the age of thirty-eight.

tion, with the exception of Austria, that what happened to her was of the greatest importance. That someone of the personality and character of Frederick William IV should succeed to the Prussian throne in 1840 is another of those chances which no one can say were inevitable yet which demonstrably had a decisive influence on subsequent events.

Before his accession, and for some time after it, Frederick William was thought to be favourable to the hopes of the liberals. Some of his actions indeed encouraged these hopes. One was his restoration of the old liberal Arndt to his professorship at Bonn; another was his gracious reception of the poet Herwegh.* However, Frederick William was no liberal, he was not even a progressive in the sense Pio Nono was when he first became Pope.

Frederick William III had promised his subjects no less than five times that he would grant a constitution, but had done nothing further about it. His son, though determined not to grant a constitution in the sense understood by liberal opinion of the time, nevertheless did seek to enlarge the role of his subjects in Prussian affairs. An incentive for his initiative was a law of 1820 which declared that any new loan or increase in taxation would be illegal without the agreement of 'the future representation of the people.' Frederick William wished to raise such a loan or to increase taxation to pay for the construction of railways.†

Frederick William's plan was to develop the traditional Estates of the various Prussian provinces and he called all the seven provincial Estates to Berlin to constitute a United Diet in the spring of 1847. However, liberals in the Diet voiced demands for a free press and a constitution and refused to grant the king the loan that he wanted. Metternich commented on developments to the king of Württemberg in a letter at this time: 'Where the evil appears it is unmistakable and Prussia has come to grief. Already the king has been drawn on to a path along which he did not mean to venture.'

Historians sometimes seek to explain Frederick William by portraying him as a romantic, dwelling on his artistic enthusiasms

* Herwegh was the current hero of German democracy who a couple of years previously had escaped from Prussia to Switzerland after difficulties during his period of service in the army, and there had published *Poems of One Who Is Alive.*

† Engels looked upon this as mere subterfuge and saw the king's financial difficulty as the outcome of his own extravagance and incompetence.

and abilities, and then pointing to his mental instability which culminated in insanity. The warped romanticism which this might imply does, of course, accord with Frederick William's love of the medieval and his respect for the historically established. His employment of an essentially feudal institution, the Estates, his attachment to the view of his being 'the Lord's Anointed' and his great respect for the Habsburgs as the traditional leaders of Germany exemplify this romantic atavism. 'His commercial embarrassments were the sharpest satire upon his medieval proclivities' was the somewhat unkind comment of Engels.

Frederick William was artistic and romantic but, what is sometimes forgotten, he was also very intelligent. Metternich, seeking to explain Frederick William's policies, painted him as trying to create foundations for his government without endangering his sovereignty 'by a form of popular representation after the fashion of modern constitutions.' Instead he was trying to secure liberties for his subjects by resting them on traditional foundations. In his desire to resist the revolution which had overtaken Europe he was seeking to return to the previous order; in his attempts to combat the desire to sever society from her links with the past, he strove to strengthen those links. But the question Metternich asked was, 'are the isolated will of one prince and the purity of his intentions enough of themselves to ensure the success of undertakings which make a direct appeal to the mind of men?'; thus highlighting the failure of Frederick William to see that mankind will not necessarily accept ideas which are self-evident to their author.

When it is remembered that Frederick William was brought up as a prince, and a prince in a rather provincial and unsophisticated court, it is not surprising that he might have come to overvalue his considerable talents and intelligence. With his assurance in his own ability and understanding he grew to believe that he was always right. When it came to implementing his ideas, to translating the core of the theory into practice, Frederick William lost interest. He failed to understand that compromise and hard bargaining were essential and either hectored and blustered or gave up, sometimes the two in turn. His creative, artistic streak may perhaps have inhibited him from gladly acquiescing in the second best, but often his subsequent indifference contributed to his failure to obtain even that.

People who knew the king talked of his impatience, his naivety over politics and personal behaviour, his lack of stamina. Metternich likened the difference between him and his father to that between a fairy story and an epic; his mother is claimed to have seen him as 'a prey to the passing moment'. He disdained the need to be painstaking and careful, holding to his own ability to comprehend in a flash. 'Where careful scrutiny will reveal only insurmountable difficulties, the king with a whimsicality all his own sees only a task calling for genius,' opined Metternich. 'The king reckons too much on the power of his genius,' claimed the Chancellor.

He was not prepared to relate his attitude to circumstances or to subordinate his personal feelings to reality, as is so clearly shown by his rejoicing over the downfall of Louis Philippe in 1848. This unwillingness to face a situation also characterizes his paintings which have been described as 'for the most part southern land-scapes, done in the cool north with a pen inspired by longing ... the visions of a restless brain, striving to escape from the hideousness of everyday.' Too much exposure for a mind like this to such a reality as the events of 1848 were to bring, was always likely to lead to the total retreat from this reality provided by insanity. This is precisely what happened in the case of Frederick William.

But his accession was certainly important in the growth of the hopes of German nationalists. Although attached to the idea of a German nation, Frederick William was inhibited from really bidding for German leadership because of his sincere belief in the historic role of the Habsburgs as Germany's 'Arch-Dynasty'. Nevertheless, Prussia did begin to play a more prominent part than under Frederick William III in military matters, in trying to secure the repeal of the Federal Press Law of 1819, and finally in pressing Metternich for a conference of princes to discuss constitutional reforms for the Confederation.

However, it was the parliamentary liberal and democratic move-ments, the former goaded by the latter, which voiced nationalist aspirations most loudly. A meeting of liberal opposition parties from the constitutional states of south-west Germany took place in the autumn of 1847 and decided to summon a larger gathering the following spring to discuss further measures for securing German unity by parliamentary means. Meanwhile, at first in Baden, deputies in the constitutional states sought to push their own rulers into forwarding a German parliament.

The growth of German nationalism can also be followed in

German reaction to foreigners. The surge of patriotism resulting from what was seen as a French threat in 1840, and which produced the mood of 'Wacht am Rhein' and 'Deutschland über Alles' as well as German-Danish hostility over the future of the Duchies of Schleswig and Holstein, was both cause and symptom of the growth of national feeling.

Nationalism was also challenging the established order in the Habsburg Empire. In Bohemia, opposition came from two directions although it might seem like one single force on impact. First there was the old aristocratic opposition to the central government. Operating through the Estates it sought to curb the government's powers to allocate and dispose of taxation; it claimed the right to initiate legislation and demanded the restoration of ancient freedoms. This was a feudal, provincial opposition and was in no way specifically anti-German but it became tangled with Czech nationalism which was.* The nobles looked to this growing movement for support and were influenced by it, adopting some of its policies. These were much more radical, socially and politically, seeking equality for the Czech language and a unity for the old lands of St. Wenceslaus: Bohemia, Moravia and Silesia (though the latter was in the main inhabited by Germans).

The tradition of independence in Hungary had never been lost, as the fate of Joseph II's attempts to germanize it had so clearly shown. Hungary, as the 'Kingdom of St. Stephen', consisted of Croatia and Transylvania besides Hungary proper. The magnates in Hungary who composed the Upper House in the Diet thought of themselves as Habsburg nobles, often living in Vienna for much of the year and marrying into the other noble families of the Empire. The Lower House represented the remainder of the nobility; a much more numerous class than in most European countries— being about one in fifteen of the population—they varied enormously in their wealth and the quantity of land which they owned. They, along with the magnates, had the privilege of paying no taxes and held a virtual monopoly of political power. The lesser nobles were fiercely proud of being Magyar and jealous of Viennese attempts to wrest control of the country from them. However, not only did they

---

* An example of this is the way in which Czech nobles patronized Palacky. He edited the *Museum Journal* and began to publish his *History of Bohemia* in 1836. This work portrayed the political past of the Czechs and demonstrated the large part in it played by conflict between Czech and German.

fight for the right of the Magyars to run Hungary but they also pressed for Croatia and Transylvania to be brought under Hungary.

Nevertheless it was one of the great magnates, Count Széchenyi, who by 1830 was leading the nationalist movement. At the same time as fighting for a full restitution of the Magyar language he, familiar with western Europe and Britain, sought to develop the economy as well. But Széchenyi wished to avoid hostility to the Imperial government and this clearly inhibited his nationalism. The lead instead passed to Kossuth who came from the minor nobility and was more extreme and radical in his ideas. The Diet of 1847 saw those who were fighting for national reform produce a common programme.

They asked for a more equitable system of taxation—implying a sacrifice for themselves, the abolition of serfdom with compensation for the landlords, a parliament elected on a wider franchise than the existing Diet, a government which would be responsible to it, and the incorporation of Transylvania into Hungary.

Meanwhile, however, a counter-Magyar nationalism was emerging. The determination to extend the use of the Magyar tongue had led to the declaration of Magyar as being the exclusive state language. In the past the Croat nobility had made common cause with the Magyars to resist Vienna but the growth of Magyar chauvinism was bringing about a reappraisal. The abolition of Latin as the official language for government business and the substitution of Magyar particularly incensed the Croat nobility and led to their increasing support for the Croat nationalist movement, although it was as yet much less developed than its Magyar counterpart.

1846, the year Pius IX became Pope, saw a revolt in Galicia, a Polish province of the Austrian Empire. It was a nationalist revolt, seeking to re-establish an independent Poland. In Poland as in Hungary national consciousness was really confined to the gentry which, again as in Hungary, constituted a larger proportion of the population than in many European countries. Extending from rich landowners to people living much as the peasants, the gentry embraced nearly all the educated classes. In this way they took the place of the middle class of most western European states, with the added point that their background and traditions made them much less timid and more used to fighting.

The 1830–1 revolt in Poland had demonstrated that the peasantry as a whole, and not merely the non-Polish Ruthenes (or little

Russians), were largely untouched by the ideas of nationalism. The Polish Democratic Society held that revolution had failed in Poland because the peasantry had never been mobilized on its side and they set out to remedy this by incorporating social reform into the revolutionary programme. Even so, in 1846, there was little understanding between the classes; enormous mutual hostility and suspicion was the rule.

The accession of Frederick William IV in 1840 had encouraged the Polish nationalists and a revolt was planned in 1846 against the three partitioning powers. However, the leader, Mieroslawski, was much too open in his preparations and was arrested in Posen by the Prussians at Russian instigation. This event broke the revolt in the Prussian and Russian provinces, but scattered outbreaks did occur in Austrian Galicia. However, these were totally submerged by a jacquerie against the landlords on the side of the Austrian government in which some 2,000 of the Polish gentry were killed. It is not clear just what part the Imperial authorities had in these events; despite the stories of local officials promising payments 'per capita' for slaughtered gentry, involvement has never been proved. Certainly the government was forced to promise to abolish the Robot (compulsory labour rent) in Galicia. The small free state of Cracow containing about 136,000 people, which was all that 1815 had left of an independent Poland, was occupied by Austrian troops and subsequently annexed to the Empire in October 1846. It might seem that the Galician revolt at least had been successfully dealt with but the manner of it was most disturbing to an Empire whose structure was based on land ownership. At the same time the fear of revolution in Europe became stronger.

It was not only the political aspects of revolution which were straining the fabric of the European Order—the World of the Restoration—by the 1840s. The economic revolution was also bringing dislocation and difficulty. The competition of large-scale industry in Britain, and in its early stages elsewhere, was slowly strangling traditional handicrafts. Even in the Austrian Empire, much more economically retarded than France, there were over two hundred spinning mills with more than 250,000 spindles by 1847. The Silesian silk-weavers had felt this sort of competition in 1844 and risen in revolt, but all over Europe similar distress existed even if it did not always have such spectacular results. Masters and journeymen were forced to abandon their crafts and seek employment in the new factories. Sometimes they were overtaken by competition from abroad before the advance at home had reached the stage of providing factories to offer them jobs. Considering also the problems created by the enormous increase of population discussed earlier, it is easy to see why towns were swelling with people who were often without work; for instance the population of Vienna nearly doubled between 1815 and 1848. Although there was a great rise in emigration to the United States from Germany and France, this escape was not always an easy one for the landlocked.

1845 saw a disastrous potato crop and a poor corn harvest over much of Europe. The following year the failure of crops was still more widespread. For the countryside, already undergoing the decline of its handicraft industries, which organized as cottage industries had played an important part in the peasant economy, the crop failure resulted in catastrophe. In the towns while wages stayed the same, food prices climbed abruptly, and with mounting unemployment destitution set in.* In the prevailing conditions of malnutrition it is not surprising that disease should add its ravages to a situation that was already intolerable. Thus in many parts of Europe food riots occurred among growing disorder; in Vienna attacks on foodshops and bakeries were frequent events.

'So when 1848 opened, all Europe was restless and hungry,' wrote Clapham. However he went on to say, 'it was also in financial difficulties', and this is the aspect of the crisis that is not always so clearly understood. It was, in this context, the first of those modern crises of finance and credit that were to occur over the next century and a half, and of which 1931 is probably the best known example.

During 1847 a financial crisis shook Europe. In England, where it was most severe, the recent Bank Charter Act had to be modified to allow the fiduciary issue (bank notes issued in excess of gold backing the bank held) to be increased, so short was cash. The current railway mania and the growth of industrial investment generally had created a situation of overstrain in which too high a proportion of capital was tied up in fixed assets. This position, one of over-extended credit, produced a scare and a headlong demand to turn the credit back into cash, a demand which obviously could not

---

* The common labourer's wage in 1847 was reckoned to be inadequate to allow him to procure essentials. Also at this time a third of the population of East and West Prussia had ceased to eat bread and had come to rely entirely on potatoes.

be satisfied. The bad harvests had been followed by high imports of corn from outside Europe which had to be paid for in gold, thereby further denuding the reserves. Naturally bankruptcies were frequent, each aggravating the situation further, and the credit crisis spread across into agriculture. Further bankruptcies came in 1847 in England when a better harvest caused corn prices to sag, thus catching speculators. This financial crisis in Britain, as well as resulting in an economic slow-down, set off a chain-reaction all over Europe as British investments abroad were cashed and brought home; thereby, as it were, exporting the liquidity problems.

The general economic and financial gloom of 1847 was perhaps lifting a little in 1848—certainly it was in Britain—but it still hung heavily over Europe. It was small wonder that the American Consul in Amsterdam, discussing the German emigrants passing through, could write: 'All well-informed people express the belief that the present crisis is so deeply interwoven in the events of the period that "it" is but the commencement of that great Revolution, which they consider sooner or later is to dissolve the present constitution of things.'

However, economic distress of itself rarely produces revolution. Nowhere in 1848 were the conditions worse than in Flanders with the hand-loom weavers in total distress, yet there was no revolution in Belgium; Britain also survived the 'Hungry Forties' without revolution. And in 1831 the Lyons silk-weavers, their wages forced down because of foreign competition, had broken out in rebellion only to be suppressed by the troops of Marshal Soult. A vital factor in the lack of revolution in England and Belgium and the earlier suppression of rebellion in Lyons was the attitude of the governments concerned. It is to these we must turn; especially to the government of Vienna, the lynch-pin of Restoration Europe.

Chapter IX

THE DECAY OF THE OLD

IN THE early nineteenth century the Austrian Empire had, in the words of a contemporary observer, been 'called upon to discharge the function of ballast in the European ship of state', and her condition was therefore of vital importance for the stability of the ship. Metternich had no doubt as to her condition by the 1840s: 'I am no prophet, and I know not what will happen; but I am an old practitioner, and I know how to discriminate between curable and fatal diseases. This one is fatal; here we hold as long as we can; but I despair for the issue.' His daughter said of him at this time that he had never seen, during the long period of his public career, 'so dark a future, such sombre clouds'. Why was Metternich so gloomy?

The short answer is that, at a time of increasing difficulty in the Empire and in Europe generally, the Habsburg government appeared to be paralysed. 'Creaking wheels revolved lazily, and their motion was uncertain, unequal and difficult,' was how Count Hartig, a minister in the Habsburg government at the time, described the situation. Two successive Prussian diplomatic representatives at Vienna sent home despatches describing the hopeless confusion round the Emperor. In the face of mounting unrest in Italy the government was unable to reinforce the army to anything like the extent that commanders requested. It was necessary to borrow heavily to cover current expenditure, the government feeling it an unpropitious time to seek an increase in taxation; so there was no hope of increasing expenditure. Metternich wrote to Radetzky, the Austrian commander in Italy and a fellow survivor of the struggle against Napoleon: 'We are destined by Providence not to spend our old age in repose. The past called for great efforts from us, but it was better than the present.' The Chancellor, at this crucial juncture, had suffered great physical decline; he was becoming deaf and was somewhat blind in one eye, no longer did the old resilience remain. '*Ich bin so lebensmüde*,' he wrote to his wife in 1847.

But perhaps the most important contributory cause to this decline of the Habsburg government had been the death of the Emperor Francis in 1835. Bigoted, narrow and inflexible as he was, he did represent a determined will: so long as he was alive the Empire was governed. His death transformed the situation, for his eldest son, Ferdinand, was physically and mentally an invalid, subject to epilepsy, 'as unfitted for willing as for thinking', according to the historian Treitschke. Baron Hügel who visited Ferdinand in 1849 after his abdication has left a revealing account of the meeting. 'I found the Emperor as usual, exceedingly gracious and affable.' After some discussion the Emperor asked if the visitor wished to see the Empress, and the reply being in the affirmative, went to fetch her. 'I could see him run with great nimbleness, along the inlaid floor, slippery as a looking-glass.' Hügel's conversation with the Empress was terminated when word came that the Emperor had already taken himself to dinner. The undignified and rather grotesque figure that emerges from this account (a piece of writing it should be said which in no way sought to attack or denigrate the Habsburgs) goes some way to justifying Palmerston's remark about a 'government where the sovereign is an idiot.'

Although not quite the mental defective he has sometimes been portrayed as, Ferdinand was obviously not going to be able to take the dominant role in the running of the Empire played for so long by his father. 'We now have an absolute monarchy without a monarch' was the judgment of Baron Kubeck, a government official. Francis had recognized this problem and there had been thoughts of passing over Ferdinand in the succession. However Francis's attachment to the principle of legitimate descent, together with the fact that his younger son Charles Louis was not really very much more suitable as a potential Emperor, caused Francis to resign himself to Ferdinand as his successor, after fortifying him with the precept to rely upon Metternich and change nothing. At the same time the old Emperor adjured the Chancellor not to desert his son.

The member of the royal family chosen to assist Ferdinand was Louis, Francis's youngest and favourite brother. The Archduke Louis, perhaps the least able of the brothers, was described by an American diplomat in Vienna as 'advanced in years and still more antiquated in his opinions and policy'. He had had great affection for his eldest brother and over the years had come to model himself upon Francis. Thus he was a firm adherent of leaving everything as it had been in Francis's reign, and naturally pursued the same sort of immobile policy with the same hostility to experiment and fear of change: 'letting it lie is the best way of dealing with it' was one of his maxims. However, he was by no means as strong as his brother had been, and could be influenced, especially by members of his family, into a state of indecision and doubt.

Soon after Ferdinand's accession a Council of State was in-stituted, composed of Ferdinand himself, the Archduke Louis, Metternich, Ferdinand's brother Charles Louis, and Count Kolowrat. Kolowrat had been a minister under Francis and long a rival of Metternich. While not of outstanding ability, he did possess some technical understanding of the business of administration and his work in charge of the finances had earned the old Emperor's gratitude. However, the rivalry between Metternich and Kolowrat had developed into bitter dislike and distrust. This had gone so far that for long periods the two would not speak to each other and only communicated in writing; behaviour hardly likely to facilitate the transaction of State business. As the personal rival and enemy of Metternich, Kolowrat was believed opposed to the Chancellor's policies, and therefore of liberal or progressive tendencies in contradiction to the Chancellor's immobility and reaction. How-ever, this was not an accurate assessment; the hostility was personal rather than philosophical.

Of course other members of the royal family, not of the Council of State, were influential. Although frequently opposed to one another in their aims, they were united in their jealousy of Met-ternich and were determined to prevent him from becoming too powerful. Perhaps most important in the Court was the Archduchess Sophie, the Emperor's sister-in-law. She was an extremely lively and vigorous woman, the most outstanding of six sisters, Bavarian princesses, all of who were cultivated and intelligent. Sometimes known as the 'man of the Imperial Court' Sophie had early come to see that her husband, Charles Louis, was not a satisfactory vehicle for her ambition and hence centred her hopes upon her son, Francis Joseph.* If Ferdinand was not to have children, which

---

* Although the future was to demonstrate her ambition for other members of her family such as her son Maximilian who was to meet his death in a forlorn attempt to win the crown of Mexico.

seemed certain, this boy would succeed to the Imperial throne and
Sophie was determined therefore to preserve her son's inheritance.
At this time she believed it endangered by the refusal of the government to consider an accommodation with the forces for change in
the Empire and she felt that Metternich was inhibiting such an
accommodation. She was, however, at no time a progressive, whatever might have been believed of her.

The Archduke John, himself not innocent of personal ambition,
also advocated concessions by the government in the face of growing
dissatisfaction. John, an uncle of the Emperor, was disappointed
at his own share of power and resented the position of his less able
brother, the Archduke Louis. He too saw Metternich as a reactionary and an impediment, and manœuvred to secure his downfall. In this aim he had the support of the Archduke Stephen, the
Palatine of Hungary.

Metternich thus was in no position to dictate policies and in fact
often found himself having to intrigue to maintain his place and
influence. This state of affairs probably explains his apparent
change of heart over the Church; long a sceptic he now began to
favour the Church and assist it to gain more power in education.
It was certainly a departure which Sophie and the Empress wanted
and could well have been an attempt on the Chancellor's part to
appease them. Confronted by a situation that demanded the choice
to be made between concession and firmness, adaptation and
toughness, the Habsburg state was weak and lacking direction.

There have been several examples in history of a strong,
centralized state finding itself numbed by the death of its ruler and
the succession of an incompetent. If the entire bureaucracy and the
decision-making machinery operates through the ruler his ability
is crucial. Sometimes a strong minister backed by his king has been
able to maintain the momentum of state. Cardinal Richelieu
managed to perform this function under Louis XIII in seventeenth-
century France. However, Ferdinand was no Louis. He was
completely incapable of giving the kind of consistent support to his
minister as the French king had to Richelieu and he was frequently
incapacitated at a critical moment, never having the dignity and
command which Louis could summon. The Archduke Louis was
nearer the French king in character, but a member of the royal
family, even if officially regent, can never hope to have the authority
of a king, and the Archduke was not even regent.

Above all, Metternich was no Richelieu. The Chancellor possessed exquisite timing and the capacity to distinguish and register
the nuance. He was extremely perspicacious in his reading of
character and thus anticipating behaviour. But this consummate
diplomat, whose career one contemporary fellow diplomat claimed
to be the 'longest, the most difficult, and (for his own principles) the
most triumphant in the annals of modern diplomacy', lacked the
will and determination of Richelieu. Metternich might have great
powers to reason and analyse, powers that might let him discern the
way forward, but he did not have the ruthless will to hack away all
that might obstruct it. Confronted with the overwhelming dangers
that menaced the Habsburg Empire in the 1840s, impeded by the
jealousies and contradictory ambitions of the various members of
the Court, dogged by the rivalry of other ministers, and backed
only by an invalid Emperor and the uncertain Archduke Louis,
Metternich would have had to possess the qualities of a Richelieu, a
Bismarck and a Cavour as well as his own, to have any chance of
surmounting the dangers and emerging triumphant. Instead the
Chancellor was ageing, tired, rather dispirited and alone: he had
reason for his pessimism.

'Fear ever produces inactivity; while hope prompts action', wrote
an Austrian minister at this time. The inactivity of the Habsburg
government was certainly accompanied by growing hope and
activity among the opposition.

In Austria there was no nationalist cause which opponents of the
government among the nobility could espouse to gain support
from other social classes, in a struggle against 'foreign' domination,
as there was in other parts of the Habsburg Empire. Therefore to
find allies the nobles were committed to pursuing policies favourable
to the wishes of the liberals among the middle class. In their turn,
many of the liberals of Vienna turned to the members of the Lower
Austrian Estates (Vienna was part of Lower Austria); seeing the
Estates as the only channel through which reforming policies could
be urged upon the government with any chance of success.

Among several societies formed in Vienna where members of the
middle class came together with liberal nobles of the Lower
Austrian Estates such as Baron Doblhoff, two stand out in importance; the Lower Austrian Manufacturers' Association which was
started in 1840, and the Legal-Political Reading Club which opened
in 1842. The Reading Club in theory existed to provide its members

with important scientific and artistic works and periodicals, but in fact it acted as a forum for discussion of contemporary problems as well as providing a platform for visiting foreign celebrities. The Manufacturers' Association also ranged widely over the whole field of current issues besides trying to further modern industrial techniques.

At the same time the students at the University of Vienna became increasingly active in social and political matters. 'These young people, whose pursuit should have been study', in the words of Hartig, formed fraternities which corresponded with the students of other German universities, tried to keep abreast with the political literature of the time, and even sought to associate with the unemployed and working classes living in the suburbs of the city.

Under the police minister, Count Sedlinitzky, the tight censorship, the host of police spies and informers, the constant interference with correspondence combined with the rigid system of education had done much to stifle intellectual life.* However, by the 1840s the picture was changing. Although there was still a thorough control over what was printed in the Empire, more and more Austrian publicists were able to have their work produced elsewhere in Germany and smuggled back to Austria, where it stimulated and strengthened the movement for reform.

Engels was not far from the truth when, talking of the revolutionary elements in Austria by the end of 1847, he listed nearly all groups of the population:

'The peasant, serf or feudal tenant, ground down into the dust by lordly or Government exactions; then the factory operative, forced by the stick of the policeman to work upon any terms the manufacturer chose to grant; then the journeymen, debarred by the corporative laws from any chance of gaining an independence in his trade; then the merchant, stumbling at every step in business over absurd regulations; then the manufacturer, in uninterrupted conflict with trade guilds, jealous of their privileges or with greedy and meddling

---

* There were twelve censors in Vienna to whom everything that was to be published had to be shown. An example of their work was the statement 'a band of youthful heroes who flocked around the glorious standard of their country' becoming in their hands, because of its nationalist implications, 'a considerable number of young men who voluntarily enlisted themselves for public service'.

In the Book Catalogue of the Leipzig Easter Fair of 1839, out of the 3,127 titles listed of German publications only 180 were Austrian.

officials; then the schoolmaster, the savant, the better educated functionary, vainly struggling against the ignorant and presumptuous clergy, or a stupid and dictating superior. In short, there was not a single class satisfied. . . .'

Radetzky, the Austrian commander in Italy, was to claim. 'Milan has been lost at Vienna', but long before revolution broke out in Vienna the Viennese situation of a decaying government being confronted by increasing opposition was present in Lombardy and Venetia.

After the Austrians were expelled from Milan in 1848, the Milanese issued a manifesto 'to the European Nations', in which they listed the wrongs they had suffered under Austrian rule: 'The Austrian government levied immoderate taxes on our property, on our persons and on our necessary articles . . . it forced on us shoals of foreigners, avowed functionaries and secret spies, eating our substance, administering our affairs, judging our rights, without knowing our language or our customs . . . [it] spread around us nets of civil, ecclesiastical, military and judicial regulation all converging in Vienna, where lay monopoly of thought, will and judgement . . . it gave the police full power over liberty, life and property, and then threw the patriot into the same prison with the assassin.'

Nevertheless Lombardy and Venetia were the most prosperous, the most free and the best governed of all Italian states in the Restoration period. D'Azeglio spent, of his own volition, ten years of his life in Milan rather than his native Turin, and he explained: 'I, who was a professional hater of the foreigner, am compelled with shame to admit that, if I wanted to breathe, I had to return to Milan.'

The Lombards may have complained about their taxes but they were lighter than those they had to pay when they became part of a united Italy, and the Austrian government, on the whole, was honest and well-meaning, if unimaginative.

With the death of Francis and the succession of Ferdinand, despite the latter's journey to Italy in 1838 and his coronation with the Iron Crown of Lombardy, the anti-Austrian feeling grew. The very virtues of the Austrian administration made its deterioration more marked. Metternich, well aware of the growing difficulties, in August 1847 sent Count Ficquelmont to Milan as an adviser to try to strengthen the government's position.

However the effects of Pio Nono's actions were continuing to be felt in Lombardy, and an affray broke out over the arrival of the new Archbishop of Milan in September. The latter was Italian (his predecessor had been a German), and his enthronement was greeted with great excitement. The rejoicings, the exhibition of the Papal colours, and cries of *Viva l'Italia* heightened feelings and a mêlée ensued in which police intervened with drawn swords. Trouble continued and further disturbances occurred, leading to more casualties.

The police redoubled their efforts to check the manifestations of discontent and tightened their regulations. Several fashions adopted by the young Italians were forbidden. Hats of an odd shape, waistcoats of a peculiar cut or the dressing of the hair and beards in a certain manner, were all seen as emblems of revolt and prohibited. However, as soon as one fashion was banned another was adopted.

Trouble came to a head in Milan at the beginning of January 1848 with the 'Tobacco Riots'. These followed the decision taken by many Milanese to stop smoking and to prevent their fellow citizens from doing so.* On January 1, the boycott began peacefully enough and accounts vary as to how and why the situation got out of hand. However, violence was always likely to arise from the determination of the Milanese to discourage their less ardent compatriots from smoking, if necessary by force, since obviously the police and soldiers would feel called upon to intervene. It also seems that at least one Austrian soldier had a cigar snatched from his lips by the crowd, and returned immediately to report the incident to his fellows.

The counter-action of the army seems not to have resulted from the orders of Radetzky or the higher ranks, but rather to have arisen more spontaneously at junior officer and N.C.O. level. Groups of soldiers went into the streets, inviting interference as they blew smoke in the faces of bystanders, holding fistfuls of cigars, sometimes smoking two at a time and probably forcing the odd passer-by to smoke. This provocation naturally resulted in fighting and the soldiers seized the chance to attack civilians. The worst fighting was on January 3; although casualties were not heavy, a few people were killed, some of them certainly innocent of lawless behaviour.

Although the fighting stopped and the soldiers were confined to

* The sale of tobacco was a state monopoly and the decision to boycott it was derived from the refusal of the American Colonists to drink tea, which had led to the Boston Tea Party.

barracks, the outcome was an enormous heightening of tension. 'A great iniquity has been committed in Milan,' wrote D'Azeglio. The American chargé d'affaires in Vienna believed it 'evident that the day of combat rapidly approaches'.

The 'Tobacco Riots' feature the Austrian army and no account of the state of Austrian rule in Italy would be complete without a description of it. The army not only supported the civil authority in Lombardy and Venetia, but units were stationed in Parma and Modena, and of course it had, since 1815, intervened to quell revolt and disturbance in all the Italian states. It was the means of Austrian domination in the peninsula and its shadow hung heavily. In 1848 it consisted of about 70,000 men, only half the number that its commander, Field Marshal Radetzky, considered necessary for its task. There had been some reinforcement at the end of 1847 but the weakness of the government in Vienna, on top of the chronic financial difficulties of the Empire, precluded this being on the scale requested.

Despite this, however, as subsequent events were to demonstrate, the multi-national, multi-lingual army was an excellent fighting force. Much of the credit for this must clearly be given to its commanding officer, the eighty-one-year-old Radetzky.

In the succeeding year Radetzky appeared to hold the fortunes of the Austrian Empire in his hands: '*in diesem Lager ist Österreich*,' wrote Grillparzer. Yet in 1832 his career seemed finished. He had made a promising start as a young staff officer at Marengo, had been a general at Wagram and served with distinction as Chief of Staff at Leipzig. But heavy debts incurred by his wife had encumbered him and led to his eclipse. However, in 1834 he was recalled to be commander of the army of Italy.

Radetzky had had a joyless family life; his own youth, his marriage and, with the exception of his daughter, his relations with his children were all barren of love and affection. Instead this man had come to see in the army the purpose that his personal life lacked. This institution, and the state it served, captured all his loyalty. Here he derived his security; here he lavished his devotion. Very strong and determined, of enormous energy and vitality (he fathered an illegitimate child at the age of seventy-nine), Radetzky was master of five languages. The latter accomplishment assisted him in maintaining contact with his soldiers, something he felt to be of paramount importance. Enormously popular with the troops,

Radetzky had managed to build up and preserve high morale in the army during a trying period. Here, certainly, there was no sign of the decay of the old.

Just as the Quadruple Alliance was crucial to the defeat of Napoleon, so its maintenance was crucial to the Restoration Settlement. The enlargement of the Alliance by the rehabilitation of France among the victorious powers and the consequent vicissitudes of the Alliance have already been discussed. With the change of regime in France in 1830 a regrouping of the powers appeared likely: Britain and France, the two constitutional states, on one side and the three autocratic eastern Courts on the other. However, this division never hardened, partly because of the rivalry between Britain and France which developed in the Mediterranean and partly because of the Powers' refusal to allow doctrinaire attitudes to override national interests. In spite of the frequent alarms and crises the victorious allies had, in the last resort, usually continued to hang together. What challenges there had been occurred on the periphery of Europe, in the Iberian Peninsula and the Near East. However by the mid-1840s the position had altered as Britain began to challenge Austrian policies in an area where Austria considered her security vitally threatened. It was in this way that the diplomatic scene demonstrated the decay of the old.

Perhaps the best date to pin-point this change is 1846, which saw the return to the Foreign Office of Lord Palmerston. Contrary to what Metternich and other statesmen from time to time claimed, Palmerston was not a 'revisionist'. He believed in peace and the peace guaranteed in the Treaties of 1815. Where he differed from other European statesmen was in the manner in which he thought this peace might be best achieved.

Palmerston considered that the most likely way to avoid revolution in Europe was by governments granting timely concessions. 'In proportion as grievances are removed and nations become contented with their existing condition, in the same proportion each man among them devotes his mind to the improvement of his own individual condition, and ceases to think or to wish for any great alteration in the political state of the country to which he belongs.' Along with this belief in concession went Palmerston's dislike of interference by the major states in the ordering of other states'

METTERNICH
LITHOGRAPH AFTER LIEDER

MAZZINI

Photo Mansell Collection

PIUS IX
ENGRAVING AFTER
METZMACHER

Photo Mansell Collection

MANIN

Photo Mansell Collection

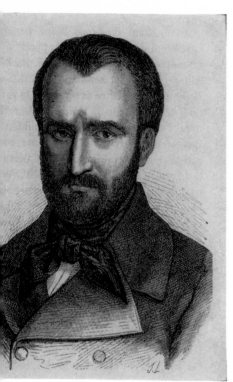

THE EMPEROR FERDINAND I
OF AUSTRIA

Photo Mansell Collection

FREDERICK WILLIAM IV
OF PRUSSIA,
APRIL 11, 1847

Photo Mansell Collection

METTERNICH FLEEING FROM VIENNA
CONTEMPORARY CARTOON FROM *ROMANTICISM AND REVOLT*

Photo Webb

CHARLES ALBERT OF SARDINIA

PAINTING BY HORACE VERNET IN THE ROYAL
GALLERY, TURIN

THE REVOLUTION IN PARIS: THE DEATH OF
THE ARCHBISHOP

VIENNA UNDER SIEGE: WINDISCHGRÄTZ'S
TROOPS MARCH IN

affairs: hence Palmerston's conviction that the peace of Europe would best be secured by moderate reforms and his determination to do what he could to forward them at the same time as he inhibited the autocratic powers from striving to prevent such developments.

Although he was powerless to do anything in 1846 when Austria, in defiance of the Vienna Treaty, annexed Cracow with the agreement of the other two eastern Powers, Palmerston was strong in his protests. However, when it came to Metternich's attempt to concert the actions of the major states against the Swiss Federal Government's attacks of the Sonderbund, Palmerston was able to thwart the Chancellor's schemes by delaying tactics, allowing the Federal troops time to win the war.

Where Palmerston found his best opportunity to influence affairs was in Italy. First, he stood by the Pope in his protests at the Austrian action in Ferrara in 1847: 'every independent sovereign has a right to make such reforms and improvements as he may judge conducive to the welfare of the people whom he governs.' Secondly, Palmerston sent Lord Minto, a member of the Cabinet, to Italy in the summer of 1847 with the object of discovering the real situation of the peninsula and of counselling him about it. At the same time he was to advise and support the Italian rulers in their reforms and progress towards liberalism: to encourage them to continue, to reassure them that Austria need not be feared and to succour them with hints of British protection.

Quite how far Minto forwarded revolutionary developments in Italy with his mission it is difficult to know. But he certainly disconcerted the Austrians and alarmed Ferdinand II of Naples while encouraging the hopes of the radicals. During his stay in Florence the streets are reported to have been hung with placards proclaiming, 'Death to the King of Naples!'

The return of Palmerston to the Foreign Office had one other important result. The entente with France had broken down in 1840 with France's anger at her isolation in a Near Eastern crisis. However, attempts had been made with some success by Guizot, the French minister, and Aberdeen, the British Foreign Secretary, to repair the damage. It is probable that rivalry in the Mediterranean would anyhow have prevented a lasting accord but Palmerston showed less interest in maintaining an entente. He was deeply aggrieved at what he felt to be Guizot's chicanery in marrying a French prince to the Infanta of Spain. The result was a personal

E

vendetta against Guizot, which included the release of politically
compromising documents to Guizot's main opponents in France.
Also, the end of friendship with England forced Guizot to turn
elsewhere for allies, as he feared a renewal of French isolation.
This search for friends pushed him towards Metternich and
Austria, a development which however satisfactory to Guizot and
Louis Philippe was anathema to the liberals in France. Thus,
although not a fundamental cause, Palmerston's policy without
doubt assisted in the undermining of Guizot's position.

While the city of Palermo was celebrating the birthday of its king
with artillery salutes and military parades, it found itself being
called upon to rise in insurrection, to cries of '*All'armi!*' and
'*Viva Pio Nono, Viva l'Italia!*' The day was January 12, 1848, the
king, Ferdinand II, and this was the beginning of the Sicilian
revolution: the first revolution of the 'Year of Revolutions'.

Remarkably, this revolution had advertised itself in advance.
Following disturbances earlier in the winter, reports were rife of an
insurrection planned for January 12. Then, two days before, a
proclamation was openly posted announcing the date to all. 'At
dawn on January 12, 1848, the glorious period of universal regenera-
tion will commence. Palermo will welcome with rapture all armed
Sicilians who volunteer to support the common cause. . . .'

Even more remarkably, the Neapolitan government did next to
nothing to prepare itself for the announced revolution, although the
situation had led to British ships standing by at Messina and
Palermo in case of danger to British interests.

In fact, the rising began rather half-heartedly, despite the
presence among the crowds in Palermo of men from the surrounding
countryside who had been sent in to assist it. Most seemed content
to watch the efforts of the handful of revolutionaries and listen to
their exhortations rather than to follow them. If prompt military
action had been taken it appears likely that order would soon have
been restored. However, the military did not act with firmness or
speed, and, fearing a general rising, after only feeble attempts to
re-assert control they contented themselves with securing vital
positions. These defensive tactics allowed the revolt to spread and
much of the city fell under the insurgents' control. The following
day the revolutionaries, though still inadequately armed, took the

offensive and began to attack bands of police and army patrols. A provisional government was formed and reinforcements rushed in from near-by towns and villages to help promote the revolution.

The artillery which the army possessed was not at first employed, and then only sporadically, in an attempt to bombard the city into surrender. This was partly the outcome of the general hesitancy and indecision which paralysed the command throughout, but in particular it was because of the protests of the foreign consuls. The role of Britain was especially important, not just because of her ships but because, ever since the period of French domination of Naples, and Sicilian independence under the protection of the British fleet, Britain had been suspected by the Neapolitans of having designs upon Sicily and being prepared to assist revolution in their pursuit.

Although Palmerston's previous policy had seemed aggressive, and undoubtedly Englishmen present in Sicily did give unofficial help and encouragement during the revolt there is little evidence of direct involvement. General Pepe (the same who led the 1820 Carbonari revolt), on inquiring of his English friends what assistance he would receive if he was to go to aid the Sicilians in 1848, was told that he 'might expect much sympathy, but not the smallest aid in arms, men, or money'. However, whether the suspicions were accurate is unimportant, their existence was what was significant. The belief that the British would intervene was enough to inhibit the already panicky and pessimistic authorities. It also increased the doubts of the Neapolitan king when he received reports that he was faced not only with rebellion in Palermo, but with a full Sicilian revolt.

The first reaction of the Neapolitan government to the outbreak had been to dispatch reinforcements, and at least 5,000 troops arrived in Palermo on the night of January 15. However, the commander of the flotilla which brought them, the king's younger brother the Count of Aquila, was disturbed at what he saw and took back discouraging reports to Naples. King Ferdinand decided that the best solution to the crisis was to try to come to terms with the rebels by negotiation; but while proposals, allowing a degree of self-administration for the island, were being decided upon and forwarded to Sicily, the hostilities continued. On arrival, the proposals were promptly rejected by the rebels, now everywhere on the offensive and driving the royalists before them. January 24 saw the

troops evacuating Palermo and soon the order for general embarka-
tion arrived. The army, much bedraggled and leaving quantities of
equipment and horses behind it, left for Naples on the 19th and over
the next few days, with the exception of the citadel of Messina, the
remaining forts capitulated and their garrisons left the island. 'Our
Fatherland is free and we are worthy of our Fatherland,' declared
the Revolutionary Committee.

Enormously encouraged, liberals in Naples began to clamour for
a constitution. An insurrection in the Cilento region and reports of
disaffection in the army deprived Ferdinand of the will to stand
firm despite the exhortations of the Austrian Ambassador, Prince
Schwarzenberg. Schwarzenberg claimed, probably quite correctly,
that those demanding a constitution only numbered a few thousand
and that the masses had no desire for such changes. The only way
that the 'turbulent minority' could achieve their ends would be if
the government gave in, frightened of a confrontation. People
around Ferdinand, however, sensed the direction in which events
were moving and their manœuvres and shifts decided the king.
On January 29, having dismissed his cabinet, Ferdinand announced
his intention of granting his subjects a constitution. 'Having heard
the general desire of our beloved subjects . . . we declare that is it
Our will to gratify this by granting a constitution.'

Schwarzenberg wrote to Metternich: 'The game is up. The King
and his ministers have completely lost their heads.' Although
Metternich commented, 'I defy the ministers to lose what they
have never possessed', the decision was momentous. The other
Italian rulers who had so far stopped short of granting constitutions
in their reforms now found themselves under irresistible pressure.
Charles Albert granted a constitution on February 9 and he was
followed by the Grand Duke of Tuscany, and finally by the Pope.

Perhaps it was fitting that the first revolution of 1848 broke out
in Sicily since this island probably had the oldest revolutionary
tradition in Europe, going back centuries before the French
Revolution and directed principally against foreign domination.
The essential difference between the revolutionaries of Sicily and
those of Naples is that the former represented the whole population
and were not confined to one group or class. Those who wished for
change on the mainland were of the middle class and nobility. At
times peasants might join in outbreaks of violence in protest
against their poverty and distress but they had no common interest

with those who wished for a constitution. The latter, both democrats and moderates, had been increasingly stirred by the reforms of the Pope in Rome. They also wished for some sort of Italian state, although like Italians elsewhere, they differed in the sort of Italy they wished for and the degree of unity it should have.

In Sicily the nationalism was Sicilian rather than Italian. What Italian nationalism there was saw an independent Sicily taking her place in a federal Italy. The resentment felt for rule from Naples was something that could be felt at the same time by those powerful and wealthy Sicilians who believed that the important positions in their island went increasingly to Neapolitans and by the liberals who saw the extinction of their constitution of 1812 as being the result of the loss of their autonomy and their incorporation into Naples; also those suffering grinding poverty and oppression could always blame Neapolitan exactions for their condition. This anti-Neapolitan feeling was capable of bursting out with extraordinary strength. Perhaps the best example was the hysteria and violence in 1837 which followed the cholera epidemic. It was generally believed that this was the result of a deliberate attempt by the Neapolitans to poison the Sicilians. Mobs took 'justice' into their own hands in answer to leaflets demanding revenge 'against the oppressors of our Fatherland and our lives'.

This hostility to rule from Naples was exploited by revolutionaries from elsewhere in Italy who maintained contacts with Sicily. September 1847 had witnessed an attempt at a co-ordinated revolution in Reggio and Messina, and previous united action in Naples and Sicily against their common ruler had been tried in 1844. However, successful co-operation would always be difficult as the revolutionary tradition in Sicily was above all separatist, whereas the constitutionalists in Naples never wanted Sicilian autonomy.

Subsequent events and one-sided propaganda have contributed to the portrayal of Naples as the most reactionary of Italian states and Ferdinand, its ruler, as the most cruel and tyrannical of Italian rulers. In fact, under Ferdinand, Naples had the first railway, the first steamboat and the first iron bridge in Italy. An odd and unintended tribute to Ferdinand's patronage of progress comes from General Pepe, the life-long revolutionary and 'Progressive'. He describes how, on his return to Naples from exile in 1848, he rode in a lift, obviously, from the description, a novel experience:

'[I] was conducted by the king to a very small cabinet where I was seated opposite him, without knowing the motive. I felt we were descending, and then I perceived that we were in a machine constructed to descend and ascend, in order to avoid the fatigues of mounting the lofty stairs.'

Naples saw consistent progress under Ferdinand, by no means an inhuman ruler. Ferdinand was certainly an absolutist by conviction and by upbringing but for the first eighteen years of his reign he showed magnanimity to his subjects and much more forbearance in punishing rebels than, for example among his contemporaries, Charles Albert. Because of the success of pamphleteers, he is known by many as one who bombarded his subjects and played cruel practical jokes on his wife. It might be more appropriate if he were remembered for his behaviour at an entertainment in his honour, in the last weeks of his life. Ferdinand had an unfortunate habit of hitching at his breeches and on this occasion he continually stood up in his box to do so. Each time the audience stood up also, thinking he was about to leave.

Ferdinand struggled above all to maintain his independence: independence from a constitution at home, independence from Austrian domination, and independence from English economic and diplomatic bullying. He had nothing to gain and everything to lose from the sort of Italian nationalism that would lead to war with Austria. If unsuccessful he would suffer at Austria's hands, if successful he would be merely helping to aggrandize Charles Albert and Piedmont. Consequently Ferdinand was trying to maintain the status quo while bettering conditions in his kingdom.

None the less there were enormous failings in the personnel of government for which the king must take some of the blame. Also by 1848, although still a young man, he had lost much of his earlier energy and decisiveness. His actions and those of his government in the last weeks of 1847 and the first of 1848 show all the signs of 'the decay of the old'.

An account of the collapse of the Orléans regime, the 'Bourgeois Monarchy', might seem out of place under the heading, 'the decay of the old'. Born in revolution, it was after all a constitutional regime at a time when so many other European states were without constitutions. However, Louis Philippe's France had, long before 1848, become the despair of those who looked for change and radical development in Europe. It was evident that if European revolution required French support and patronage for its success, such a revolution must wait for the departure of Louis Philippe. Thus Louis Philippe personified the 'old' to many in Europe who awaited the end of his reign.

In fact Louis himself was as much as Metternich a man of the eighteenth century. His portrayal as the 'Bourgeois Monarch' misleads when it implies a mid-nineteenth-century businessman. Louis Philippe could never be classed as one of Matthew Arnold's 'Philistines', even if he was no 'Barbarian'. He was an extremely cultivated man, in the words of Tocqueville, 'enlightened, subtle, flexible'; the product of a very wide education. It would be difficult to find a man, and especially a monarch, who shared Louis Philippe's combination of academic training and practical experience. The former was the result of his father's liaison with the remarkable Mme de Genlis who acted as his 'director of studies'. The latter came from his varied and often hazardous progress through the Revolutionary and Napoleonic epic, in which he was, by turns, revolutionary soldier, unloved exile, son-in-law of the reactionary King Ferdinand of Sicily, participant in futile royalist expeditions and traveller in many lands including America. But not only was Louis Philippe knowledgeable and experienced, he was also intelligent and physically brave. It is not difficult to see why the Duke of Wellington discerned in him 'a prince of the most estimable character, great talent and deserved reputation'.

It was largely as a result of his experience allied to his reasoning that, although he was prepared to sanctify his regime with the *Tricoleur*. Louis Philippe was firmly opposed to policies of movement and revolution. He sought to build order and prosperity at home, and at the same time strove to preserve peace abroad. Louis Philippe was not affected by the temptation, felt by many of his countrymen in 1830, to impel France on a revolutionary crusade in Europe; he realized that such a policy was totally impractical in such an age. From then on he struggled against any such enterprise in his efforts to keep France at peace with the major European powers, as was instanced in 1840 when he dismissed Thiers, whose forward policy in the Near East was threatening to involve France in a conflict without allies.* This fear and distrust of foreign adventure

* In fact, whatever they might say in opposition, French statesmen when in

was certainly an important reason for Louis Philippe's determination
to hold on to the Guizot ministry, believing that a change of minister
might result in foreign entanglements that could lead to war.

Guizot, the dominant personality in the Soult–Guizot ministry
after 1840, remained in power until 1848, much the longest period
of government enjoyed by any of the king's ministers. A leader of
French Protestantism, a distinguished historian, a great orator,
Guizot achieved eminence in a variety of ways but was never
popular and has had little subsequent acclaim from historians.
Under the restored Bourbons Guizot had been a frequent critic of
the government but during the July Monarchy he was considered
the leader of conservatism. He, like his monarch, opposed further
concessions to reform and to liberalism. His attitude to reform,
along with his personal unpopularity, made him hated as a barrier
to progress and led to a combination of his enemies determined to
secure his downfall.

It has frequently been argued that the July Monarchy was
enormously corrupt. It has been said that the elections to the
Chamber were controlled by government bribery and influence, and
the freedom of the Deputies was constrained by the fact that many
of them were government servants. The government, 'a Joint Stock
Company for the exploitation of France's national wealth' in
Marx's words, is accused of doing nothing to help the great mass of
the people in the towns, particularly those in Paris, who found
themselves subjected to the effects of economic crisis as well as the
trauma of the gestation of the Industrial Revolution. From this
view of the 'Bourgeois Monarchy' the revolution which overthrew it
appears as one of contempt: 'the contempt into which the governing
class, and especially the men who led it, had fallen, a contempt so
general and so profound that it paralysed the resistance even of
those who were most interested in maintaining the power that was
being overthrown,' wrote Tocqueville. No longer would France
stand by and watch herself raped by the middle class, busy with its
own enrichment.

However, it is misleading to talk of the middle class as quite
such a homogeneous body. It contained many different categories
of people from various parts of France, whose interests, far from

power were to find it difficult to depart much from the line of Louis Philippe.
Lamartine during the Second Republic was to adopt an inactive policy,
claiming that *un règne négotiateur* might be as worthy as *un règne conquérant*.

being the same, were sometimes mutually opposed. There was, for instance, considerable opposition amongst some of the middle class to the industrial and economic changes taking place, and hostility for this reason to a government which allowed and even encouraged such changes. In this sense an entrenched section of the bourgeoisie can be distinguished, linked by reaction in their opposition to the government.

Again, there is little evidence of bribery being used extensively by the government to secure suitable electoral results: certainly succeeding regimes failed to produce any documentation despite their freedom of access to all information. It is also strange that 1846 was the only election under the July Monarchy in which the parties favourable to the ministry increased their representation at the expense of their rivals: hardly a story of successful corruption.

Of course, revelations of scandal and corruption did increase the unpopularity of the government and the governing class. 'A few glaring instances of corruption, discovered by accident, led the country to presuppose a number of hidden cases, and convinced it that the whole of the governing class was corrupt,' explained Tocqueville. There was a feeling of alienation from the governing class among many Frenchmen, but this should not be accepted as the explanation of the revolution which followed to the exclusion of other, more vital, factors.

Why then did a revolution break out in Paris in February of 1848? An enormously important factor was the revolutionary tradition of France: the tradition of the Jacobins, the Sans Culottes and the Enragés as well as that of Babeuf handed on through Buonarotti to Blanqui and the secret societies. Since the 1790s revolution was seen in France as a route, open to man, to improve his lot and right his grievances. What Heine, in Paris at the time, called *Guillotinomanie* was growing among Frenchmen in the 1840s. 'Depend upon it, dear Sir, that your revolution of July and our Reform Bill have made it impossible to stop the democratic machine which they have set in motion,' wrote Croker to Guizot. This democratic machine in France was seen as one that could be driven by revolution. Michelet, Lamartine and Louis Blanc published their histories of the French Revolution at this time; these books, though perhaps symptoms of the revolutionary tradition, strengthened the cult enormously. The economic crisis and the growth of socialism of course contributed to the current revolutionary

E*

attitude of mind, but they should not be detached from the older revolutionary tradition. The tradition was also infused with nationalism and was therefore offended by the apparent failures and lack of dynamism of the monarchy's foreign policy. The decline in the frequency of outbreaks and attacks against the king and his regime after 1840 should not be allowed to conceal the advance of the revolutionary tradition. It is against this tradition that the immobility of the regime should be viewed. Faced with demands for reform, the ministry feared that concession would be exploited by revolutionaries who advanced the cause of reform not for its own sake but as a convenient form of attack.*

The occasion of crisis was a proposed banquet in Paris, one of a series of such celebrations that were part of a campaign for parliamentary reform and the extension of the franchise. The campaign was led by moderates who formed the left opposition (the dynastic left) in the assembly as well as by Republicans, both moderate and radical, who wished the end of the monarchy: both those who wished to change the government and those who wished to change the form of government.

The growth of agitation and excitement generated in Paris by the proposed banquet led the government to decide to take firm action and prohibit it. The moderate opposition leaders had no wish for a trial of strength, and in addition, were disturbed by the extent and the nature of the support they were receiving. So it was decided that only a token demonstration would be held and the matter would then go forward to the Law Courts.

However, others took a more determined line, *Le National* and *La Réforme*, rival republican newspapers, printed on February 21 full plans of the demonstration for the following day, thereby ensuring that it would be more than a mere token. The decision of the majority of the opposition leaders to call off the banquet, printed in *Le National* on the 22nd, was too late and was unable to prevent the demonstration. Huge crowds thronged the city, there were outbreaks of violence and uneasiness grew as the day progressed. The following day began with increased agitation in the

---

* Some writers have stressed how little room for manœuvre the regime possessed. Abroad the diplomatic problems of 1846–7 posed by the increase in confidence of liberalism and nationalism, and at home the financial crisis and the need for a loan, together made the government tread warily and eschew experiment.

streets, but more important was the attitude of the National Guard, who were now called out. This middle-class body was unenthusiastic at best, and at worst, frankly hostile to the government. In theory they were there to stiffen the resolve of the regular troops, in fact their manner led to a crumbling of morale. Badly led, the National Guard and the army did not prosecute with vigour the existing plans for dealing with insurrection and in the mounting crisis the king wavered before deciding to dismiss Guizot.* However, his replacement, Count Molé, was unable to form a government, and as Guizot had foreseen, the shifts of policy increased the feeling of the breakdown in government.

Even so the situation was not yet hopeless. But the mood of the people became ugly when a procession, carrying the Red Flag, came into confrontation with soldiers guarding the Foreign Ministry. A shot was fired—it has never been satisfactorily established why and by whom—and in the ensuing panic the troops fired into the crowd, killing over forty people. A procession with some of the corpses paraded Paris, increasing acrimony and inciting anger. Molé meanwhile reported his failure to form a government to the king around midnight. Louis Philippe now called in Thiers and appointed Bugeaud as commander of all armed forces.

The start of the third day, the 24th, saw the troops under the direction of Bugeaud begin to clear the barricades which had sprung up in the streets. But lacking a really decisive lead and with the clear unwillingness of the king to accept bloodshed the advance of the troops began to peter out. Orders for withdrawal were followed by the crowd pressing forward to the Tuileries. The king, wishing to make a last attempt to retrieve the situation, decided to review those detachments of the National Guard and regular troops at the time in the precincts of the Tuileries. Meeting with a luke-warm reception and some cries for reform, Louis Philippe abandoned his review, and soon after returning to the palace, decided to abdicate in favour of his grandson. While the king fled Paris and the people celebrated their victory inside the Tuileries, a final attempt was made by his daughter-in-law before the assembly to save the monarchy for her son. However, this endeavour failed; the

---

* How much Guizot's actual resignation was due to his own pique, how much to the demand of the king, is in doubt, but certainly Louis Philippe had come round to the idea of a change of ministry as being the best way of dealing with the crisis.

assembly did not give her the backing she desired and moreover pressed on to nominate a provisional government.

The revolution was completed that evening outside the Hotel de Ville with the declaration of the Republic. The Provisional Government emerged after long discussion as an amalgam of those chosen by the assembly and the heroes of the two reformist opposition newspapers, *Le National* and *La Réforme*. The dominant personality was the poet Lamartine; it was his voice which proclaimed the Republic to an impatient crowd and his eloquence which saved the *Tricoleur* as the flag of the revolution when the crowd wished to adopt the Red Flag.

Three days of mounting insurrection in Paris had seen the downfall of Orleanist rule and the creation of the Second Republic. There was certainly a quality of spontaneity about the revolution; a people bursting into revolt with leaders who, almost until the last, thought they were mounting an attack upon the government of Guizot, suddenly to find that they were being swept in a revolutionary and republican current, with no other choice but to be borne along with it or to drown. Obviously, the revolutionary traditions of the people were of great significance in this outcome. Also important, clearly, was the lack of a legitimate base, hallowed by time, for the Orleans Monarchy to rest upon. Brought into existence by revolution, it followed a variety of governments which had been born and had perished in force.

Nevertheless, the part of the king was of supreme importance. The lack of a firm lead, the failure to back Guizot, the hesitations, and in the last resort, the refusal to fight for his throne, were the reasons for his fall. 'In 1848 he let the sceptre slip voluntarily from his hand,' admitted the socialist Louis Blanc. Tocqueville writes of the 'senile imbecility of King Louis Philippe' and 'his weakness'; perhaps this weakness was the product of age (he was seventy-four), perhaps a result of a lack of ruthlessness. 'If he did not fall as a king he knew how to fall as a human being' was the opinion of Blanc.

History has many examples of how the breakdown in government in times of rebellion can turn crisis into disaster. Conversely, by a steeling of the will and a regaining of nerve the insurrection can be quelled. The course which events took in Paris in the February of 1848 is perhaps best expressed by Flaubert: 'quietly and rapidly, the monarchy was disintegrating all by itself.' This was indeed the 'decay of the old'.

PART FOUR

IMPACT—IMMOVABLE MOVED

Chapter X

THE FALL OF METTERNICH

6 'O NE MIGHT have understood the possibility of the throne becoming vacant in France by the assassination but not by the expulsion of King Louis Philippe,' wrote the Austrian minister Count Hartig, demonstrating his surprise at the outcome of the February revolution in Paris. Everywhere in Europe those who wished for reform were immeasurably heartened, those who sought to preserve were filled with gloom.

'One morning toward the end of February 1848, I sat quietly in my attic chamber, working hard at the tragedy of *Ulrich von Hutten*, when suddenly a friend rushed breathlessly into the room, exclaiming: "What, you sitting here! Do you not know what has happened?"

' "No; what?"

' "The French have driven away Louis Philippe and proclaimed the Republic."

'I threw down my pen—and that was the end of of *Ulrich von Hutten*, I never touched the manuscript again. We tore down the stairs, into the street, to the market square, the accustomed meeting-place for all the student societies after their midday dinner. Although it was still forenoon, the market was already crowded with young men talking excitedly. There was no shouting, no noise, only agitated conversation. What did we want there? This probably no one knew; but since the French had driven away Louis Philippe and proclaimed the Republic, something, of course, must happen here too.'

Carl Schurz, who wrote this description, was a student in Bonn at the time but he captures the mood of students in many other European towns as well. All over Germany governments found themselves giving way before liberal demands, in Baden, in Württemberg, in Saxony and Bavaria. Some of the pressure had a nationalist flavour, as in Württemberg where the king was entreated

135

to summon a German assembly. At the same time fifty-one liberals were meeting in Heidelberg to draw up preliminary plans for a national assembly which would be able to promulgate a constitution for a free and united Germany.

The Hungarian Diet had opened in the previous November but the news from Paris and elsewhere inspired Kossuth to lambaste the Imperial government. Not only did he demand a constitutional government for Hungary at once, but he claimed that a lasting constitutional Hungarian regime would only be possible if there were constitutions in Vienna and elsewhere in the Empire. It was not only in Pressburg (modern Bratislava), where the Diet was meeting, and elsewhere in Hungary, that Kossuth's speech aroused support and excitement. It considerably added to the agitation in Vienna itself.

Here the growing political interest of the previous few years reached a new pitch of intensity. Groups of people began to forgather at street corners and in cafés, excitedly discussing developments: there was a rush, to change paper money and bank credits into gold, amounting to a 'run' on the banks. The price of government stock fell by nearly a third and a surge in demand for essential foodstuffs, such as meat, forced prices to rise steeply.

The students of Vienna at this time were, for the most part, extremely poor. The sons of the aristocrats and the very rich did not usually attend the university, and of course, there were no grants or state assistance. The majority were forced to live in squalid conditions on insufficient food, seeking to eke out their existence, where possible, with a little private teaching and coaching. Living at this subsistence level, the students were particularly affected by the general economic conditions, although they found little sympathy or understanding from their teachers.

It was natural that the students, already politically active, should become more militant with the news from Paris. Medical students refused to accept posts as surgeons in the Austrian army, hitherto looked upon as desirable opportunities, as a token of their disenchantment with the regime. A group of forty students, drawn from the various societies and fraternities met on March 9 to take an oath of brotherhood. Meanwhile, some of the medical students, previously more independent than the majority of their fellows, assembled in secret to try to decide upon the reforms they thought most necessary, such as the abolition of censorship and freedom for teaching. They determined to call a full student meeting for March 12. A professor at the time attributed the political involvement of the medical students to the 'antiquated and dogmatic' courses of other departments in the university which stifled their initiative.

However, it was not only the students who were meeting and pressing for reform. Early in March a group who called themselves 'the Party of Progress', many of whom were members of the Legal-Political Reading Club, met under the direction of Bach, a liberally minded government servant. The outspoken proclamation which set out their programme attacked the oppression of the absolute government, blaming the failures and the absolutism upon the 'present councillors' of Ferdinand who, it claimed, came between the Emperor and his subjects.

It demanded a widening of the membership of the Estates to the middle class and even the peasantry; at the same time enlarging their functions and making public their working. Police despotism and censorship were attacked and the right was claimed for the people to be armed.

Meanwhile a memorandum was produced by the more liberal members of the Lower Austrian Estates; it painted a dark picture of the state of the monarchy and claimed that improvement could only come if the government listened to the advice of the Estates when they assembled. This view was also advanced in a petition of the Lower Austrian Manufacturers' Association. However, many were distrustful of the less progressive of the members who might effectively wreck all attempts to work for reform through the Estates. This was the background of the decision to draw up a petition taken by progressives under the lead of Bach on March 9. The aim was to circulate the petition as widely as possible in order to gain signatures and then present it to the Lower Austrian Estates for their opening on March 13, thus seeking to confirm them in their desire for reform.

The petition asked if the people of the Empire might assist their beloved Emperor to steer through the present troublous times. As well as expected points such as liberty of the press the petition sought constitutional advance through a new United Diet which might represent a wider selection of the people: 'the representation of the agricultural, industrial, commercial, and intellectual elements which are imperfectly or not at all represented in the existing estates.' The Diet would have the power to refuse taxation and legislation.

This petition was distributed for signature in all likely places, such as the Legal-Political Reading Club and the Manufacturers' Association, as well as various public buildings. Bach even solicited support for it in the streets.

Finally the petition, with several thousand signatures, was laid before the Estates to be submitted to them upon meeting.

The students had also planned to obtain massive support for their petition to be sent to the Emperor, and this was the purpose of the meeting they had arranged for February 12. The police, forewarned about the meeting, were disturbed and asked the Rector of the university if he wished for their assistance. The Rector, however, saw that police presence would merely serve as provocation and instead promised that he and other professors would seek to restrain the meeting.

By eight in the morning on February 12 the Aula or Great Hall of the university was already alive with students. Many had just been fortified by a fiery sermon from the Professor of Theology, delivered at Mass earlier in the morning. In it they had been recommended to act with courage and hope, confident that truth would conquer and that better times would come.

The excitement of the students increased and there was a great press around the tables to sign the petition. Attempts by the professors to calm the agitation failed, even that of Professor Hye who had enjoyed the goodwill of liberal elements since his stand against the annexation of Cracow in 1846.

All that the professors were able to achieve was the concession that the petition should be taken to the Emperor by themselves (one of the delegates being Hye) rather than by the students. The professors, having presented themselves before the Archduke Louis, were summoned later in the afternoon for an audience with the Emperor. He informed them that he accepted their petition and agreed 'to take it under consideration'. Of course the students were not satisfied with such a transparent attempt at evasion. It was determined that another meeting should take place on the following day, to precede a march to the meeting of the Lower Austrian Estates at the Landhaus.

In the face of this mounting unrest the government fumbled and did virtually nothing. Those who looked to concession and the dismissal of Metternich as the only way to secure the dynasty, saw all these events as so much evidence for their case. Those who believed in immobility on the other hand, such as the Archduke Louis, felt the need for a more determined stand and feared any concession.

Whether it was, as rumour at the time had it, that the anti-Metternich elements at Court were conniving at the agitation, hoping to exploit it for their own ends, or that a government, for some time semi-paralysed, was now totally incapacitated, is not clear. What is evident is that the Imperial government's actions, or lack of them, would have been little different if it had been bent on its own destruction.

Seeking to explain the apparent calm that prevailed in the drawing-room of Princess Metternich despite the mounting difficulties of January and February, a frequent visitor there suggested: 'We have enjoyed fair weather for so long in Austria that we can no longer conceive a tempest. The inclement conditions of the beginning of the century are now forgotten. The younger generation has only known blue skies.'

However, with the fall of Louis Philippe and the coming of March all this changed. Metternich wrote to his ambassador in London to say that it was 'not Austria alone but Europe that is thrown back more than half a century'. 'The calmest minds among us are profoundly shaken,' wrote Princess Metternich in her diary.

Certainly March 13 did not awake to 'blue skies'. Though soft and mild the day was overcast and grey. During the night some students had been busy in the suburbs, seeking to gain the support of the workers who lived there, and early in the morning other students were making from the Polytechnic and the Medical Schools for the university, where at nine o'clock they were due to hear the answer of the Emperor to their petition of the previous day.

Although lectures started, they were received with little interest and soon began to falter. Those who had reluctantly been listening moved to join their fellows who were assembling in the Aula; there Professor Hye was to report the results of his mission, which despite his attempts at camouflage was seen as a failure. Hye's counsels of caution and prudence did nothing to counteract the determination of the students to press ahead. 'As soon as I reached the University at eight o'clock in the morning I beheld the true face of Revolution,' was one professor's judgment.

Thus it was that cries of 'To the Landhaus!' were met with enthusiastic response and the students proceeded to march, gathering support as they went. Kudlich, himself a participant, later described the marchers as 'determined to cover Austria's shame with the bodies, their lives'.

Outside the Landhaus people had been gathering for some time. By nine, the inner courtyard was already filled by 'intruders of the better classes'. In no way was this a revolutionary crowd, eager to storm the meeting of the Estates; rather it was a coming together of the curious, anxious to see what was going to happen. Peaceful and fairly quiet, people gathered in groups, gradually merging into one body.

They awaited the arrival of the students for guidance as to what action to take next. As the students streamed up, the crowd parted, making way for them to approach the Landhaus. However, the students had not looked beyond their march and in the ensuing hiatus the demonstration began to show signs of sagging. It was at this juncture that a speech was delivered by a recently qualified doctor, Adolph Fischof, which restored the momentum. Hoisted up on the shoulders of some of his neighbours, he appealed to the crowd: 'This day we have a weighty mission to fulfil. What is important is that we show courage, that we are resolute, and that we resist with stout hearts.'

He proceeded to demand freedom of the press, and a freer education the better to make use of it. He concluded by beseeching co-operation from the various peoples of the Empire.

This speech was received with acclamation and was followed by a series of others, the speakers, the better to be heard, climbing up on the winter covers of the fountains in the square and in one case some steps used for dismounting from carriages. These speeches became more ambitious and daring until one demanded that they all march into the Landhaus itself.

For the time being the crowd was appeased by the Estates' offer that twelve people should be admitted to the deliberations in the Landhaus to watch over the people's interest. Meanwhile, amid the growing excitement, a translation of Kossuth's speech to the Hungarian Diet of a few days previously was produced and read to the crowd. This, although prohibited from being openly printed, had been circulating for some days but had not hitherto reached a very wide audience. Kossuth's demands for a constitution, not only for Hungary but also for Austria, agitated the crowd to a new pitch, and the cry for a constitution was taken up on all sides.

After this the contents of a note thrown from a window in the Landhaus were read out. The note set out the Estates' requests to the Emperor, but following the fiery speech of Kossuth, it was derided for its pusillanimity, each paragraph being saluted with ringing laughter. The paper was finally torn up to the accompaniment of cheers.

Attempts to secure quiet failed and instead the crowd determined to force the Estates to act as its spokesmen. A rumour—in fact false —that the twelve observers had been arrested decided the issue and the Landhaus was broken into. Stormy scenes followed and quite clearly further deliberation was impossible. Finally, about noon, the Estates decided to send a delegation to the Emperor, led by their president, expressing the demands of the people.

The accounts of participants suggest that they were surprised at the inaction of the government. Before March 13 many had assumed that the Lower Austrian Estates would not be allowed to meet, or anyhow that the opening of the session would be postponed. The demonstrators and the bystanders expected prohibition and intervention all the time. The American, W. H. Stiles, described those who spoke to the crowd outside the Landhaus as 'pale with terror at their own daring'. Thus they thought to make a gesture against authority but then found themselves, temporarily, at a loss when no answer came. They solved this problem only by making a further gesture which, in turn, was received in silence. This continued until they finally had gone so far that there was no turning back; committed now, only victory would suffice. 'There was for us all no choice,' wrote one student. Some, presumably, were from the start set on a desperate confrontation with the authorities and were determined to proceed with maximum energy in their attempt. But the great majority seem to have drifted into the 'revolution' and then found themselves so compromised that they had no alternative but to press for victory. 'I seemed to see in the hall of the revered old University none but candidates for the Spielberg, [prison]'. noted one who was present at the university during the afternoon and realized just how far events had developed.

Thus demands were stepped up from mild reforms to a constitution, a National Guard and, above all, the overthrow of Metternich. It was this last item that explains the immobility of the

Court. Even if the anti-Metternich party at Court had not played a part in stirring up agitation before the 13th, clearly it was prepared on the day to see the Chancellor become the object of resentment and the symbol of repression and reaction. It trusted that in the popular clamour capital could be made out of Metternich's discomfort, his dismissal might be secured and others might escape censure in fastening all blame upon him. Several days earlier Princess Metternich had written, 'today they all look to poor Clement for help; at the same time they want to make him responsible for the mistakes of others in previous years.' There were enough troops in Vienna to have dispersed the crowds at the outset, before public opinion had hardened. Incompetence alone cannot explain the failure to break up the demonstration at its birth.

With the arrival of the deputation from the Estates, claiming quite correctly that they were unable to continue their meeting, the government was at last forced to take notice of events. The crowds extended much further than merely around the Landhaus, in fact the greatest press was now near the Hofburg and in Ballhaus Square; however, despite shouts and insults, the people were still not violent. The Archduchess Sophie and her husband were cheered by the people as they strolled about and Metternich himself was able to walk to the Hofburg to attend the meeting of the government. Conscious of his style as always, the Chancellor moved slowly, dressed immaculately in light grey trousers, a green tail coat, black silk cravat and carrying a gold-headed cane. However, whatever his carriage and appearance he soon despaired when he arrived at the palace. In place of firmness and decision he found dither and doubt. Faced with disturbance and demands voiced from the streets, Metternich's reaction was wholly in accord with his philosophy: absolutely no concession to the rioters. Whether some of what they demanded was right or not did not matter; what did matter was that the government must not surrender in the face of insurrection. 'Monarchies disappear when they lose confidence in themselves,' he said. He alluded scornfully to the 'rabble' outside and advised clearing the streets, restoring order and making sure that the United Diet be brought speedily into existence in an atmosphere of calm and peace. For the reformers he had no patience; 'when I think of all the imbecilities I heard in the course of that famous 13th of March I often ask myself whether the people were mad or merely drunk,' he was later to write.

Amid the recriminations and mutual accusations that were thrown back and forth, no clear line emerged at the State Conference. It was all very well for Metternich to urge firmness and the appointment of Prince Windischgrätz as commander of the troops in Vienna, but every minute that passed the greater the force that would be required to restore order, and Metternich knew that the government was incapable of facing the issue with the necessary determination and unity. The answer that was given to the petitioners from the Estates was merely an attempt at prevarication; the time for such a course was long since over. The accounts of several people who were in the palace testify to the increasing chaos there; as well as the mental breakdown of nerve there was a growing physical breakdown as more and more people were able to burst, unheralded and uninvited, into the Court and harangue any member of the government they there encountered.

Nevertheless, belatedly, troops were called out and Archduke Albert was commanded to restore order, using, however, the minimum of force, and that only with great reluctance. Key points were to be occupied and the gates of the city were to be shut to prevent any more of the workers arriving from the suburbs. Several hundred who had already responded to pleas for help from some of the rioters were causing grave unease to the more prosperous demonstrators.

Archduke Albert himself, seeking to persuade the crowd to disperse, was forced to retire when an object was hurled at him.* Troops were now ordered to clear the streets and after several salvoes overhead shots were fired into the crowd. The first victims of the revolution had been claimed. At once the situation grew worse. Demonstrators became violent at many different points and barricades were thrown together, which the troops then tried to clear. Attempts were made to storm the gates into the city, and in the suburbs customs posts and factory machinery were attacked. Troops outside the Landhaus were pelted with stones from upper windows and forced to retreat while other soldiers were pressed back by the crowds outside the palace. It was here that some troops hesitated before firing on the crowd; the delay alarmed the govern-

* Usually said to be a piece of wood, but one contemporary claimed that it was an iron lantern bracket from the scaffolding of a new police building. Again opinions vary as to whether it struck the Archduke or his companion and whether he was thrown from his horse or not.

ment and led to suspicion that the army could not be depended upon.* The army did manage to clear some streets but failed to restore confidence and calm; other parts of Vienna were held firmly by the insurgents. The government action was in the classic pattern of how revolution should not be treated: enough violence to create martyrs and arouse bitterness but not enough to cow.

Sometime after five in the afternoon a deputation of the Civic Guard arrived at the palace, there being augmented by those deputies who had remained after the unsatisfactory reply to their petition. The Civic Guard, a mainly ceremonial body drawn from the more prosperous bourgeois, offered to prolong until nine o'clock the unofficial truce which was prevailing. If by this time Metternich had not been dismissed, the students armed and the soldiers withdrawn from the city to the suburbs, they themselves would side with the revolt. At the same time they argued for more concessions to appease the people. Archduke Louis, weakened by the Emperor's dislike of any measures which would lead to bloodshed, sought to temporize while refusing their demands. However, the anti-Metternich faction at Court added their influence on the side of dismissal. The conference chamber 'had become a public thoroughfare into which everyone who chose could penetrate; an indecent clamour was kept up on all sides'. It was no place for a calm decision. A deputation from the university, led by the Rector, besought the government to permit the arming of the students to help defend the city and maintain order, so that they, 'the hopes of so many families', would not be involved in bloodshed if the truce was allowed to expire. The government gave way and the Academic Legion came into existence.

Sometime about six Metternich was summoned and he returned to the Hofburg, the Archduke Louis having more or less decided that the Chancellor must go. However, argument continued and to some it seemed that the result was still in doubt. Windischgrätz argued strongly in favour of the garrison being allowed to attempt to gain control and restore peace; he suggested also that the Archduke Albert be replaced as commander. The Council seemed to agree to this, deciding to defy the ultimatum. The general left to put on his uniform preparatory to taking command himself, but in his absence sometime after eight the decision was finally taken to

---

* Although in fact it was subsequently claimed that the delay was due to uncertainty over the orders rather than conscious disobedience.

dismiss Metternich. Pressed to accept the situation, Metternich stipulated that, as he had promised the Emperor Francis to stand by his son Ferdinand, he must be released by Ferdinand's personal decision. 'Tell the people that I accept everything,' was Ferdinand's reply.

Thus Metternich resigned from the office he had held so long. Returning, the uniformed Windischgrätz was just in time to witness the end. He is said to have stood still as if struck by lightning, exclaiming, 'This must not be!' But it was some months before Windischgrätz was listened to. Now that the decision was taken, Metternich was icily calm. 'With unmoved tranquillity, and dignified composure' he brushed aside the gushing compliments from courtiers and deputies over his 'sacrifice'. 'This moment, Prince, crowns your glorious career,' exclaimed one petitioner. 'You see things from too subordinate a point of view,' replied Metternich, always the patrician. 'You forget that Austria proper is but the smallest province of the Empire, and that, if you rob the monarch of the halo which surrounds him, the various kingdoms will fall asunder. Have you considered, as yet, how you will control the movement in Hungary?' 'Oh, all those matters will easily come right.' 'To that,' answered Metternich, 'there is no reply.'

And so the Chancellor left office and returned home to his wife who described him as 'resigned, calm, almost happy'. However, a man who had struggled, who had expended so much effort and ability, to maintain the order in Europe to which he was accustomed, could scarcely be 'calm, almost happy' at seeing the fortunes of the Empire pass into the hands of those who believed that 'all will easily come right'.

Hartig summed up Metternich in his misfortune as one who had 'to witness the clouds of incense in which he had been enveloped, by sincere as well as by hypocritical reverence, suddenly dispersed by a gust of wind; to reap the basest ingratitude in return for his ceaseless exertions to promote the interests of the state and the welfare of his fellow citizens'. And Hügel was surely near the mark when he later accounted for his support of the prince that evening: 'I could not, in the moment of imminent danger, forsake the very old man with a broken frame and a broken heart.'

Metternich had fallen; an era had closed. The following day, under the care of Hügel, the Metternichs were to flee Vienna in a cab on the first stage of their long and hazardous journey which was to bring the refugees to London, where their arrival was announced by *The Times* on April 21.

Meanwhile, as the students armed themselves from the arsenal on the night of the 13th, the sky was lit up over the western suburbs by the glow of fires. Police buildings, toll gates, shops, factories and the hated machines were attacked by the desperate workers, as symbols and causes of their poverty and distress. At the same time many of the gas lamps on the land just outside the city wall had been broken and the gas which rushed out of the exposed pipes caught alight and flared fiercely. The concern felt by the more prosperous bourgeois at this turn of events was summed up by one at the time who spoke of 'plunder, arson and the commission of every kind of abomination'. However, such feelings were overborn by the sense of release and emancipation which the citizens experienced with the fall of Metternich.

At first sight, it is amazing that the fall of one elderly minister, physically somewhat incapacitated and well past his prime, should be seen as of great consequence. Yet nevertheless it was. In Vienna, throughout the Empire, in the German Confederation and all over Europe, the news of Metternich's fall was seen as momentous.

Man likes to trace his problems to simple causes, partly because of the desire to blame something other than himself for his misfortunes but particularly because it is only by reducing the number of agents of his ills that cure seems likely or even possible. The African villagers of the 1950s came to believe that all their woes were brought about by colonialism; the Castilians of the early seventeenth century were persuaded that the presence amongst them of the Moors was the cause of Spain's decline. Independence and expulsion therefore become the elixir. By 1848, Metternich was seen as the architect of misfortune all over Europe.

The craftsman in Vienna suffering from the first effects of industrialism, the peasant who had unsuccessfully come to the town in search of employment, the indigent student who lacked prospects, the bourgeois who resented his political impotence, the noble who wished for more say in government, the member of the Habsburg family who chafed at the prominence of one who was merely a state servant, all came to see in Metternich the barrier obstructing the pursuit of their aims. Farther afield he was blamed by the German who resented the weakness and particularism of his Fatherland; the Magyar who was irked by Austrian predominance, and the

Italian who wanted more political liberty, the end of Austrian rule or merely to become wealthier. He was seen by those who suffered from the Industrial Revolution as being responsible for its spread while he was blamed by others for its failure to spread fast enough. Above all he was attacked everywhere as the evil spirit of reaction by those who sought their future happiness in revolution and change. Thus his fall assumed enormous significance wherever it was reported.

The viability of governments, like that of currencies, is largely a matter of confidence. When once the confidence in a currency is lost—and it may be lost because of quite trivial reasons—it is no use discussing whether the reasons for the collapse having occurred were valid; the collapse makes them so. It is much the same with governments; the fall of Metternich was seen as a great event, a turning point, something different from the mere dismissal of a minister. It does not matter whether it was, the fact that it was thought to be so made men act accordingly. 'The last beam of the old system has given way,' wrote *The Times* on March 21. For all this, the success of the revolution was not yet assured and this soon became clear to the people of Vienna.

If the government had added other concessions to the fall of the Chancellor peace might have been restored at once, but instead it seemed to wish to carry on more or less as before. Talk of Vienna being put under a state of siege, rumours of the powers given to Prince Windischgrätz to 'restore order', added to the sense of insecurity. The dismissal of the detested chief of police Sedlnitzky and Archduke Albert, who had commanded the troops the previous day, were not enough, especially as the latter was replaced by Windischgrätz. Mounting agitation was temporarily quieted by the announcement of the formation of a National Guard and the definite promise to end censorship. However, the respite was only transitory and on the 15th the people of Vienna, partly out of fear of counter-revolution, partly spurred by previous success in the face of government weakness, redoubled their demands. By the early evening the Court was forced to promise a constitution, and to agree to a general Estates from the Austrian lands, with augmented middle-class representation. It was to be called forthwith to assist in the working out of the terms of the constitution.

This news, 'received with the utmost favour and joy', seemed to signal the success of the revolt. A delegation from the Hungarian

Diet under Kossuth, which had come to argue for a separate ministry for their country, found that they had no battle to fight; their request was granted. Instead they were fêted and cheered, swallowed up in a sea of rejoicing. Symptomatic of the general euphoria was the claim of Fischof, the young doctor whose speech outside the Landhaus had been so important: 'The world was made in six days, Austria in two.'

The 17th saw a new ministry appointed; Kolowrat, trading on his reputation for opposition to Metternich, remained for the time being at its head. Some members, such as the Foreign Minister Ficquelmeont, were by no means to the taste of reformers but the Minister of the Interior, Pillersdorf, was held to be in sympathy with liberal demands and accordingly his appointment was acclaimed.

In its very success the revolution began to lose its unanimity. The Court party which had been prepared to use the revolution to get rid of Metternich was by no means well pleased at the turn of events; the continuing demands of the people were seen as outrageous, just as the continuing concessions were seen as humiliating. 'I could have borne the loss of one of my children more easily than I can the ignominy of submitting to a mass of students,' was the comment of the Archduchess Sophie. It was now that the Archduchess emerged as the strong personality of the Court, holding it together and giving it will, and she rapidly ceased to be the darling of the liberals. At the same time those members of the nobility who had participated in and encouraged the revolution became frightened, since events were no longer under their control. This falling away from the revolution was perhaps predictable; what was more significant was the increasing concern at developments felt by the more prosperous of the bourgeois.

The lawlessness in the suburbs on March 13, repeated the next day, had affected some members of the middle class directly since it was their factories and shops that were being destroyed, but a much larger group were dismayed by the attacks on property and the increasing militancy of the workers, who were showing themselves no longer willing to accept passively the appalling conditions to which they were subjected. Symptomatic of this division in the unity of revolution were the arrests that were being carried out at the behest of the middle class, of people thought to be concerned with attacks on factories and buildings—before the end of the month the gaols proved inadequate to house all the suspects awaiting trial.

Another weakness in the revolutionary movement was appearing by the end of March: what can be described as the national question. The events in Vienna had quickly been communicated to all parts of the Empire and had set off accompanying revolts. 'The convulsions in the capital communicated themselves contagiously to all parts of the Empire,' wrote the Minister of the Interior, Baron Pillersdorf.

Revolution in Budapest, in Pressburg, in Venice, in Milan and Vienna might all be against the government expressed by Metternich, but once the Chancellor had been driven out, different issues were raised: above all Austria's relationship to Germany. Vienna, as Metternich had said, did not fulfil the same role in the Austrian state as Paris did in the French. From March 13 the colours of Germany (black, red and gold) began to replace the old Austrian colours of black and yellow; the majority of the liberals and radicals in Vienna saw their revolt as part of a wider German one.

However, once it was asked what part Austria should play in the creation of an integrated Germany awkward implications arose. If a true German federation was to be created, what was to happen to the non-German parts of the Austrian Monarchy? Were Hungary and Italy to be abandoned, all connection with them severed? At first it seems many of the Viennese thought that the rest of Germany would be glad to form up behind Austria, as a constitutional state with the Emperor as its monarch, while the non-German parts of the Empire would likewise become constitutional states, still under the Emperor. But very soon it became clear that Vienna would not be able to have it both ways like this. Once it was realized that participation in the German federation would mean the loss of much of the traditional role of Austria, people were not lacking to suggest that a looser unit, a confederation, was the best expression of German unity.

But the loss of concord among the victors of March 13 must not be taken to suggest that the revolution was faltering. On the contrary, its momentum was increasing as was exemplified by the government being forced to promise a unicameral assembly which would be chosen by universal manhood suffrage. This body, acting as a constituent assembly, would draw up the final form of the constitution. The powerlessness of the government in the face of radical and democratic demands was also revealed in the way popular opinion was mobilized to force the resignation of members of the government, such as Ficquelmont, who were disliked, and generally to intimidate those who were suspected of opposing the revolution. This popular pressure was partly expressed in newspaper attacks but also in the practice of 'serenades'. These consisted of a large number of people—frequently in their thousands —gathering outside the house of the victim and there indulging in jeering, wailing and the shouting of abuse and threats.

The collapse of the government's power and the general breakdown in law and order were behind the flight of the Emperor and the royal family on May 17. The fugitives journeyed to Innsbruck— in theory the Emperor's health no longer permitted his residence in Vienna. This action shocked opinion in Vienna and cooled some of the revolutionary ardour; many of the revolutionaries who had no desire for a republic saw the withdrawal as a personal affront.

In the story of the revolution it was the students who played the dominant role; they 'formed the nucleus, the real strength of the revolutionary force,' wrote Engels. The workers in the suburbs, totally lacking leaders of their own, turned instead to the students as their guides and protectors. All grievances were referred to the students, from the public to the purely personal and private; the trust placed in their judgment was often pathetic. The students' importance was recognized outside Vienna and they were lionized by their fellow students elsewhere in Germany. At a student conference at Eisenach it was said that 'all competition with the Viennese for the favours of the fair sex was in vain'.

Thus it was perhaps appropriate that the climax of the revolt in Vienna should have come over the question of the Academic Legion. The government, at last determined to make a stand, resolved to disband the Legion and thus reduce the power of the students. It thought that it could rely on a considerable body of support from the more moderate citizens and decided to act in the forthcoming university vacation. However, once again it handled the situation badly. The result was the disturbances of May 26. Barricades were erected, paving-stones pulled up and on all sides citizens and students prepared to fight the authorities; meanwhile they were reinforced by workers who flocked in from the suburbs. Faced with the opposition of the National Guard and such determined resistance from the students themselves the government had to give way. It had to accept not only the continued existence of the Academic Legion but also the withdrawal of nearly all troops from the city. Finally it agreed to try to persuade the Emperor to return to his capital. Pillersdorf was described at this time as having 'looked like a corpse, terribly worn and grey as ashes'.

It is difficult to judge just how much the government was to blame for the outcome of events. Engels pointed to the ill-timed government offensives as repeatedly cementing the alliance between the revolutionaries which was otherwise about to come apart. Pillersdorf himself argued that the government's task was an impossible one. He instanced the way in which the people 'usually concludes, that the boldest, most resolute, and courageous individual, must at the same time be the ablest and most suitable commander'. He saw the cause of the trouble in these words: 'A transition so sudden and unprovided for, from one system to another, diametrically opposite, has left in its train an agitation in the capital which gave rise to extravagant and unattainable demands and raised the most adventurous hopes.' One of the main difficulties of the government was knowing who they were really responsible to. For this the policies, or non-policies, of the Court were largely to blame. The difficulties of the government *vis-à-vis* the Imperial family were high-lighted by the flight to Innsbruck, about which it was told nothing.

Nevertheless, wherever the fault lay the fact remained that the authority of the government had now gone. A Committee of Safety was created and took over the running of Vienna, watching the activities of the police and trying to maintain the peace.

The revolution had occurred at a time of economic crisis and had itself deepened the crisis. The damage and destruction of machines and factories had increased unemployment among the workers; the general unease and sense of insecurity had severely lessened trade. Finally, in an economy in which demand was to a large extent expressed by the wants of the rich, the flight of the Emperor and members of the nobility had had a catastrophic effect on the small shopkeepers and craftsmen. At the same time, many domestic servants lost their means of employment. All this led to an increase in agitation for the authorities to bring work to the poor and unemployed. Consequently the Committee of Safety found itself responsible for a vastly extended public works policy and having to grapple with all the attendant problems of such a policy.

Although in no sense a proletarian revolution against the bourgeois, these social and economic demands as expressed in the 'Right to work', when coupled to the radicalism and the first stirrings of republicanism, implicit in the change of attitude towards Ferdinand, show just how far and how fast the revolution had developed since the fall of Metternich.

Chapter XI

THE FLOOD TIDE OF REVOLUTION

'THE REPUBLIC meant bloodshed, expropriation, terror and war,' wrote the Duc de Broglie in his memoirs. Certainly, whatever it meant to French aristocrats, to revolutionaries across Europe a new French republic was the first stage in their long-awaited great revolution. French armies, it was hoped, would drive the Austrians from Italy and liberate the peninsula; French armies would break down the German Confederation and create republics in the place of the reactionary club of princes nestling in the pocket of Austria; most important of all, French armies would lead a crusade against Tsar Nicholas and Russia, which would leave all Europe free to develop and in particular would allow the rebirth of Poland. The 'System of Metternich' in European affairs would be destroyed.

Today, from the high ground of history, it may seem that by 1848 France had lost her ability to dominate Europe, that her armies were in no position to challenge the rest of the Continent and that she had no intention of campaigning for other peoples' liberties. At the time, this was by no means clear.

Since the defeat of Napoleon all the major European powers had continued to think of France as the great danger, whatever temporary conflicts and rivalries they had become involved in. Tsar Nicholas's ejaculation, 'Sellez vos chevaux, messieurs', as he announced the new republic to his Court was not just a declaration of bellicosity; it reflected a widely held view that France would attack, and that fact being inevitable, it was better for the war to be fought on the Rhine than in Russia. The same attitude explains why Charles Albert had so many of his best troops guarding the Alpine frontier: what had happened was what European governments had been dreading for thirty years.

However, times had changed and in France Lamartine, who was directing the foreign policies of the new republic, wished to do nothing that would bring Europe down upon his country. His 'Declaration to Europe' was preceded and accompanied by diplomatic and unofficial advice that France meant no harm. Even the Declaration itself, despite its proud boast that 'the Treaties of 1815 exist no longer as law in the eyes of the French Republic', seeks to reassure elsewhere. 'Nevertheless the territorial circumscriptions of the treaties are a fact which it admits as a basis, and as a *point de départ* in its relations with other nations.' The manifesto was in fact largely designed to still the clamour for aggression from radicals inside France.

Palmerston saw that if France was left to her own devices she would do nothing to endanger European peace, and he therefore counselled moderation to other statesmen. In the last resort Britain could afford to 'wait and see' behind the Channel, just as Russia could across Europe, but Prussia and Austria were in no position to take chances.

Metternich, of necessity, had been forced to try to arrange an alliance against France, even if it were only defensive: 'I shall now create between Berlin, Vienna and St. Petersburg a nucleus for thought and action.' His fall prevented any chance there might have been of intervention against France. The 'international conspiracy' against revolution was no more.

The already-growing movement for reform in Germany was immensely heartened by the news from Paris. In state after state throughout the Confederation public meetings were held and petitions drawn up as Germans pressed forward with their demands for concessions from their rulers.

The ultimata varied from one state to another, depending for instance upon whether there was already some measure of representative government or not, but broadly they can be classed as the usual liberal demands of the time. If there was no constitution the desire for one, with a representative assembly, took first place; then came the demands for trial by jury, and the arming of the people in the form of the creation of a Civic Guard. In addition, rulers everywhere were asked to pledge themselves to do everything possible to bring about the meeting of a national parliament in order to secure German unity.

Some rulers accepted at once, such as those of Württemberg, Baden and Hesse-Cassel; others refused at first but then gave way, as with the King of Saxony. In Bavaria, where the Lola Montez

The German Confederation

N

HOLSTEIN

MECKLENBURG

R. Elbe

H A N O V E R

P R U S S I A

Königsberg

Berlin
Potsdam

Leipzig

SAXONY

R. Rhine

P

Cologne

Bonn

HESSE-
CASSEL

HESSE-
DARMSTADT

Frankfurt

R. Elbe

BOHEMIA

Heidelberg

B A D E N

Stuttgart

WÜRTTEMBERG

BAVARIA

R. Danube

Munich

Vienna

AUSTRIA

H U N G A R Y

LOMBARDY

VENETIA

R. Po

A D R I A T I C   S E A

——— Boundary of the
German Confederation

PRUSSIA

HABSBURG
EMPIRE

Scale 50 0 50 100 miles

affair had become entwined with the movement for reform, and in Hesse-Darmstadt, rulers gave way to their sons to carry out reforms that the fathers were not really prepared to accept.

Clearly the chances of the German states being able to operate and develop their reformed governments successfully depended upon the acceptance, or at any rate acquiescence, of the two major powers Austria and Prussia. In the same way, whatever the kings, princes and grand dukes of the medium and smaller sized states might promise, there was little likelihood of any effective German parliament meeting to secure the unification of Germany without Austrian and Prussian agreement. The events of March 13 in Vienna and what followed upon them had broken the power of the Habsburgs to prevent change in Germany, both in the constitutional developments of the smaller states and the move towards unification. Prussia was in a similar state of flux.

Although Frederick William was, in March 1848, to find himself on the defensive before the demands of his subjects for reform, this was not, as with most of his fellow rulers, because he had no positive policies of his own and therefore merely waited upon events. On the contrary, after the palpable failure of his plans for the United Diet in 1847, he was busy with schemes to secure a real federal unity for Germany. The reason for the Prussian king finding himself overtaken was that, as with many men in the spring of 1848, the sheer speed and scale of what happened overwhelmed him.

The Prussian towns, in common with most other German communities, witnessed mounting excitement after the fall of Louis Philippe. 'I was dominated by the feeling that at last the great opportunity had arrived for giving to the German people the liberty which was their birthright and to the German Fatherland its unity and greatness,' wrote a student in the Prussian Rhineland.

In Berlin large public meetings early in March urged a free press and the recall of the United Diet, with the promise that in future it would be summoned at regular intervals. However, in addition, a mounting opposition to the army became noticeable.

Everywhere the army was seen as the symbol and agent of reaction but in Prussia it meant something more as well. This was partly the outcome of history; the Prussian army had always been disproportionately large in relation to the size of the state, with the result that it had been particularly influential in the life of Prussia. Moreover the rigid class basis of the officer corps had provoked the resentment of the middle class. Law and order in the cities of Prussia was in the hands of the military, and particularly in Berlin, as resentment mounted so the maintenance of public order became more difficult. Troops were hooted and insulted by the Berliners and in their turn they used more force than was necessary in the performance of their tasks. The result of this violence was a desire among the people for the troops to be withdrawn and for they themselves to be armed and to act as police.

Despite this sort of agitation among his subjects, Frederick William was undoubtedly presented with an enormous opportunity at this time. In sharp contrast to the Habsburg government, the Prussian administration was quite clearly efficient and not in decay. Then, the goodwill felt for the Prussian king at his accession as one who, however erroneously, was supposed to favour a policy of movement and change in Germany, still lingered. A gracious surrender to some of the demands of the reformers together with a really decisive bid to put himself at the head of Germany might have been outstandingly successful.

However, Frederick William, although impulsive, was not the man to stretch out and seize an opportunity if to do so meant acting in a revolutionary manner; he was too much the traditionalist for that. In the nervous bid he did make he continued to see the Habsburgs, over his shoulder, as the rightful leaders of Germany. As he grasped for the new with one hand he clung to the old with the other.

On March 18 the excitement of Berliners came to a head. The streets were full from mid-morning and the square about the palace was packed. It was generally expected that the king was to make pronouncements on the changes he envisaged. Although extremely animated the crowds were not hostile to the king and there were reports of knots of people repeatedly cheering him. The shops remained open and windows around the palace square were occupied by ladies of fashion: expectancy rather than dread was the dominant emotion.

By midday it was known that the king was changing his ministry; men of the mercantile classes such as Camphausen were to serve in the new one. In the early afternoon two royal proclamations were made public. They promised freedom of the press—subject to certain provisos with regard to newspapers; the prompt summoning of the United Diet (scheduled for April 12), and a series of rather vague affirmations about the transformation of Germany into a federal state.

These were greeted with enormous enthusiasm and pleasure, 'so violent that it might almost have been taken to be the result of intoxication': to some extent the product of satisfaction that so much had been achieved without fighting and bloodshed. Yet in a matter of minutes the mood had changed; barricades were going up on all sides, 'paving stones seemed to leap from the ground', and citizens were engaged in violent and bitter fighting with the military. 'In one hour,' reported an observer, 'the appearance of the city was entirely different, its physiognomy quite transformed.'

Workers and members of the middle class laboured together to construct barricades out of any materials that came to hand, strong in their united determination to resist the soldiery. The army meanwhile replied with brutality; all the pent-up fury and anger of the last few days was released. One cavalry officer told of how he 'rode at a gallop right through the crowd, riding down several', merely on his way to join his squadron. Soldiers who fought their way into houses, from which all manner of projectiles had been hurled down at them, had no mercy on whoever they found; the defenders of one house were finally thrown from the roof into the street below.

Prisoners were treated with revolting brutality. A prisoner's story of how a column was marched to Spandau, all the while being clubbed and beaten by their captors, is backed up by the account of one officer who described the reaction of his soldiers to prisoners who were brought before them. After saying that the prisoners provided 'entertainment enough' for the bored soldiers, he continues: 'The drivers with knout or whip, and the gunners with sabre or sidearms, encircled every batch of prisoners, and did not take their eyes off the accompanying squad for a moment . . . awaiting a chance of getting in a smart blow at the prisoners to make them feel their hatred.'

On through the evening and into the night the battle raged in the streets as the soldiers sought to capture and demolish the barricades. How had this extraordinary turn-about occurred; why had a peaceful and jubilant scene been transformed in this way?

Military leaders in the circle of the Court were adamant that the rising was premeditated and planned, largely the work of foreign agitators. One piece of evidence used to justify these assertions was the discovery of turves used to block windows, which had, clearly, been cut and stored for some time. But, in the main, the theory rested upon the speed and scale of the rising.

Even so, the haphazard way in which barricades were built, the positions where they were constructed, and more important perhaps, the vital points where they were not, backed by the overwhelming majority of contemporary accounts, suggest the lack of any plan.

Among both the military and the people there were extremists who wanted violence and were prepared to exploit any chance that arose to introduce it. However, the prevailing moderation of public opinion meant that the small body of republicans and socialists would have no chance if they rose on their own accord. If though, in the climate of suspicion and odium existing between the citizens and the military, the troops seemed to act provocatively, then the situation might easily deteriorate. The start of the trouble seems to have been two shots fired by a contingent of infantry going to the assistance of cavalry who were clearing the square in front of the Palace. No orders had been conveyed to the crowds to disperse or move back and they, seeing the cavalry and hearing the shots, assumed the beginning of a treacherous attack on unarmed people by the hated military. Neither shot in fact injured anyone; it was later claimed that both shots were fired in error and were the result of jostling and pushing by the crowd. Nevertheless, it is easy to see why people should believe the worst.

What happened, though, might have been avoided if a stronger hand had been in control of affairs. The king, knowing that what he was doing in the direction of German unity and greater liberalism at home was angering the traditional Prussian outlook of many of his officers, felt the need to act in a way that would reassure and appease the military. Consequently he gave the command of the troops in Berlin to General Prittwitz, a man of a hard and authoritarian stamp, described during the fighting as 'quiet, cold, resolute and clear-headed as he always was'. Prittwitz may have reassured the military but he certainly did not allay civilian fears. Then, the king was not prepared to intervene in order to control the fighting once it had started; his repeated consent to his officers' demand to be allowed to storm barricades—'Yes, but don't fire!'—is pathetic evidence of this irresolution.

The army, naturally, used methods of war, such as full scale artillery bombardment, when forced to deal with the insurrection.

They should not be blamed for this since it is the political power that must decide whether the tactics necessary to secure a military victory are politically justified: this the political power, Frederick William, notably failed to do.

Assailed from two sides, by liberals who counselled the withdrawal of the army and accession to popular clamour, and by the conservatives and orthodox military opinion, backed by his brother Prince William, who urged that the attack on the barricades should be pressed home, Frederick William was in turmoil. He had been greatly upset by events before the 18th and the fighting that day had distressed him beyond measure. Horrified by the bloodshed and disorder he drafted a proclamation, 'To my dear Berliners', during the night. This demonstrates all the king's impetuous love of the grand gesture and his lack of political acumen in knowing how to make it. 'Listen to the paternal voice of your king, you inhabitants of my true and beautiful Berlin . . .' he pleaded, but the people were not impressed by promises.

The king finally decided to recall the troops on the 19th. At first it seems to have been envisaged as a phased withdrawal (if any barricades were dismantled by their defenders the troops nearest to them would be ordered back at once, so that gradually all the barricades would be down and the troops either in their barracks or on the way out of Berlin). However, to the end, muddle prevailed and what happened instead was a full, unconditional withdrawal of all troops that in fact left the king very much at his people's mercy.

This was clearly demonstrated by the events of the afternoon when a huge crowd forced the king and his fainting wife to come out of the palace to pay their respects to the corpses of dead fighters, assembled for a parade around Berlin. The signs of the victory of the people were everywhere to be seen. With the troops out of Berlin, the people armed themselves and took over the task of maintaining order in the capital. A liberal ministry under Camphausen was installed and when the United Diet re-convened it quickly drew up plans for an assembly to meet to help produce a constitution for Prussia. Finally Prince William of Prussia left for London after March 19th; his presence was seen as too provocative.

The army was shattered by its withdrawal and saw what had occurred as a humiliation. 'We officers embraced each other, sobbing. We knew not what else to do. It was the expression of impotent despair,' was a typical reaction.

However, the army had not been defeated. Amidst the general sense of victory and rejoicing in the immediate aftermath of those March days one who was less blinded wrote, 'I could not get rid of the feeling that everything which was there called a victory, was nothing but a something taking place by the condescension of the authorities.' Away from Berlin the army was able to regain its morale and by the end of March the king, having left his 'dear Berliners', was in Potsdam, a vantage point from which they would seem less 'dear'.

One result of the happenings in Berlin, however, was that the King of Prussia was in no position to resist the call for a German parliament.

On March 5, at Heidelberg, fifty-one liberals met together, determined to do all they could to secure a National Assembly for the German people as the first step towards their unification. Because these men were by no means representative of the German Confederation as a whole—no less than twenty-one were from Baden—it was decided that a much larger body should be assembled in Frankfurt which could hope to organize the creation of a German parliament.

This larger body, which met on March 31, became known as the Vorparlament. Invitations to it were sent automatically to all who had at any time been members of a German state assembly, and in addition to other people distinguished for their liberalism. However, this body still did not represent Germany fairly; some areas such as Austria with only two members were hopelessly under-represented, while others, like Baden with seventy-two, were just as clearly over-represented.

Of course, without the great changes taking place all over Germany the meeting of the Vorparlament would probably never have taken place. Even the old Federal Diet had come to see the need for constitutional change and had inaugurated a committee to prepare a new German constitution. The result of this, to a large extent inspired by Professor Dahlmann, was swept aside by the meeting of the Vorparlament, but several of the committee, such as Dahlmann himself, were also members of the Vorparlament, and subsequently helped to secure the acceptance of the Vorparlament's proposals by the Diet.*

* He had been one of the Hanoverian professors dismissed in 1837 and was later welcomed to Prussia by King Frederick IV.

F*

The Vorparlament contained people with very different ideas as to the sort of unity they were seeking and how they should set about obtaining it. The main division, however, can be drawn between those who wanted to declare a German republic at once and the more moderate majority who did not. The leaders of the former group were two democrats from Baden, Hecker and Struve, These men, although very often bracketed together, were very different in personality and behaviour. Hecker, for some time the leading left-wing liberal in Baden, was the much more obviously attractive leader: large, handsome and extrovert—he habitually wore a blouse and carried a pistol—he was described as 'a meat-eater and a full blooded, healthy man'. This was in contrast to Struve who was portrayed by the same writer as 'wizened . . . bloodless and boneless . . . the monk of the German Republic'. Struve was much more of a fanatic than Hecker and had arrived at his social and political ideas largely from intellectual conviction whereas Hecker based his ideas more upon practical experience.

Both men wanted a degree of social revolution which was quite alien to the moderates whose wishes were summed up by an observer as 'wash my furs for me, and don't wet 'em', so timid were they of the results of change. When Hecker and Struve failed to secure the decision of the Vorparlament for a republic they decided to declare one themselves, relying on force, in the form of a popular rising, to translate it into fact.

Hecker's hopes centred on his belief that the soldiers would not fire upon fellow Germans, in this case the column he was gathering in Constance before marching into Baden. This was not such a foolish hope in the Baden of April 1848 as it may sound today. In the event the soldiers did fire, but only after their commander, Friedrich von Gagern, was killed, leading from in front to ensure that they would fight rather than fraternize. Hecker was easily defeated, although he himself managed to escape into Switzerland.* Struve, who had organized another band, was also cut off and routed. The end of this south-west German rising came when the 650 or so of the German Legion, who had come from France under the poet Herwegh and whose offers of help had only been grudgingly accepted by Hecker, found themselves alone and were speedily overcome.

* Though elected to the Frankfurt Assembly he was not allowed to take his seat and he emigrated to the U.S.A.

Herwegh, who really did measure up to all the rather trite clichés about romantic poets turned revolutionary leaders, was a most incompetent commander. 'Herwegh is a poet, and has all the faults of one,' complained one who served under him on this occasion. However, he was not the coward in this affair that many reports claimed. 'Notwithstanding his unfitness for the position he had assumed, I became attached to Herwegh for his amiable qualities,' was the opinion of Corvin who fought with him, had no reason to love him, and would certainly have seized on any cowardice.

While this rising was being contained the election for the National Assembly was proceeding, supervised by a 'Committee of Fifty', acting for its parent, the Vorparlament. The members were elected by near universal suffrage but, contrary to the recommendation of the Committee, the majority were chosen by indirect election. On the basis of each state being allowed to return roughly one member for 50,000 of population, some 605 members were anticipated; however, in no sitting was this number ever reached.

The assembly which first met in the St. Paul's Church, Frankfurt, on May 18 was not a cross-section of the German people. No representative of the urban working class was elected and only one peasant, whereas one-third of the members were government officials of one kind or another: there were large numbers of lawyers, university professors and teachers.* After the first day the assembly convened under the presidency of Heinrich von Gagern, recently appointed the chief minister of Hesse-Darmstadt. Heinrich was one of three brothers who played prominent parts in the events of 1848, another being the commander of the troops who was killed defeating Hecker.

Von Gagern's leadership was to have an important bearing on the early struggles of the assembly; certainly he was enormously admired by many around him. He seemed the 'embodiment of all in the way of great resolve and noble passion that revealed itself in that Assembly,' according to one witness. However, another comment, 'his talent for presiding is certainly not nearly so great as his disposition for it', points to the failings behind the impressive exterior which showed themselves more clearly with time. Nevertheless it would be wrong to underplay this impressive exterior:

* It has been estimated that over 95 per cent of the deputies had had a secondary education and over four-fifths a university education.

Gagern's gravitas and moral dignity were able to elevate the whole working of the assembly after the petty spitefulness and rancour of the opening day.

Among the other better known figures at the Frankfurt parliament, Robert Blum was from the Left. A man who had made his way from very humble origins to become a member of the intellectual circle in Leipzig, the great centre of the German publishing business, he was not really an extremist, believing in peaceful advance. It was perhaps this as much as anything which led Engels to chastise him as being 'too fond of the shallow declarations of a German dissenting preacher . . . [whose] arguments wanted both philosophical acumen and acquaintance with practical matters of fact'. Blum's dislike of the path of violence is clearly demonstrated by an attack on the rising of Hecker and Struve: 'They have betrayed the People by their mad rising; the People has been checked in the midst of its victorious progress; that is a horrible crime.'

On the Right of the assembly the most celebrated and probably the most hated member was von Radowitz. He was described at the time as looking 'like a sealed book containing the secret of reactionary politics'. After an extremely varied earlier career, which had included a period in Napoleon's army, he had become very influential in Prussia, being extremely close to Frederick William IV and being used by him for important diplomatic assignments.

Also from the Right was the colourful and flamboyant Prince Lichnowsky. Very intelligent and frequently a scourge of the Left in debate, he is perhaps best known for the manner of his death. It was of him that the fine comment was made, 'he belonged to those men who seem gifted with everything for this world, and this world only'.

The members included some who, although not very important in 1848, mattered greatly because of their actions in the past. Such a man was Thurnvater Jahn, the fighter against Napoleon and Arndt, the old patriot poet who was besought to stand before his fellow members a second time so that he could be properly seen and acclaimed by his admirers. Other members still, such as Jacob Grimm, the fairy story writer, and the constitutional historian Dahlmann, whatever they were to achieve in politics, were important for reputations won in other activities.

The problems which faced the assembly were enormous. At a time of great turmoil, both political and social, international as well as domestic, it was seeking to unite a group of states and then to act as the legislature for the unified state: all this was to be accomplished peacefully by processes of discussion and majority decision in a land where there was no parliamentary tradition and when, throughout, the assembly's powers were never clearly defined.

It has long been fashionable to mock at the men of Frankfurt and to regard them as windbags; Engels for instance called them 'old and worn-out political characters [who] exhibited their involuntary ludicrousness and their impotence of thought'. The fact is that their general level of ability was high but that they were taking on an impossible task.

Although there were no parties in the modern sense, like-minded men tended to congregate together in various hotels and these became the centres of particular ideas and attitudes.

The Left saw the assembly much as the Convention in France after 1792, the representative of the Sovereignty of the People, and therefore clearly entitled to create the Germany it wanted. The Right believed that the decisions of the assembly would have to be enacted by the existing state governments. However, the degree of co-operation looked for between the princes and the assembly varied enormously and gave rise to grouping in between the extremes.

Clearly an executive power was required for the new Germany, but there was great disagreement as to what it should be and how it should function. Finally, on von Gagern's urging, the assembly decided to create a provisional executive in the form of an Imperial Regent who would appoint a ministry responsible to the assembly, to direct foreign policy, control the armed forces and generally manage the security and welfare of the German people.

Their choice as Imperial Regent was the Habsburg Archduke John, the uncle of the Emperor but a man with a liberal reputation. When this decision was followed by his arrival in Frankfurt and the setting up of his ministry, the old Federal Diet simultaneously dissolving itself, on July 12, the new German state appeared to be launched.

Perhaps nowhere did the news of the fall of Metternich and the revolution in Vienna provoke a more immediate response than in the Italian provinces of the Austrian Empire. The mounting antagonism to Austrian rule, manifested in the Tobacco Riots, had been further nourished by the granting of constitutions in the other Italian states. Austrian power stood clearly revealed as the barrier to constitutional progress: there was a general air of expectancy abroad that some showdown was imminent and necessary. A student in Milan wrote of this mood: 'The lectures of the schools were neglected even by the most studious; wild discourses and extravagant hopes absorbed our excited imaginations. Collected in groups, we passed the day in practising military evolutions, and night found us congregated and busily occupied, in some remote chamber, in melting bullets and preparing cartridges.'

Even Venice, seemingly politically asleep, had begun to awake and stir uneasily under Austrian rule. News of the constitutions in Sicily and Naples provoked excited demonstrations in the theatre when a Sicilian dance was passionately encored and the police had to be called in an attempt to restore calm. Thus when reports arrived of events in Vienna it was at once assumed that the opportunity to demand concessions had come. Of course there were different ideas as to what concessions should be sought, but it was assumed on all sides that concessions there should be.

Rumours first reached Venice on March 16 and were confirmed the following day. A demonstration followed; a few hundred men made for St. Mark's Square with banners hurriedly improvised from their handkerchiefs tied to sticks. The main demand was for the release of Manin and Tommaseo, the one a lawyer the other a writer, who had been imprisoned as political prisoners despite the failure of the authorities to prove any case against them.

The Habsburg government in Venice was in the charge of two Hungarians, Palfy and his military commander Zichy. Their conduct, at a time when governments were distinguished for their lack of fight almost everywhere, was inexplicable in its feebleness. Pestered for the release of the prisoners, already somewhat taken aback at the news from Vienna and frightened by his wife's stories of being insulted and hooted in the streets, Palfy surrendered with the engaging but hardly helpful phrase, 'I do what I ought not to do.'

After this weak start the government never regained its nerve. An Italian tricolour, hung in front of St. Mark's, defied attempts to remove it despite the arrival of men with ladders urged on by the soldiers; the great bell of St. Mark's was rung in defiance by a group of citizens who broke into the tower during the night. Then Manin's request for an armed Civic Guard was acceded to after troops, who had been tormented by the assembled crowds, fired on and killed unarmed citizens. Even though Palfy's qualifications as to its character and construction were straight away disregarded no firm stand was taken. For several days a joyful Venice celebrated its victories and no clash between the city and the Habsburg representatives resulted. However, the Venetians would clearly not rest content with what they had gained.

The next crisis occurred over something which owed little to nationalism. The great arsenal, in effect, was run by a naval officer, Marinovich. He was a tough man and had become very unpopular because of his vigorous measures: in particular he had tightened up on the all-pervading practice of looting by which employees were able to construct whole houses from stolen materials. Iron bars had been fitted, wages docked, and men dismissed in an attempt to curb the abuse. At the same time Marinovich had recommended cutting the men's pay while his own had been increased by a grateful government. He had kept his head in the current collapse of authority and sent the ships of the Austrian fleet, largely manned by Italian sailors, away from the contamination of Venice; and otherwise demonstrated his intention of preserving his authority.

On the 21st, an attempt was made by the arsenal workers to murder their hated 'master' by ambushing him on his way home, a plan that was described later as 'to watch the wild beast as it issued from its lair, to assail it with stones and brickbats, and to knock it down and drown it'. This plan failed but the next day Marinovich was seized and murdered, his body being subsequently mutilated. Under the leadership of Manin, a general assault on the arsenal was then made. Although in the event little resistance was offered this fact should not be allowed to detract from the bravery of an action that, at the time, seemed to verge upon the foolhardy.

Now that the arsenal was in the hands of the Venetians the final confrontation with the government had arrived. Palfy surrendered his authority into the hands of the military in the person of Zichy. The latter faced with demands for a total transfer of power and instant withdrawal of all non-Italian troops, gave way with only a pretence of resistance. Unkind gossip of the time had it that Zichy retired to bed upon hearing of Marinovich's death but, when he realized that only his signature rather than his life was required by the revolutionaries, he sprang up with the words, 'Now, thank God, I shall eat my dinner in peace.'*

Amidst enormous excitement Manin proclaimed the Republic of Venice, of which he became president, and by the evening of March 22 Austria's authority was no more.†

The fall of Metternich was known in Milan on March 17 and here, the centre of opposition to Habsburg rule in Italy, energetic action was at once decided upon. A vast and excited public meeting on the next day developed into a procession to the Palazzo del Governo to demand reforms. One who took part wrote of 'that disordered and fluctuating movement of the living mass; the hurried strokes of the tocsin; the countless handkerchiefs fluttering from the balconies thronged with females flinging down cockades which, tossed about in the air, were caught and struggled for by hundreds of upheld arms'.

In the concourse were both moderates and extremists in the patriotic cause. Of the former, Casati, the mayor of Milan, had already used his influence earlier in the day to dissuade the Austrian civil authorities from calling in the military, on the grounds that such intervention usually provoked rather than prevented violence.

The procession proceeded amidst enormous enthusiasm until confronted by a handful of sentries before the palace. The temper of the crowd was clearly shown when the sentries, having fired at the mass of approaching people who had disregarded their challenge, were swept aside like chaff. The appearance of the Archbishop, sporting a tricolour cockade and distributing blessings and salutations, in no way satisfied the throng which flooded into the palace, looting and destroying. The leaders meanwhile surged into the Council Room and there confronted the senior Austrian government official available.

Under pressure, he accepted their demands which centred on the determination of the Milanese to form a Civic Guard. Having got their way the revolutionaries took the unhappy official with them

* The surrender was described in the official treaty in these words: 'His Excellency Count Palfy, desirous to prevent bloodshed . . . has recommended to Count Zichy all possible regard for that beautiful and monumental city, to which he is deeply attached. In consequence of his recommendation and in consideration of the urgent circumstances, and to save the city from the horrors of bloodshed he . . . agreed upon the following treaty.'

† It is interesting that in a dispatch to Palmerston he was described as 'a man', some details of who the new president was being left to a later dispatch.

as security for their gains. However, there was no question of matters being allowed to rest there. The returning procession was fired upon and Radetzky evidently had no intention of accepting promises extracted by force. This was clearly realized by the Milanese who soon began the construction of barricades in the town. At first, though, these were of a temporary nature; one of the earliest was a large waggon overturned with its load of empty barrels, and others were hurriedly felled trees.

Radetzky launched his troops into the city and commanded them to seize important objectives; barricades they took were thrown into the canal. However, a stiff resistance was mounted, available projectiles were hurled down upon the troops from upstairs windows and the barricades were manned gallantly. After a night of drenching rain the fighting continued on the second of what were to become known as 'Milan's Five Glorious Days'. The British vice-consul reported that by eight o'clock in the morning 'every part of the town was in full insurrection'. Many more barricades were built: it was reckoned that there were nearly 2,000 by the evening and they were more scientifically constructed than those of the previous day. The contents of houses, such as 'costly furniture, bureaus, damask sofas and even pianos', were brought into the streets and there joined post-chaises and omnibuses. Even when, after bombardment and a charge, the Austrian troops had seized such a barricade, little had been accomplished since a new one was promptly built, and in any case, what was one lost among the thousand?

By the third day it was clear to Radetzky that, with the fierce resistance of the townspeople, coupled with disturbing news of affairs elsewhere in Lombardy and Venetia, he would have to change his tactics. Consequently he decided to withdraw his soldiers from their more exposed positions and concentrate them upon holding the walls of the city, thus starving it into surrender. At the same time he tried to parley with the more conservative leaders of the revolt.

However, the formation of a War Council under the republican Cattaneo, although at first somewhat at cross purposes with the lead of Casati, injected more determination into the defence, refusing to countenance a truce. There were plans instead to go over to the offensive and break out—an idea was put forward for draining an underground sewer to re-establish connection with the surrounding countryside. On the 21st determined efforts were made to smash through the gates; movable barricades were constructed to provide cover for those in the assault and behind these great bravery was shown. From young aristocrats such as Dandalo and Manara to poor workpeople there was evident a solidarity which cut across class. Dandalo himself said that the insurrection 'owed its success to the unanimity of the combatants, much more than to any preconceived plan of action'. Wounded were at once taken into houses, and valuable china was sacrificed by its owners to be thrown at troops in the street. The successful assault on the Tosa Gate was watched by some young ladies on a balcony: 'each time an Austrian was brought down they clapped their hands as at the theatre, and gave "vivas" for the lucky marksman; but when the aim was wrong, and no mischief done, they saluted the failure with a general hiss.' Radetzky grasped the new determination of the resistance: 'The character of his people has altered as if by magic, and fanaticism has taken hold of every age group, every class and both sexes.'

Fears that Charles Albert was about to attack and cut him off, added to mounting concern at the state of his soldiers who had been subjected to continuous fighting, determined Radetzky to withdraw right away from Milan. So, on the 22nd, he began what might have been a disastrous retreat. It is to the enormous credit of Radetzky and his soldiers that the operation was accomplished so successfully. Laden with wounded and encumbered by wives and families, the troops had to fight their way out of the town at a time when their morale might have been expected to be zero.

Radetzky ordered a long artillery barrage to provide some cover and there was a great bonfire of furniture, hay and straw in the castle to serve as a distraction; but the chief reason for success was the order and discipline of the troops coupled with his ability as a commander. 'You are not conquered, you are not going to be. I have withdrawn before the enemy, not you,' Radetzky told his troops. There were few men in authority prepared to shoulder this degree of responsibility during February and March 1848.

Meanwhile among the Milanese, despite the circulation of atrocity stories concerning the departing troops, the feeling of triumph led to a mood of euphoria.* It was assumed that the Austrians were totally defeated and in headlong flight back to Vienna; Piedmontese troops who arrived were assured that they

---

* One story told of little boys found nailed up on doors, another of captured soldiers, discovered to have hands and fingers among their effects, severed and taken for the rings with which they were adorned.

had little to do. A great memorial service in the Duomo, which echoed in the packed square outside, was held for those patriots who had fallen in the fighting. This for a time maintained the patriotic excitement but in general life returned to normal.

The correspondent of *The Times* described this return to normal in a passage which also throws light on the spirit which had animated the resistance:

'The barriers are being actively demolished, and, while nobles at one end claim their magnificent carriages, a good housewife at the other asks for the kitchen table, which she contributed for the same patriotic purpose. The managers of the Scala, and other Theatres, are looking for their benches, and the malle-poste and diligence owners are entreating that the heaps of straw and manure stuffed in at their doors and windows shall be removed. In one place, a crowd of honest women are disputing the right of ownership to several mattresses and feather beds which have been exposed, in the common cause of the country, to the last week's rain, and in another, the greengrocer and the oil-man, alternately laying hold of a counter which the cloth-dealer finally carries off. The only things unclaimed were the sentry-boxes of the Austrians, which in these strange days had been employed to exclude the very men they were constructed to shelter.'

Whatever had been his original intentions, Radetzky soon decided that his only course was to withdraw his embattled troops on to the Quadrilatero, the area of land dominated by the four fortresses of Mantua and Peschiera in the west and Verona and Legnano in the east. Although by no means of equal strength, the fortresses together constituted a formidable barrier. Radetzky ordered the other Austrian troops in Italy to retire as best they could upon the Quadrilatero and there concentrate, he himself setting up his headquarters in Verona.

With most of the towns in revolt, the march at first proved far from easy. However, after the village of Molignano had been bombarded and assaulted, following the seizure of Radetzky's interpreter by the inhabitants, the warning was heeded and less opposition encountered. In this situation, with the Austrian troops struggling back to the Quadrilatero, the towns and cities in Lombardy and Venetia in insurrection, and news arriving of continuing unrest and confusion in Vienna, reactions in the rest of Italy were not always predictable.

Nowhere was the problem so immediate as in Sardinia-Piedmont, especially when it is remembered that, as in other Italian states, a constitution had recently been granted which gave public opinion more say in affairs. Whatever the enigma of Charles Albert's character and intentions, whatever is believed of the sincerity and the selfishness of the Piedmontese, one fact stands out clearly: the sad misfortune for Piedmont and Charles Albert that the collapse of the Austrian position in Italy coincided so exactly with the coming of constitutional government.

Cavour wrote to a friend, just after the constitution had been granted, of the 'happy revolution' which had occurred. There had been no real loser and the Throne had not been degraded or lost its moral authority. But he went on to say that the one fear he had was of the international situation, particularly the hatred of Austria and the wish to expel her from Italy: it was this that might blow Piedmont off course.

Charles Albert, on the other hand, had for some time seen the future in terms of war with Austria. His attitude had been made abundantly clear during the interview with D'Azeglio in 1845, when the latter, who was informing his king of the opinions he had gleaned in a tour of Italy, was astonished by Charles Albert's reply: '[Those gentlemen] can rest assured that when the opportunity arises, my life, my children's lives, my arms, my treasure, my army; all shall be given in the cause of Italy.' But, if there was to be fighting, Charles Albert did not want interference in the direction of affairs from his subjects, interference which, he felt, could only inhibit the efficient prosecution of the war.

It was at this juncture that the Milanese liberated their city, and popular feeling clamoured for war. Cavour wrote in his paper *Il Risorgimento*: 'The supreme hour of the monarchy of Savoy had sounded, the hour of decisive resolutions, the hour upon which hangs the fate of the monarchy and the people. In the face of events in Lombardy and Vienna, hesitation, doubt or delay are no longer possible.'

Allowing for journalistic hyperbole this assessment probably did sum up the situation accurately. As emphasis of the perils of delay Charles Albert knew that there was a considerable body of opinion in Milan which wished for a republic, and if he did not move at once, despite the support of such as Casati, Lombardy might be lost to him. Finally, there was always the fear that revolutionary

France might step in to aid revolution in Italy and thus shoulder him aside.

Worried, wishing he had had more time to prepare, and nagged by his dislike of constitutional government, Charles Albert declared for war and his troops crossed into Lombardy with the flamboyant declaration, 'People of Lombardy and Venice! The destinies of Italy are maturing; a happier fate awaits the intrepid defenders of inculcated rights.'

Elsewhere in Italy the same excitement prevailed. By the middle of April all the Italian states seemed to be contributing to the war effort and King Ferdinand of Naples was forced to declare war on Austria; troops were soon marching north commanded by General Pepe, the veteran Carbonaro. Regular troops and volunteers from Rome under Durando and D'Azeglio were on their way to the frontiers and Parma, Modena and Tuscany were all despatching contingents. The Milanese had acted as if their part were accomplished but they too had volunteers formed under the young Manara, one of the heroes of the Five Days, and more troops were to follow.

Notwithstanding the hesitations and doubts expressed by some, and the lack of enthusiasm for war against Austria among many Italians, it really did seem, in the words of the Grand Duke of Tuscany, that 'the period for the regeneration of all Italy had arrived'. Mazzini, among other exiles, thought so and hurried across the Alps: romantic that he always was, he stopped to pick the first flower he saw on his descent from the snows into Italy and sent it to a friend in England.

News came in of the success of Charles Albert's forces in seizing the town of Goito and with it a bridgehead across the river Mincio, between Peschiera and Mantua. An American woman, married to an Italian and living in Rome, eulogized: 'I have been engrossed, stunned almost. . . . A glorious flame burns higher and higher in the heart of the nations.' It was small wonder that Garibaldi, already on his way back from South America, should write with such optimism of the news he learnt on arriving off the Spanish coast: 'The Piedmontese army was pursuing the scattered remnants of the Austrian; and all Italy, replying as one man to the call to arms, was sending her contingents of brave men to the holy war.'

Along with the Italians, many Poles were awaiting a wave of

revolution in Europe as the best hope of creating their own state. Particularly was this so among the many thousand refugees who had come to western Europe after the failure of Poland's revolt against the Tsar in 1831. Believing in the need for French help they had ceased to have faith in Louis Philippe and looked instead to revolution in France: the failure of 1846 had done nothing to change their opinions. The Polish poet Mickiewicz's cry 'for the universal war for the freedom of nations, we beseech thee, O Lord' expresses this sentiment.

At first the spread of revolution in 1848 seemed to justify these Polish hopes. Governments and popular feeling combined to express the desire that Poland should be reconstituted. In Prussia where Mieroslawski, the unsuccessful plotter of 1846, was released from prison by Berliners, the government appeared to bless the Polish cause, allowing the Grand Duchy of Posen to be used as a base for a crusade against Russia. Meanwhile Polish *émigrés* in France set out for Posen to join the attack upon the Tsar.

But the bellicosity of those who were championing Poland began to dwindle as it became clear that Russia did not intend to lauch a counter-revolutionary attack westwards. If Russia was to attack anyway, a Polish revolt would serve to embarrass her and could only help: if Russia was prepared to tolerate the changes to her west, a Polish revolt might lead to war with Russia after all and thus could only harm. However, the Poles continued to organize themselves in Posen and excitement ran high as an army was assembled.

In Austrian Poland the force of revolution was not so great as might have been anticipated. Perhaps the ability of the Governor of Galicia, Count Stadion, had something to do with this and certainly the memories of the abortive revolt of 1846 must have militated against the success of revolution in 1848.

Nevertheless, on the receipt of the news of Metternich's fall in Vienna, agitated demonstrations took place, both in recently annexed Cracow and in Galicia. In Lemberg, Stadion was badgered to grant liberal, social and nationalist reforms. He released political prisoners and allowed the citizens to form a National Guard but referred the majority of the demands to the Imperial government.

In contrast to 1846 the Polish nationalists realized that some attempt must be made to secure the backing of the peasants but even so they were forestalled when the Vienna government gave Stadion the right to declare the emancipation of the peasants from the Robot, compensation for those losing by this decision to be paid by the state. In this way the movement for revolt in Galicia was kept just below the surface. But in Cracow it did break through, with the influx of *émigrés* unable to reach Posen and the formation of a National Committee which claimed to speak for all Galicia. Plans for the subversion of Austrian authority miscarried but street fighting continued in Cracow for a couple of days before the Imperial troops were able to restore order. The authorities took this opportunity to expel those Polish *émigrés* who were not Austrian citizens and to dissolve the National Committee. Meanwhile in Russian Poland there was no revolt at all.

In comparison to the hesitancy of the Polish revolt, the Hungarian movement for reform flowed fast. Hungary had been staunch in its refusal to be integrated into the Habsburg Monarchy in the past. 'Though united with Austria by the link of the Crown, [Hungary] has nevertheless been separate and distinct from Austria by its own complete constitution,' was how Lord Palmerston described Hungary's situation to the House of Commons. Clearly at a time of revolt and rising nationalist aspiration, the Hungarians would not be backward in voicing their demands.

The 1830s and '40s had witnessed increasing nationalist agitation in Hungary, and the Diet which met in November 1847 contained a party of opposition to the government with something approaching a coherent reform policy.

However, in Hungary, virtually alone in Europe at this time, the government had its own reform programme. Under the vigorous leadership of Count Apponyi, himself a Hungarian magnate, the Habsburg government had come to consent to the principles of reform in the amelioration of the conditions of the peasantry and the extension of taxation to the nobility.

The Polish revolt in Galicia in 1846, and the jacquerie which followed, had had its greatest impact in Hungary. Fear of a repetition was behind both Apponyi's determination that the government must offer measures of reform and also the acceptance of these reforms by conservative magnates. These projected reforms had the effect of releasing some of the pressure of opposition, to an extent where it might have been safely contained; this despite the fire and ability of Kossuth.

A revolutionary of 1848-9 who met Kossuth afterwards wrote: 'The whole romance of the revolutionary time found in Kossuth's person its most attractive embodiment.' Again and again those who came in contact with him spoke of Kossuth's charm and ability to convince: recently described by an historian as 'one of the most persuasive men ever to be born', Kossuth had equal facility with his tongue and his pen. It was this power to attract which first gave him his opportunity. For, although noble, his family were indigent and the young Kossuth was faced with having to make his own way in the world. He became factor to a wealthy, titled woman who, widowed, fell in love with him. It was she who later secured for him the chance to attend the Hungarian Diet as a proxy for one of her friends. From here he exercised his talents as a publicist to such good effect that he had soon built up a personal following.

He was determined not to be seduced, by the prospect of collaboration with Vienna, from his attempt to secure Hungarian liberties, and he devoted his energies to persuading his colleagues to the same view. The lesson he learnt from the Galician revolt was that a nationalist policy could only be strong if it was supported by a wide section of the population. This conviction led him to demand the emancipation of the serfs 'lest the nobility will be put to the scythe and this moment will be simultaneously the fatal day of Magyar nationality'. 'I know nothing of socialism. I have never occupied myself with it,' he continued, 'my aim is to secure for the Hungarian people national independence and free political institutions. When that is done my task will have been performed.' This was his motive for urging equality for all before the law, much wider representation in the Diet and the end of the nobility's immunity from taxation. But even these demands of Kossuth's were met by the Habsburg government in the spirit of compromise and he found it most difficult to convince his fellows that they should refuse the government's offers.

It was at this stage that the news came from France of the fall of Louis Philippe. The alarm and excitement, financial as well as political, that this caused created the opportunity for Kossuth to exploit. On March 3, in a violent denunciation of the Viennese government he portrayed the Austrian state as a building upon rotted foundations; drawing the conclusion that Hungary must secure her own future by gaining control of her internal affairs. He went on to state that the only guarantee of Hungary's future would be the granting of constitutional government for the other Austrian provinces.*

However, despite a favourable vote for Kossuth's proposals in the Lower House, the magnates stalled when their turn came to ratify them. This was the situation when reports of the revolution in Vienna and the fall of Metternich began to arrive.

Again, this news was decisive. Action was at once taken; the new Palatine, the Habsburg Archduke Stephen, convened the House of Magnates, who voted an extended reform programme. Full autonomy for Hungary under the Habsburg crown, with a responsible ministry at Budapest, along with union with Transylvania was demanded: a deputation including the Palatine set out for Vienna to press these demands on Ferdinand.

The magnates at Pressburg had partly been influenced in their acquiescence by news from Budapest. The largest town in the kingdom, Budapest had had its political excitement channelled into a more radical direction by the students, who led demands for annual Diets elected by universal suffrage and the abolition of feudalism.

Reports of what was happening were considerably embellished with stories of a large body of country-people armed with scythes, gathering together in the first stage of a peasant revolution. Rumours of this sort, while helping to persuade the Diet to agree to the reform demands, explain the coolness with which the leaders from Budapest were received when they reached Pressburg.

When Ferdinand came to Pressburg in April and gave his assent to the new constitution, the 'April Laws', it seemed that Hungary had gained her autonomy; the revolution was victorious.

The Hungarians and the Germans were not the only subjects of the Habsburgs to revolt in 1848. The Grand Principality of Transylvania, one of the regions which the Hungarians were seeking to bring into direct union with Inner Hungary, was another location of rebellion. Naturally, events elsewhere in Hungary excited Transylvania and united with mounting Roumanian nationalism— the Roumanians were numerically the preponderant people of the principality—to produce a revolutionary programme compounded of nationalist, liberal and social reform. However, the revolutionaries

* It was this speech which when publicized in Vienna was such a stimulant to revolution there.

remained tied to belief in Austria and the wish to find a future inside the Austrian Empire.

The Roumanian nationalism in Transylvania was closely involved with that in the Danubian Duchies, Moldavia and Wallachia, still under Turkish sovereignty but now enjoying a measure of self-rule. In both duchies a chronically unstable situation developed into a revolt with the news from Paris. The Wallachians were at one time promised help by Lamartine, and the rising featured a considerable section of the population. In Moldavia, the revolution never really spread beyond the Boyars—the noble class—despite attempts to build barricades in Jassy, the principal town of the duchy.

Revolutionary sentiment spread to other peoples of Hungary, public meetings were held, resolutions passed and programmes drawn up. There were stirrings among the Slovaks, and the Serbs held a great 'National Congress' in May; but perhaps the most significant development came in Croatia, where a certain Jellacic, who had been prominent in debate, was appointed to the position of Ban which happened to be vacant at the time. A great meeting at Zagreb saluted Jellacic, who early in April had assumed absolute power for Croatia.

1848 found Bohemia, like so many other parts of the Austrian Empire, trying to extend its rights. Nationalism, on the level of hotel-keepers in Prague refusing to serve those who ordered in German, was linked with far-reaching demands for more power for the Bohemian Diet. News of the revolution in Paris, and the confusion it led to, 'afforded the Czechs of Bohemia a favourable opportunity for the indulgence of their national sentiments as well as dreams of freedom and independence', in the words of the American chargé d'affaires in Vienna at the time.

On March 11, a public meeting was held at the Wenzelbad Hotel in Prague and a petition drawn up to be presented at Vienna. It contained the liberal demands of the time and in addition sought the extended use of the Czech language in government and law as well as requesting that Bohemia be administered in common with Silesia and Moravia, the old lands of St. Wenceslaus's kingdom.

Although the Emperor agreed to some clauses of the petition, those who had borne it to Vienna were not received in Prague as heroes. Again, the fall of Metternich had transformed the situation. A second petition demanded that Bohemia, Silesia, and Moravia must be governed as a separate state, responsible to an assembly which would be elected on a democratic franchise. Bohemia wanted home rule along the lines which Hungary enjoyed. At the end of May the governor of Bohemia, on his own authority, proclaimed a provisional government in Prague: here revolution once more was victorious.

Revolution was indeed triumphant on all sides; from end to end of Europe governments were being overturned or forced to accept change. In the Low Countries there were riots in the large towns and a Belgian Legion set out from Paris to promote the struggle. However, in both Belgium and Holland revolt was stilled when reform, including some diminution of their powers and an extension of the franchise, was granted by the monarchs. At the same time the Legion was defeated; one section of it, arriving by train, was towed away after a timely change of locomotive, and thus rendered harmless.

But the virus of revolt continued to spread, with barricades and cries of *Viva la Republica* in Madrid, demonstrations in Athens, crowds out in the streets of Copenhagen and democratic banquets in Stockholm. Truly Europe was in revolt. The break-down of society, so long foreseen by Metternich seemed at hand.

PART FIVE

IMPACT—IRRESISTIBLE RESISTED

Chapter XII

REVOLUTION HESITANT

ONE HISTORIAN saw 1848 as 'the turning point at which modern history failed to turn'. It is open to question whether history proceeds in single, regular movements as the notion of a turning point implies. Even if it does, the metaphor is somewhat misleading in this case. Perhaps 1848 can more accurately be portrayed, to retain the metaphor of a journey, as the moment when a dark road is illuminated, exposed as having been all the time a cul-de-sac. So long as Restoration Europe survived it was possible to see development temporarily checked by reaction—by the blind and stupid policies the authorship of which was so often attributed to Metternich.

Once the pressure of frustrated progress had built up beyond a certain point it would be able to thrust aside the obstruction and the advance might be resumed. This advance-progress could be presumed to be in a single direction. However, once it had been resumed it soon became clear that far from there being one objective there was a multiplicity; far from the various forces behind the advance being complementary they were contradictory. The road that men had been struggling along together had now clearly ended; there was no single way forward. Some might find a way round the blank wall, some might retrace their steps, some might even decide to stand uneasily where they were, but as for pressing on together, that was now obviously impossible. Scarcely a month after the fall of Louis Philippe the contradictions and incompatibilities of the revolutions were coming out into the open.

Early on in the 'Five Glorious Days' the cry had been taken up in Milan of *Viva Pio Nono! Viva l'Italia! Viva la Republica!* To many it must have seemed that these cries meant the same thing: the cause of nationalism expressed by a reforming Pope, the cause of nationalism expressed in a new Italy and in republicanism. Metternich had resisted all these aims and now that he had fallen they seemed likely, at last, to be realized.

It was perhaps fitting that the illusions which lay behind such views should be first exposed by the actions of Pio Nono, he who had done more than any other man to generate in Italy political excitement of the sort which led men in 1848 to demand, and fight for, concessions or submission from their governments.

The problem which confronted Pius was that of what role he should play in the war that was being fought in north Italy. The commanders of the Papal troops and volunteers who marched north from Rome were quite certain about this: Durando, D'Azeglio (being Piedmontese themselves) and Ferrari believed that the contingents from the Papal States must throw themselves into the fray against Austria at once. On the one hand Charles Albert needed what help he could get if he were to be successful; on the other hand the nationalist cause demanded the co-operation of all Italians in the great effort. Durando intended to march the troops northwards against the Austrians and force the Pope to accept the situation by declaring war.

The constitutional government in Rome was not quite so certain but it too wanted to join in the war, partly because it believed that a regime in Rome which did not pursue a war policy would have no chance of survival. So both these groups, though their tactics might have been different, saw the future in terms of participation in a war against Austria for the liberation of Italy.

The position of the Pope was very much more complicated. As a man, Pius was sympathetic to the Italian cause and certainly did not wish for an Austrian victory. But he was being called upon to proclaim a Holy War or crusade, not as a man but as the Pope, and against a staunch Catholic power. However, the fear of causing schism in the Church, although real enough, was not the most important objection in Pius's eyes to a declaration of war. This, in his own words, was because 'We, albeit unworthy, are upon earth the vice-regent of Him that is the Author of Peace and the Lover of Charity. . . . We reach to and embrace all kindreds, peoples and nations, with equal solicitude of paternal affection'. Whatever Popes in the past might have done, Pius had no business in declaring war and acting the aggressor and he knew it.

Although he was adamant on what he could not do, Pius was less clear on what he could do. Did he intend to allow the troops to cross the Po, claiming that he could not prevent them from exceeding his orders to defend the frontier, or did he always mean to make his position plain? It is here that the charges of equivocal behaviour may be justified. In the event, the proclamation issued by Durando to his troops but written by D'Azeglio made such a policy of silence impossible. 'Italy is condemned by the Austrian Government to the pillage, rapes, and cruelties of a savage soldiery, to incendiarism, assassination, and total ruin,' wrote D'Azeglio. He went on to state that the Pope 'has blessed your swords, which, united to those of Charles Albert, must act together for the extermination of the enemies of God and Italy'.

If Pius remained dumb on the issue of the war it could be assumed that it had his support. His answer was to publish the Allocution of April 29 in which, after justifying his policies as the execution of reforms long enjoined upon the Papacy by the European Powers, he dissociated himself from the war against Austria.

This declaration had an enormous effect once the news had been absorbed. Angry crowds were out in the streets and Rome was at once near to revolution. What was the position of those Papal troops who had joined the war? Were they mere bandits in the eyes of the Austrians? Did the Pope intend to revoke his constitution? Those who wished could easily exploit such doubts, and many such there were. Power rapidly deserted the government and fell into the hands of popular clubs and the Civic Guard. The position Pius had held in the eyes of Italians since 1846 was gone for ever. This decline is brought home poignantly by a passage in a letter from an American woman living in Rome, who apologizes for her failure to get a rosary blessed as requested but goes on to say: 'I suppose she would not wish it, as none can now attach any value to the blessing of Pius IX.'

Even so, it is absurd to see Pius as guilty of some terrible treason. Casati had written from Milan to a Papal minister a few days before the Allocution was published. He asked: 'Is it not the cause of humanity, religion and the Gospel which we are defending? Why should the Pontiff, benevolent, holy, and just man as he is, hesitate to consecrate by his word of authority the righteous cause of Italy?' These questions have only to be asked for answers to jostle one another in reply.

Pius's position was impossible. Count Pasolini, who had loyally supported the Pope, told his son that in 1848 Pius had 'hoped for impossibilities'. Metternich from the opening of the Pontificate had seen that the course Pius had embarked upon was bound to lead to

G

disaster. He had recognized this so clearly that he could not believe any Pope could follow such policies, and he had not allowed for such an eventuality in his plans.* While the Pope was an absolute ruler in the Papal States, if an issue arose in which there was a conflict between his temporal and his spiritual interests, he made the decision as to which should give way. What was intolerable in the new situation was that the Pope as constitutional monarch would find such decisions taken out of his hands. It was in fact impossible for him to be, at the same time, a constitutional ruler of a temporal state and the autocratic head of a world-wide Church.

However, for two years Italy had been swept along in the train of Rome, not because of what Pius did and said but because it was he as Pope who was doing and saying it. Perhaps nothing more clearly illustrates Pius's political naïveté and his failure to grasp the consequences of his manœuvres than his reactions to the public rumpus which followed the Allocution. At first he believed that he was misunderstood and determined to have the Allocution translated into Italian. Then he pathetically asked, 'My People, what have I done to you?' D'Azeglio could have told him. He had written: 'If the Pope . . . consents to be what opinion is making him, the Papacy is definitely the guiding force of the world.' When the favourite loses, the punter always blames the horse or the jockey, never himself.

The Allocution did not prevent the Papal troops from fighting; when it was issued Durando had already crossed the Po. It did, however, make reinforcement and further recruitment difficult. The essential unity of the effort against Austria, even if it had been essentially spurious, was now exploded. Many who had felt constrained to participate in the war, but had no real liking for so doing, now remained at home justifying themselves by the Allocution.

The most important consequence in this respect was that it established a firm precedent for Ferdinand II of Naples to withdraw his troops from the conflict. Ferdinand had not wanted to fight Austria. True he had always wished to remain independent of Vienna but that was something very different from dispatching his

* 'In his heart, the Pontiff always came before the Prince, the priest before the citizen,' wrote Farini. Farini in fact thought that it was the belief that the temporal power must not be corrupt and abuse-laden in the interests of the spiritual power that had set Pius on the road to reform in the first place.

armies in a war of aggression. Also, he saw no advantage in waging a war whose main purpose seemed to be the aggrandizement of Sardinia-Piedmont, particularly when, after his own deposition, the Sicilians offered their throne to the son of Charles Albert. However, Ferdinand was a constitutional monarch and was not now in a position to make such a decision himself. A new situation was created by the meeting of the assembly, when arguments over procedure developed into a confrontation with the king.

The great changes that had occurred in Europe since Ferdinand had agreed to a constitution had made many Neapolitans dissatisfied with what they had obtained. Far from the charge of perfidy, which was later made against Ferdinand, being fair, it is clear that it was the liberals and radicals who were determined to disregard the constitution if they were able to force more concessions from the king. It was their attempts to do this that led to the wrangle with Ferdinand at the opening of the assembly and to the attempts of the liberals to enlist popular support.

Such support proved to have a will of its own. When the assembly, its immediate claims satisfied and worried at mounting lawlessness in the streets, demanded the dismantling of the barricades it was totally ignored. Social motives began to assert themselves and the situation became one of disorder. It was at this stage that the king intervened with his troops. May 15 witnessed vicious and bloody fighting with atrocities on both sides, but by the end of the day the king had reasserted his authority. 'They have given him what he lacked, the knowledge of his power. He feared us: now he defies us,' recorded one liberal.

It was not therefore surprising that on May 18 Ferdinand should recall his troops from the north and cancel plans to send others to join them. He wanted the soldiers at home to maintain order and also to help him regain Sicily. General Pepe refused to lead the soldiers back but managed to persuade well under a tenth of them to cross into Venetia with him. The loss of the Neapolitans—somewhere in the region of 40,000 had been promised—was a serious blow to Charles Albert, the more so because it was regular, trained troops which he lacked.

It was not just from Naples and Rome that Charles Albert received less help than he had hoped. Nearer home as well, the response was disappointing. First, the quality of those who volunteered to fight the Austrians was very varied. One volunteer from

Milan described his colleagues as 'crowds of turbulent spirits, seeking nothing but impunity to plunder'. Such men were frequently impossible to discipline and had no stomach for hard fighting. Even when the Milan government sought to organize a professional army, commissions were handed out to unsuitable people; some junior officers who had been discharged with infamy from the army of Piedmont received senior rank in the Lombard army. Of course, there were fine men who volunteered as well—'the flowers and the dregs of society,' it was claimed. But not only were the volunteers deficient in quality, their quantity was also unsatisfactory. One reason was that both in Milan and Venice there was a body of opinion that supported a republic. In the main this favoured some sort of federal association with Piedmont but there were extremists who from the start wanted only a unitary republic for Italy; they looked to Mazzini, who arrived in Milan in early April.

There were many in Milan who treated with disgust the entry of Charles Albert into the war; those who would have echoed the cry, 'We have driven out the Croats—here are more of them!' Such people were not unhappy to see Charles Albert fail and even if they did accept him it was usually because there was no real alternative. D'Azeglio tells how he sought to persuade doubters to put themselves behind Piedmont: 'You need force; and where is yours? If you haven't got it, you must find someone who has. Who has any in Italy? Even some? Piedmont: because at least she leads an independent life.'

However, this support was of a kind which would only last if Charles Albert gained the victory and would desert him upon defeat. Also, because Charles Albert had been brought in to provide force, many believed that this absolved them from having to do anything further. One who fought continuously for the next year and more talked of those who assisted only 'by parading their theatrical costumes in crowded towns, whilst they spent, in sneers and declamations, that time their duty called them to employ in a far different scene of action'.

But the lack of support for Charles Albert was not just the outcome of republican scruple, it owed much to distrust of the man. A monarchist such as D'Azeglio describes how, when meeting Charles Albert in 1846, he kept having to tell himself, 'Don't trust him, Massimo,' so scared was he of being hoodwinked. Della Rocca, someone close to Charles Albert, also speaks of the prevailing evaluation of him as untrustworthy. It is difficult to over-estimate the importance of this ability to create a lack of belief in the cause which he headed. Both Venetians and Lombards saw him as a man who would sell them if necessary, just as they believed he had sold his fellow-conspirators a quarter of a century before. Della Rocca admittedly felt that Charles Albert had gained this reputation without fair cause. He thought that he had been deliberately compromised by conspirators in an attempt to force his hand and that, ever afterwards, he refused to trust anyone. 'I was constantly with him afterwards, and do not think he ever opened his mind to, or felt any affection or tenderness for, anyone.' It was this manner which, in its turn, had strengthened people's distrust for him.

However, besides dislike for the Sardinian monarchy and for the Sardinian monarch, another very important factor in the failure of northern Italy to rally to Charles Albert was an acceptance of Austria, particularly by the peasants. To some extent this was because the appeal of nationalism had not really touched all classes. It was also the outcome of a dislike for war among the peasants who so often had to pay for it, whichever side they might support: hence their opposition to any invader, even if he claimed to be liberating them.

Della Rocca tells of how the peasants of Borghetto refused to allow the troops of Charles Albert to camp in their fields, and threatened to flood the land by opening the sluices from the canals. Unmoved by appeals of nationalism, they only finally bowed in the face of threats to destroy their village. And another campaigner writes of reaction in the Tyrol to a withdrawal of some Lombard volunteers which left the local inhabitants to face the returning Austrians: 'Seeing themselves thus carelessly abandoned, they battered down the tree of liberty in our presence, cursing the day in which they had been induced to declare themselves in favour of the insurrection.'

Thus only two months after Radetzky had been forced out of Milan and all Italy seemed on the march against him, what had seemed a united movement was really far from being so. 'The time of illusions was drawing to a close', as one of the revolutionaries put it. The uprising in Italy was still powerful but the torrent of March had spent much of its force by the end of May: the revolution was hesitant.

Historians have often pointed to the hypocrisy of the revolutionaries of 1848, above all as displayed in the matter of nationalism. For example, the German liberals at Frankfurt, who were seeking to create a German state by consent, denounced the Czechs and the Poles who were trying to do the same, in the name of freedom denying them freedom. It is true that there may have been some Germans for whom a double standard operated, who were indeed hypocrites, but there are other less sinister explanations of their conduct. Metternich had been as much the enemy of Czech as of German liberals and as a consequence these Germans had considered the Czechs as their allies. Thus it is possible to explain, if not to justify, the outrage felt by the German liberals when their former allies seemed to be thwarting them, for the division did endanger the recently won victories. From there it was only a short step for the Germans to see the Czechs as the willing agents of Habsburg reaction. This angry reaction, allied to what was often a sincerely held belief that in eastern Europe Germanization was synonymous with civilization, explains the agreement expressed by many with Engels when he described the Czech revolution as a 'movement which intended nothing less than to subjugate the civilized west under the barbarian east, the town under the country, trade, manufactures, intelligence, under the primitive agriculture of Slavonian serfs'.

On the other hand the Czechs, coming to believe in themselves as a distinct people, felt menaced by the growing confidence of the Germans. The German assumption that Bohemia would naturally wish to find its future in the new Germany frightened the Bohemians but was also behind the letter of the Committee of Fifty in Frankfurt to Palacky, inviting him as a distinguished man of letters to join them.

Czechs such as Palacky saw that this new Germany would bring about the end of the Habsburg Empire, and that this would mean either that the Czechs would be swallowed up by the new Germany, or that, if they remained outside, they would be enveloped by Russia. 'Assuredly,' replied Palacky to the invitation, 'if the Austrian state had not existed for ages, it would have been a behest for us . . . to endeavour to create it as soon as possible. . . . I am not a German . . . I am a Czech of Slavonic blood.' This refusal by Palacky to participate in the developments at Frankfurt was followed by a general refusal by Czechs to co-operate in returning members for the new German parliament; in hardly a fifth of the constituencies of Bohemia were elections properly held and, even where they were, only minorities recorded votes and some of those elected refused to attend the parliament.

Such a development was naturally intensely resented by the Germans, especially when the constitutional government in Vienna discovered the Czechs going over its head to the Emperor. At the same time Czech nationalists encountered opposition on much more practical grounds—for instance, demands that all administration and government should be transacted henceforth in Czech as well as German faced many officials with the unpalatable choice of either becoming proficient in Czech or abandoning their jobs. This was why German liberals found themselves applauding the efforts of Prince Windischgrätz to stamp out the Bohemian revolution while Bohemian liberals turned to the Habsburg Emperor against his supposedly liberal and constitutional government.

Much the same problem arose over Poland, or at least those parts of Poland under Prussian sovereignty. The scheme was to allow Poles to use Posen as a base for the liberation of their fatherland, but this had been decided upon by the Prussian government without any reference to the Germans living in Posen. Although a minority, they comprised nearly a third of the population and in fact a majority of the town dwellers; clearly their opinion could not be disregarded if any plan for Posen's future was to work peacefully. The Posen Germans were horrified at developments: the creation of a Polish National Committee, the arrival of Polish *émigrés* and the recruitment of a Polish army. The Prussian government sent General Willisen to preside over the national reorganization of the province. At this move the Germans living in Posen heartened to find the Prussian troops stationed among them totally opposed to the Poles, besought their government to change its policies. Despite the efforts of Willisen, a tolerant and liberal aristocrat who was accepted by the Poles, clashes broke out between Polish and Prussian soldiers in which, at first, the Prussians were worsted. However, very soon the Prussians recovered and by the middle of May the Poles were forced to submit. Willisen, finding his attempts at compromise impossible, had resigned and been replaced by someone much more pro-German in his outlook. 'The promises given to the Poles in the first days of excitement were shamefacedly broken. Polish armaments raised with the sanction of the government were dispersed and massacred by Prussian Artillery,' was Engels's comment.

The Prussian parliament still favoured Polish hopes for Posen but the Frankfurt assembly took a more chauvinistic view. 'Do justice to your ill-treated German brethren before you do it to a foreign nation'—the remark of one deputy neatly sums up the majority view. Although the extreme Left still championed the Poles, former left-wingers joined with the Right in condemning them.

Although West and East Prussia had not been part of the German Confederation, it had been assumed from the time of the Heidelberg meetings that they should participate in the creation of the German state. Posen's status was not clarified, however, and had been left by the Committee for subsequent decision. By the time that the Frankfurt assembly met, Posen had already been partitioned into German and Polish sections; successive partition lines had been drawn up by the Prussian authorities, each one favouring the Germans more than the last. It was decided at Frankfurt by an overwhelming majority to accept the partition and welcome twelve deputies from the province. When later the plans for partition collapsed and Posen remained a single state under Prussia the deputies stayed at Frankfurt.

In the kingdom of Hungary national differences at once made themselves felt, thus inhibiting the progress of revolution. In fact the Habsburg Court has been unfairly criticized for deliberately inciting the nationalism of the non-Magyar peoples, particularly the Croats, in order to contain Magyar demands. The Habsburgs did employ the Croats and the Serbs against the Magyars, but they were exploiting a situation, not creating one.

There was some hesitancy in Transylvania at the prospect of the union with Hungary and there were murmurs among the Slovaks in northern Hungary in favour of a federation. It was, however, among the Serbs and the Croats that suspicion of the Magyars was strongest. Croatia, although for centuries part of the Hungarian kingdom, had had an historic existence as an independent kingdom, and it still preserved some of the trappings of its identity such as its Ban or Viceroy. It was not surprising, therefore, that in March 1848 there should be attempts to reconstitute the Croat kingdom and claims that the provinces of Slavonia and Dalmatia should be incorporated. A petition to this effect was sent to Vienna at the end of March and the new Ban, Jellacic, added his voice to the demands.

The position was further complicated in that a very long, thin strip of territory, lying adjacent to the Turkish border and known as the Military Frontier, including a slice of Croatia and Slavonia and being also the home of many of the Hungarian Serbs, had been treated as a separate entity. Entirely the product of its strategic position—all able-bodied men were liable to conscription, and women and old men could be called upon to defend the land—it was directly under the government in Vienna and had strong loyalties, via the military hierarchy, to the Imperial authority.

With the April Laws the Hungarians clearly expected to re-incorporate the Military Frontier into the state. However, Vienna was reluctant to relinquish it and the War Ministry maintained direct links. Thus, though the April Laws presumed that delegates would be elected to the Hungarian Diet from the Military Frontier, its transfer was not formally agreed to by the Emperor. With their military traditions and degree of organization, political in the case of the Croats and religious in that of the Serbs, these peoples would present difficulties to the Magyars whatever part the Habsburgs chose to play.

In fact, the Habsburgs were not at all clear about what part they should play. There was something to be said for the encouragement of the Croats and Serbs as a counterweight to the Magyars, but the army in Italy contained a large contingent of Hungarians whom it would have been unwise to antagonize. At the same time it has to be remembered that Habsburg affairs were by no means under single management: the government itself was divided. There existed one party favouring autonomy or even complete independence, but on the other hand the War Minister, Count Latour, was determined to do what he could to hold all the Habsburg lands together and preserve the Empire in something like its pre-revolutionary shape. Then again, the Court had no wish to preside over the break up of the Monarchy and lent its weight against separatism. The Emperor Ferdinand was tossed from side to side, agreeing to requests then renouncing his decision, all too often the victim of the last man to give him advice. This indecisiveness produced the sort of situation where the Emperor agreed that the orders of the Hungarian Ministry of Defence should be obeyed in the Frontier Districts, while accepting Latour's demand that the administration of the Frontier was not to be taken out of his hands.

Probably, therefore, the Habsburgs would have preferred to have no policy at all with regard to the Croats' and Serbs' struggle with the Hungarians, but found themselves increasingly involved. Very

G*

often their apparent duplicity was the result of divided counsel rather than of premeditated chicanery.

One man who became increasingly important in these events was Jellacic, a Croat officer who had served under Radetzky in Italy and then held a command on the Frontier. In his role as the newly chosen Ban of Croatia, he began this period as an anti-Magyar Croat nationalist. But he soon became less the Croat nationalist, while remaining anti-Magyar, and started to favour the policy of a restoration of Habsburg power—which may have had something to do with his favourable treatment at the Habsburg Court.

Amidst rescripts signed and petitions refused, Hungarian demands acceded to and then partially countermanded, some developments became clear. First, whatever promises the Hungarians were given that he would be relieved of his command and functions, Jellacic was confident of support from the Court and the War Minister. He refused to accept the orders of the Hungarian government and even to contemplate serious negotiations with them; instead he presided over a Croat Diet and accepted military equipment and supplies from Latour.

Secondly, guerilla warfare began in south Hungary. Here, the Serbs were assisted by fellow-Serbs outside the Habsburg Empire, from the Principality of Serbia, and were moving towards a closer alliance with the Croats.

Thirdly, faced with this situation, the Hungarians were beginning to arm themselves and raise a force for their defence, the Honved or Home Defence, to be financed by Kossuth at the Ministry of Finance. In Hungary, certainly, the revolution appeared to be losing its way.

The national problem in Germany was a particularly difficult one which produced conflicting views as to its solution. This is not surprising when it is remembered that the two major German powers were states which extended considerably outside Germany; the Habsburg Empire and the Kingdom of Prussia. Obviously no Germany could be created which ignored the German lands of both these states, but could a Germany be created which ignored the lands of one of them?

If both states had totally collapsed in 1848 it might have been possible to create a German state consisting of the territories of the

Confederation but even this solution would not have been popular with the many Germans who lived in lands traditionally under German rule which nevertheless were outside the Confederation. If Prussia and Austria were not to disappear the matter became more complicated. A Prussian government which entered the new German state would be unlikely to leave its non-German provinces outside, nor would other Germans want it to do so: increasingly, during the summer of 1848, it became clear that the entire Prussian state would form part of the new Germany, whatever its non-German subjects might feel.

With the Habsburg Empire there was less certainty. The Austrian lands had always been part of Germany and the old Holy Roman Empire; the choice of a Habsburg Archduke as Imperial Regent at Frankfurt testified to the viability of the relationship. However, the other section of the Habsburg Empire, the Kingdom of Hungary, had not belonged to the Confederation and clearly could not become part of Germany in the way a Polish province of Prussia could. Therefore if the Habsburg Germans were to join the new Germany it could only be through the Habsburg state ceasing to exist in its present form, and through the union between the two sections of the Monarchy being dissolved. This the Habsburg family, many of the nobility, and the army commanders were determined to prevent; the Germans living in the Habsburg Empire came more and more to share their view. A separate question, but one which became closely involved with the first, was raised when the Czechs demanded a Bohemian state; for Bohemia had been part of the Holy Roman Empire and was looked on by Germans as very much part of their future state and not at all like Hungary.

At the same time the assumption by the Germans, including those enlightened, liberal Germans who were members of the Frankfurt Assembly, that the non-Germans, who lived in those lands which they thought to incorporate into their new state, would happily acquiesce came up against and stimulated counter-nationalisms. In fact it was the pressure on the Czechs and Slovenes by the Germans, allied to Magyar policies in respect of the Slovaks and other Slav peoples, that led to the decision to summon a Pan-Slav congress to Prague at the beginning of June.

The antagonism which they encountered from these Slavic peoples mystified and horrified the Germans, and gave rise to what can only be seen as aggressively nationalist and bellicose sentiments.

As it transpired, the first opposition the Germans encountered was not from a Slavic people but from the Danes and it arose over the Duchies of Schleswig and Holstein. The heart of the dispute was that these duchies, declared indissolubly joined together, were ruled by the King of Denmark but in his person rather than in his office: Holstein was almost entirely German and a member of the Confederation, Schleswig was over a third Danish and not in the Confederation. 1848 saw the succession of a childless Danish king. The existing situation of Denmark and the duchies being ruled by one man now seemed unlikely to be perpetuated because although, under the law of Denmark, inheritance could pass through the female line, under the law of Schleswig-Holstein it could not.

Attempts were therefore made by a mounting Danish nationalism to incorporate the duchies into Denmark. This move was countered on March 23 by a rising in Schleswig-Holstein and the creation of a rebel government which called for assistance from Germany. Volunteers rushed to help the insurgents, and the Frankfurt Assembly espoused their cause; Frederick William of Prussia directed his army to go to their aid in staving off the invading Danish troops.

Although doubtless sincere enough in their patriotism the majority of the members of the Frankfurt parliament were essentially frivolous in their clamour for war against Denmark, having little idea of what really was involved. Volunteers appeared in large numbers to fight the Danes but their quality was poor. One man who fought in this capacity admitted that, despite his enthusiasm, he was never sure which side he was firing on. It was perhaps as well that the Prussian troops did intervene to drive back the Danes.

Even so, the war with Denmark was more than a military engagement in Jutland. First, it was a naval war, and a Danish commercial blockade soon produced difficulty in north Germany since the Germans had no ships to fight it. Secondly, the war had European implications; Britain, Russia and France all eyed a Prussian victory with disfavour. Probably historians have sometimes exaggerated the part played by fear of foreign intervention in Frederick William's growing disaffection with the war but it certainly was a factor. Perhaps more important was his dislike of being used as an agent of German radicalism, combined with his realization of the complexities of fighting a war with Denmark which included a blockade. Anyhow, his enthusiasm cooled and on August 26 an armistice was concluded at Malmö between Denmark and Prussia, acting on behalf of the German government as well as for herself. By the terms of the armistice the duchies were to be put under joint administration.

There was a great outcry in Germany at this armistice and in the Frankfurt parliament, but, the fact was that there was no hope of prosecuting the war without Prussia and, failing a further revolution in Prussia, there was no hope of the Prussian government continuing to fight.

The Left in the assembly had been determined in its refusal to accept the armistice, and democrats outside the assembly at once showed that they had no intention of accepting the decision. A large outdoor meeting was held near Frankfurt at which the thousands attending agreed to a motion declaring those who had voted for the armistice were traitors to Germany. Agitation developed in Frankfurt and, as there seemed no way of defending the assembly without outside help assistance was requested from the Austrian and Prussian troops stationed in the Federal fortress of Mainz.

On September 18, with the arrival of some troops and disorder in the street bitterness grew. An attempt was made to storm the assembly, and, in fact, some of the crowd did break in by a back door. However the members showed surprising determination and coolness, no doubt fortified by the bravery and presence of their president, von Gagern. The hall was cleared and parliament was saved. However, in the town barricades were built and heavier fighting developed. By nightfall a state of siege was declared. Fighting continued until an unconditional surrender was agreed to by the revolutionaries, despite the efforts of radical deputies to secure a truce.

Among the casualties were Prince Lichnowsky and his fellow Prussian, General von Auerswalde. These men, both members of the assembly, had ridden out to view the action when they were set upon by the crowd. They managed to reach a near-by house and there hid. However, despite the help of the occupants they were both discovered, pulled out and murdered. The death of the two deputies served to justify the determination of the assembly to fight the insurrection and made it harder for the Left to avoid discredit; although it is by no means certain that it had any part in the rising. Robert Blum, the most prominent member of the Left, demonstrated the despondency felt by many in a letter to his wife at this time: 'Never have I been as tired of life and of work as I am now; were it not a shame to desert one's comrades in misfortune,' he goes on to say, he would 'emigrate, buy a mill in a quiet corner . . .'.

However, it would be incorrect to see this division in the German revolution as purely the product of nationalism: the chagrin felt over the armistice of Malmö was as much the occasion as the cause of the disturbances. To a large extent the cause lay in the breach between the moderate liberals and those further to the Left, the democrats and socialists. This fact becomes plainer when other events are kept in mind. The middle of September saw communist and socialist agitation in the Rhineland,* then, after the failure at Frankfurt, Struve led a second revolt in Baden. He crossed over from Switzerland on September 21 and proclaimed a German republic. This was really a second wave of his democratic revolution in conjunction with Hecker and was even less successful. Though several thousand enlisted in his army, the majority lacked something of the idealism of those involved in the earlier attempt. 'The republicans of April had behaved like feather-brained adventurers, those of September like robbers and footpads,' was one comment. At any rate they were speedily defeated by regular troops. The effect of these uprisings was to cleave through the unity of the revolution in Germany and create in many of the middle class a fear of anarchy and disorder, thus pushing them back towards the old ruling class; class divisions as well as national divisions began to destroy the unified purpose of revolution, and nowhere more so than in France.

The tradition of socialist thought had alerted men's minds to the existence of class interest and the revolution of 1830 had left a fear among many that they might be exploited and betrayed by those who claimed to be their leaders. Thus, even in the excitement and euphoria that followed the proclamation of the republic, fear and suspicion were present.

'The Republic is only the route to the destination of social reform,' claimed one newspaper in February. There were many in Paris at the time who believed this. The secret societies, such as the Society of the Seasons which had been led by Blanqui and Barbes until their imprisonment, had preached social revolution and with

* Marx was editing the *Neue Rheinische Zeitung* in the Rhineland at the time.

the February uprising they came into the open. Barbès and Blanqui were freed and at once formed their own societies; many others were also founded and proceeded to agitate among the workers stressing the need for drastic social change.

Among the more moderate but equally determined fighters for social amelioration was Louis Blanc. He had publicized with enormous success, in his *L' Organization du Travail*, the need for 'social workshops'. These would function on the lines of workers' co-operatives and would be financed by state credit. Blanc hoped that these co-operatives would drive out private enterprise by their competition and come to function as the standard method of production in a new socialist economy.

The economic difficulties already existing were greatly enhanced in France, as elsewhere, by the revolution. There was a drying-up of credit, and a drop in demand followed on from uncertainty and the flight from Paris of many of the wealthier people, with the result that trade stagnated and unemployment grew. Clearly many would expect the provisional government to do something to improve the situation particularly when it is remembered that Louis Blanc was one of its eleven members, as was a worker Alexandre Martin (known then and to history as Albert) who had been an influential member in the Society of the Seasons. With these men in the government surely social reform would be tackled in earnest.

Deputations and petitions added force to demands for action and Louis Blanc composed the declaration, agreed by the government, that 'the Provisional Government of the French Republic pledges itself to guarantee a living wage for the worker, and to guarantee employment for every citizen'. The right to work was clearly accepted.

From the start the provisional government was an uneasy alliance. The powerful Lamartine had little time for socialist experiment, while Garnier-Pagès was actively hostile. Ledru-Rollin was rather a democratic republican than a socialist and he had scant sympathy with the economic opinions held by some of his colleagues. It is important to remember this to understand how the government went about translating its promises into action.

The best known of the measures tried, the National Workshops, were instituted under the Minister of Public Works to provide employment for the unemployed. These had no connection with

Louis Blanc's Social Workshops; far from being producer co-operatives they were agents for dispensing charity. Put under the direction of an enterprising young engineer, Émile Thomas, they tried to offer work and pay to the unemployed. Thomas found government money fairly easy to obtain but the schemes of his brilliant and inventive mind were constantly being hampered and inhibited. Increasingly, his workers—over 100,000 during May—were only allowed to tackle useless and profitless manual work, such as levelling the Champ de Mars, which from the start failed to inspire them with any sense of pride and achievement in an essential job being done.

The workers, seeing their jobs to be without purpose, speedily became demoralized. As time passed the middle class in the towns and the peasants from all over France came to resent what they believed to be a serious waste of their money—a sentiment which was strengthened when direct taxes were increased by nearly a half, thus hitting the peasantry who identified the increase with governmental extravagance and waste. Although Louis Blanc had no connection with the National Workshops some of their unpopularity rubbed off on him.

What Blanc was concerned with was the second of the government's concessions to social reform: the Commission of Labour. This commission met in the Luxembourg and consisted of delegates from both sides of industry, together with socialist thinkers and writers.* Louis Blanc was made president and Albert vice-president of the commission, a poor substitute for the executive 'Ministry of Progress' they had hoped for. In the event, besides sponsoring a reduction in working hours and the abolition of sweated labour, the commission was unable to achieve anything except plans and projected reforms. It merely had the effect of adding to the unpopularity among the middle class of all socialism and socialists.

It was not only the government's economic actions which served to focus class antagonism, however. On March 16 there was a demonstration in Paris of several thousand veterans of the National Guard. They were protesting at the government's decision to merge them with newly formed corps of guardsmen. The demonstrators, belonging to the middle class, had been members of the National Guard for some time and, proud of their uniforms and

* Proudhon, as a well-known socialist thinker, was invited to join the commission, but refused.

their esprit de corps, they resented the loss of identity involved in integration. However, democrats were horrified at the idea of an élite in the National Guard, seeing it as contrary to the ideas of the revolution.

This demonstration was followed by an enormous counter-demonstration the following day. Ostensibly, this was to show solidarity with the government but the more extreme of the societies sought to exploit it in order to force the government to adopt a more radical line. The marchers, for of such the demonstration was composed, asked for the army to be sent away from Paris; they also requested a delay in elections, both for the National Assembly and for officers for the National Guard.

Frenchmen were very conscious that a demonstration of this sort could turn into an insurrection in the tradition of the revolutionary 'Days'. Thus when it was known that a huge march was to take place on April 16 the more moderate members of the government became frightened. Ledru-Rollin found his position most uneasy, not knowing whether to side with Lamartine and oppose the demonstration or still to try and move with the party of revolution and support it. Finally he chose the former course and instigated the calling out of the National Guard to line the route of the procession. It is still not known if a plan existed to unseat the government and install a more radical one, but it is clear that the demonstration widened the split in the revolution and the marchers were jeered at as if they were communists.

The demand of March 17, that the elections should be postponed, was not a surprising one; many had realized that if the elections were held at once they would return a National Assembly far to the Right of the government. To the socialists this presented no problem; if the people were not able to know what was best for them, the elections must be postponed, perhaps indefinitely. However, to ardent republicans like Ledru-Rollin such a decision was not so easy. As Minister of the Interior he tried to 'educate and republicanize' the electorate by sending out representatives to the provinces. Nevertheless when the assembly was elected after a massive turn-out of voters it proved to be a conservative body with no time for socialist or radical policies. This development enforced some changes in the membership of the government, including the fall of Louis Blanc and Albert, which naturally added to the suspicions and dislike felt by the Paris workers for the assembly.

However, the occasion for the real clash between the assembly and the people of Paris was not over the dropping of socialists from the government or economic policies, it was over Poland. The radicals had become dissatisfied with the cautious foreign policy of the French government, particularly over their failure to start a crusade for the resurrection of Poland. On May 15, a great demonstration was planned in favour of Poland which would coincide with the assembly's debate on the Polish question. The clubs also decided to demonstrate on the same day and certainly had hoped of exploiting the situation.

The National Assembly was broken into by the demonstrators, some jumping down from the galleries into the body of the house, others bursting in through the doors. In the chaos that resulted various demonstrators jostled with one another and with the deputies, trying to speak from the tribune while the President in a futile fashion rang his bell for order and silence. The crowd, although many carried arms, seemed to have no definite plan to use them. 'Their expression was one of astonishment and ill-will rather than enmity,' wrote Tocqueville, a deputy at the time. At first, most of the speeches were in favour of Poland until Blanqui went on to attack the assembly in general terms and sought to direct attention against the policies of the government. Barbès, a member of the assembly who had so far said little, fearing to lose support by inaction, jumped up to propose war on behalf of Poland and a tax to soak the rich. Amid mounting disorder, in which an unwilling Louis Blanc was carried in triumph, an attempt was made to proclaim the assembly dissolved.*

While some of the crowd remained in the assembly others rushed off with Barbès and Blanqui to the Hôtel de Ville where a new, left-wing government was proclaimed. At this juncture the National Guard arrived and troop reinforcements were sent for from outside Paris. The assembly and the Hôtel de Ville were cleared and, although Blanqui managed to escape, Barbès was seized and imprisoned. At the same time the more extreme clubs were closed. What unity there had been since February between those who wanted social revolution and those who merely wanted political revolution was now gone: suspicion and distrust had been replaced by antagonism and hostility.

* It has been argued that the man, by the name of Huber, who sought the dissolution, was acting for the police as an *agent-provocateur*.

In Vienna, from the first days of the March revolution distrust was felt by the wealthier middle class for the workers. However, there was little or no socialist organization among the workers and thus there was little ideological backing for class warfare. Rather it was a general unease among the middle class at what they saw as the breakdown of law and order. The majority was prepared to risk this possibility at first but by the end of May, with the apparent victory of the forces for change, many felt confident enough to be more worried about anarchy than about reaction, and, in the words of Engels, 'fell more and more into that weariness and apathy, and that eternal outcry for order and tranquillity'. 'Everywhere,' observed the poet Auerbach who was visiting Vienna in the late summer, 'men with a ready tongue, but who have lost their position in society, join the democrats; and this necessarily alarms the quiet burgher.'

A more specific grievance which increasingly was voiced by the middle class was dislike of the public works programme. This had been started, as in Paris, in order to give the chance of work to the unemployed; a chance which was becoming more urgent during the summer as people continued to leave Vienna, bringing a further decline in trade and industry. The Committee of Security had agreed to provide work for any who could not otherwise obtain it in the form of construction schemes. Very soon the schemes degenerated into futile earth-moving with, in fact, less and less earth being moved. The rates of pay were fixed at the level of the maximum being paid at the time for unskilled workers, and as indiscipline grew and supervision became more difficult the wages were seen as outdoor relief. People poured into Vienna from the surrounding areas and many deliberately gave up their jobs for the soft option of public works. Finally this labour force had risen to over 50,000. It can be imagined how the whole enterprise appeared to the middle class; it not only offended their sense of economy but led many to question the system of government which could produce such a state of affairs.

In Berlin also, distrust between the classes widened into antagonism. The prosperous middle class became progressively more frightened of the workers: they refused for instance to allow workers to become members of the armed militia, who were, with the departure of the soldiers, responsible for security in the capital. As elsewhere the middle class distrusted what they believed to be public patronage of idleness at its expense, in the form of the ideas canvassed to reduce poverty and provide work for the unemployed. However, in Berlin, as elsewhere in Europe in 1848, too much motivation for events has been explained away by class feeling and class difference. Whether or not men fear violence and disorder owes as much to their personality, as to their consciousness of class interest. If man's dislike for changing the place where he lives is clearly dependent upon more than his class, why not his dislike for changing the society he lives in? In the last resort many of the divisions among the revolutionaries must have been based upon pessimistic caution and dislike of change, as against optimistic confidence in the new.

Chapter XIII

REVOLUTION IN DISARRAY

THE MILITARY problem which confronted Charles Albert when he marched across the Ticino into Lombardy was how to drive the Austrians out of Italy. The political problem was not so clear cut: it was concerned with how to create a political framework for northern Italy that would be acceptable to Charles Albert, his subjects and, of course, those who lived in the relevant lands. Was it possible to concentrate upon the military problem and then to turn to the more complicated political matters, as Mazzini at first thought? It soon became obvious that the two were inextricably bound together: on the one hand Charles Albert and Piedmont would not fight to create republics for other people, on the other hand Italian support for the war depended upon the promise of a satisfactory political future.

Thus, Charles Albert's political gaucherie in antagonizing other Italians was one important factor in his military failure; his distrust for republicanism, his demands for the ex-Austrian lands to fuse at once with Piedmont, and his reluctance to contemplate an Italian league or confederation which might lessen his own authority, were all part of this clumsiness. '*Italia farà da sè*' was his cry, but by the end of May 1848 it was clear that, far from 'going it alone', the whole of Italy was by no means 'going it' at all.

At first it might have seemed that the Austrians, after their defeat in Milan, would withdraw from Italy. On the face of it, Radetzky's position was hopeless; towns throughout Lombardy and Venetia had risen and thereby cut his communications. Many of his Italian troops had deserted him, others awaited their opportunity to do so. Most important of all, the revolution in Vienna was continuing, and by the end of May with the Court's flight to Innsbruck it cannot have been quite certain for whom or for what Radetzky and his army stood. However, Radetzky's army was an institution in itself, with its own loyalties. This was not just the outcome, as in the old marshal himself, of a lack of any other focus for affection or loyalty. A younger officer, Benedek, who was devoted to his wife, showed the same sort of affection as Radetzky for his men. In a letter he wrote home at this time, he contrasted the public outcry if a civilian was shot in a riot with the public response when 'the warm blood of the poor soldier flows in streams without his ever getting a well-earned reward'; and went on to explain that he felt constrained to help in such cases out of his own pay.

This type of army was not going to abandon its position without fighting. The effect of being driven out of Milan, far from causing the Austrian commanders to feel that they were beaten, was to make them long for the chance to prove what their men could do. Of his troops engaged in the Milan street-fighting Radetzky had written: 'It breaks my heart that such courage cannot be utilized against an open and honourable enemy;' very soon it was to have its opportunity.

Even though Radetzky would not surrender without a stiff fight, his hurried withdrawal gave Charles Albert a chance. Much criticism has, quite rightly, centred upon Charles Albert's dithering over the declaration of war and his slow advance, allowing Radetzky to get back into the Quadrilatero. A speedy advance might have found the troops in retreat and unable to regroup behind the guns of the fortresses; or at least have encouraged the citizens of Mantua and Verona to rise against the Austrians. Once he had failed to exploit this opportunity, Charles Albert's task became much more difficult. Although he outnumbered Radetzky, he had nothing like enough troops to surround and besiege the four fortress towns of the Quadrilatero. The question can be asked of whether Charles Albert should have left Radetzky in his fortresses and concentrated upon blocking his communications with Austria. These consisted of two routes: one, the inferior, north through the Alps to Innsbruck, the other east through Venetia. Radetzky had sent troops under Welden northwards in order to hold the path through the Alps, but the eastern route seemed, for the time being, effectively closed by the revolt in Venetia. If the Alpine passes could be seized and Venetia finally cleared of Austrians and held, there was every chance that Radetzky would be unable to hold out much above a couple of months.

One of Charles Albert's generals at the time (and much armchair opinion ever since) advocated such a policy, with a southern detour round the Quadrilatero and then an attack on Radetzky from the east, at the same time securing Venetia. However, although this plan might appear admirable, it was open to several strong objections. First, the political factor: Milan and Lombardy would be left unprotected from any sweep by Radetzky. In such an event Charles Albert could not rely on Milan supporting his plan and would be leaving himself open to charges of betrayal. Secondly, no one yet knew that the Quadrilatero was virtually impregnable, and there were still reports of potential revolution inside Verona. Above all, the complicated march around the Quadrilatero would impose great strain on an untried army and its hopelessly inexperienced commissariat which even a seasoned force might have found insuperable.

Nevertheless, Charles Albert was impelled by popular feeling at home to do something at once. The result was that he attacked east across the Mincio, laid siege to Peschiera and sought at the battle of Pastrengo on April 30 to block Radetzky's communications to the north. However, so long as Radetzky was secure in Verona, he could effectively maintain contact northwards with Welden by the threat of an attack, and Charles Albert failed during fighting before Verona to do anything to shake Radetzky's position.

At the same time, Charles Albert was faced by a more urgent difficulty with the attempt of an Austrian column under Nugent to fight its way across Venetia to Verona. It was at this juncture that Charles Albert's shortage of experienced soldiers was felt, since he could not spare any troops to meet the threat and had to leave it to Durando and a heterogeneous force of Papal troops and volunteers to hold off Nugent. In fact, Durando did not possess enough men to hold both the possible routes that Nugent might take, and the latter, an experienced and wily commander, was able to bluff him into concentrating upon the wrong one. Muddles and jealousy, and the final desperate breakdown of communications between Durando and Ferrari, in command of the volunteers facing Nugent, made the situation worse.

From now on Radetzky was no longer outnumbered and likely to be starved out. Using the Quadrilatero as his base he was to go on to the offensive and employ the speed of movement of his well-trained troops to crushing effect. He was, for instance, able to sweep down on the Tuscans before Mantua, and only a few days later, equally unexpectedly, to knock out the remainder of the Papal troops some fifty miles to the north-east at Vicenza, while Charles Albert thought he was still in Verona.

However, the Piedmontese did, during this period, achieve one success: Peschiera finally surrendered at the end of May. At this stage Charles Albert might have made peace; much to Radetzky's disgust the Austrian government was prepared to treat on the basis of the Adige as a future frontier and to accept the loss of Lombardy. Although Charles Albert saw that now he had little chance of victory and that these terms were generous he was unable to accept, so strong was popular feeling that the Austrians must be thrown out of Italy and that Venetia should not be deserted. There was very little chance of Austria being prepared to abandon Venetia, since she had long regarded it as strategically more important to her than Lombardy; Metternich had said as much fifteen years before. So Charles Albert continued his attempts, rather forlornly laying siege to Mantua and in the process dangerously over-extending his armies until Radetzky was given the chance to strike and break through a weakened line.

For once the Sardinian king followed a bold policy tantamount to rashness, and instead of withdrawing westwards he determined to strike north at Radetzky's flank. The resulting battle of Custoza demonstrated the quality of the Austrians, Radetzky being able to swing his line around in the course of the night to face the attack. In contrast, the Piedmontese moved very slowly and once again their supplies broke down. 'Not a drop of water could be found on the top of the hill, and the morning's rations had been infinitesimal. Our men dropped from fatigue, sunstroke, hunger, and thirst,' wrote Della Rocca. Despite brave resistance, the Piedmontese were defeated from the outset.

However, the defeat was not yet a major one and only became so when it was discovered that once more, after muddled orders and lack of urgency in command, the forces defending bridges across the Mincio had left their positions. The dispirited troops lost their confidence and the retreat became a rout, the army fleeing westwards as rapidly as possible. Milan was totally unprepared for the new situation and although there was some last-minute attempt to prepare resistance, little was achieved. The prevailing mood was one of shock, turning to outrage as the terms of an armistice Charles Albert had negotiated with the Austrians became known; these involved the handing back of Milan to Radetzky and withdrawal behind the Ticino. Against physical threats from the citizens Charles Albert was forced to defer the armistice, but soon the hopelessness of the situation was realized and after extricating himself with some difficulty from the enraged Milanese he, accompanied by thousands of Lombards, withdrew into Piedmont. On August 9, a renewed armistice was signed and Lombardy and Venetia were officially returned to Austria, scarcely a month after Venetia had merged with the kingdom of Northern Italy. Even so, the city of Venice once more proclaimed itself a republic and prepared to fight on.

A critic of Charles Albert who favoured a republic wrote that 'the concept of nationality sufficed to bring about insurrection, but it was not enough to bring victory'. This statement is, in a way, misleading: the revolution was by no means brought about purely by nationalism. In Milan, in Naples, in Venice and in Rome, just as in Paris, Berlin and Vienna, economic and social conditions lay behind the outbreak of revolt and helped to sustain the revolution. When the revolutionaries found that their new leaders were not concerned to help the poor, emancipate the peasants and find work for the unemployed, they became soured or anyhow uninterested. At the same time, many found that the political freedom for which they were building barricades, was only to be enjoyed by a minority. 'We want to bring the vote down to the small shopkeeper who has a bit put by and can afford a good pot-au-feu daily', was the hope of Cavour. Nationalism might act as a slogan for the revolutionaries but in reality it had merely served to hide their differences of aim. Now, with the betrayal of Ferdinand of Naples, of Pio Nono and the Grand Duke of Tuscany, and the military defeat, if nothing worse, of Charles Albert, many revolutionaries turned to other leaders.

So it was that the revolution lived on until 1849 in a democratic and republican form. In Venice the republic held out under Manin, in Rome the revolution rolled forward until in November, with the murder of Rossi, the Pope's friend and chief minister, the democrats took power and soon after the Pope fled to Gaeta. In Tuscany, too, the democrats under Guerrazzi had come to power by the late autumn. Even the dying embers of revolt in Lombardy were breathed on by a spirited guerilla campaign in the region of the Italian Lakes led by the already celebrated Garibaldi who, exiled for taking part in a Mazzinian conspiracy, had built a reputation for himself as a leader of irregulars in South America. Dandalo, a monarchist who had fought as a volunteer in Lombardy, said that 'the month of July drew to a close amidst the ruin of the Italian cause'. However, he too was to go and fight with great bravery in republican Rome in 1849.

Charles Albert had clearly failed; although he was to make another attempt against Radetzky the following spring it was doomed from the outset and he knew it. To what extent then was the king to blame for the failures of 1848 in Italy? If, as has often been claimed, Charles Albert had long dreamed of gaining his chance to lead a war against Austria, the state of unpreparedness and the quality of leadership in his army are a sorry commentary on his abilities. It is well known that there were no proper maps of Lombardy available, though it is difficult to see where else he expected to fight the Austrians. He had too many of his best troops guarding the frontiers with France and in no position to move against Radetzky. His army did have a fine artillery—better than that of the Austrians—and the troops fought hard and many of the officers were brave men. Nevertheless the standard of command was deplorable, the staff work almost non-existent and failure in communication widespread and often inexcusable. All the facts suggest a hurried decision to act upon the passage of events rather than the careful maturing of plans.

However, Charles Albert should not be blamed to excess. He was prepared, having set out on the road, to expend much. His fear of republicanism, and his hostility to many of the irregulars who offered their services, are surely understandable. Above all his army had absolutely no fighting experience and he had little opportunity to develop the sort of training and war simulation that Radetzky had. Without the revolutions of 1848, particularly that in Vienna, Charles Albert would not have gone to war: his defeat was not caused because the revolution in Vienna had been defeated but because the Austrian army in Italy had, after experiencing its first shock, refused to be overwhelmed by the situation and remained in a position to fight.

'Each one fervently desired to avoid the necessity of a conflict and all vaguely felt that this necessity was becoming more inevitable from day to day.' So wrote Tocqueville of the period of early June in Paris. This sense of foreboding was felt on all sides.

The occasion of conflict proved to be the determination of the government, reflecting the feeling of the assembly, to close the

National Workshops, but it would be misleading to portray this as the cause of the conflict. Tocqueville tells of a dinner at which he met the novelist George Sand who, in the course of conversation, said to him, 'Try to persuade your friends, sir, not to force the people into the streets by alarming or irritating them.' This was exactly what the decision to close the workshops did, but the previous history of 1848 in France explained why the people were so ready to be driven into the streets.

The workshops were becoming a greater financial burden to the state as more unemployed joined them, and clearly they offered no long-term solution to French economic problems. Either drastic reforms in their structure would have to be made or they would have to be closed. The government and the assembly had for some time felt that a decision must be made; they feared the growing army which the labour force constituted but on the other hand they realized that any closure could not take place without risk of insurrection.

The events of May 16 strengthened the resolve of the government to face the issue and on May 26 the director of the National Workshops, Émile Thomas, was dismissed and immediately moved away from Paris, as a preparatory step in their closure. However, the final decision was not made public until June 21. The younger and unmarried would be given the chance to enlist in the army, the older and married would be moved out of Paris on public works projects, such as land clearance, and no future enrolment would take place. Insurrection began on Friday, June 23 with barricades going up in the working-class areas. Lamartine and others in the government wanted soldiers and the National Guard to be used to storm the barricades as soon as they were built, and in this way it was hoped that the revolt would not develop. However, General Cavaignac, since April the commander of the army, opposed this plan, fearing that his troops might become scattered in detail through the city and then be disarmed. Others have seen the General's decision as caused by his desire for a full confrontation and his wish to avoid any compromise settlement. Although there were many who desired a 'final solution', it does seem more likely, however, that General Cavaignac was influenced by military considerations.

Whatever his motives, the result of the General's action in withholding his troops from battle, and instead consolidating them, was to allow a large section of the city to fall into the hands of the revolutionaries. The National Guard from the middle-class districts, the Garde Mobile and regular troops were then thrown at the barricades.* The fighting was extremely bitter and on a very large scale; 'with an exasperation unequalled in the history of modern civil warfare,' claimed Engels. 'This formidable insurrection was not the attempt of a group of conspirators but the revolt of a whole section of the people against another,' observed Tocqueville. '[It was] a struggle of class versus class, a sort of slave war.' Both sides fought believing that they must crush their opponents or be crushed. On the second day the assembly voted full executive powers to Cavaignac and declared a state of siege. The dismissal of the existing government in this way was largely the result of a feeling, not only in the assembly, but more particularly among the soldiers and Guards fighting the revolt, that its attitude was somewhat equivocal. They were disinclined to prosecute the war against the possibility that at any time the government might change its mind.

It took four days of fighting before the revolt was crushed. Troops and National Guardsmen were summoned from different parts of France to help, the railways playing an important part in the operation. Many of the provincials were itching for a chance to deal with the capital and did nothing to soften the severity of the fighting. The subsequent repression was equally ruthless. Full casualty figures do not exist but were certainly far in advance of a thousand, a great many of the insurgents being killed after the surrender. Well over 10,000 were arrested and large numbers were deported to Algeria. 'The proletarians of Paris were defeated, decimated, crushed,' mourned Engels.

The political clubs were brought under the surveillance of the authorities, new press laws were introduced, the right to work was abrogated and later in the year even the maximum hours of work were raised. Reaction flowed strongly with Cavaignac, as Minister President, retaining his powers, old monarchist politicians back in influence and the socialists totally discredited and under suspicion. Louis Blanc fled France and became one more refugee of 1848 to seek asylum in England. Even if it was not quite true to claim, as

---

* The Garde Mobile had been created early in the revolution. It was a volunteer force of young men who were quite well paid, but drawn by no means from the more prosperous bourgeois.

Lamartine did, that 'the Republic is dead', the revolution of February certainly was.

It was in Prague that the revolutions in the Habsburg lands encountered their first reverse. At the end of May the Slavic Congress began to assemble. As well as the representatives of those Slavs living in the Austrian Empire there were Poles and two Russians, one the colourful anarchist Bakunin. Their picturesque costumes and varied languages added to the excitement already felt by the inhabitants of the city. The economic difficulties experienced in Prague, which had been increased by disruption resulting from revolution elsewhere, the growth of nationalism, and the example of Vienna, all contributed to a revolutionary situation.

In these circumstances the commander of the Habsburg troops sought to take steps to deal with possible rebellion. Windischgrätz had been frustrated in his attempts to use force in Vienna in March and he was determined that, if trouble should break out in Prague, this time there should be no hesitancy.

Alarmed by reports of his preparations, popular leaders pressed Windischgrätz to withdraw troops from key points in the city, and at the same time to hand over to them quantities of artillery and muskets. Receiving only very limited satisfaction from the Austrian commander, some students began to advocate force to rid the city of the soldiers, and meanwhile the people inclined more to radical leadership.

June 12 had been chosen for the celebration of a great Mass to mark the Slavic Congress. A huge crowd, out to watch the procession, came into conflict with the troops. Some have accused Windischgrätz of seeking a confrontation as a justification for imposing military rule, but in the tense and awkward situation which prevailed taunts and insults from the crowd would have been quite enough to provoke the troops and so lead to skirmishes.

The position became even more serious when it was decided to hold a 'serenade' outside Prince Windischgrätz's residence. Troops were used to force the crowd back and fighting reached a new intensity.

The crowd began to throw up barricades which the troops then proceeded to attack. At about the same time a shot fired from opposite the Windischgrätz residence killed the prince's wife while she was standing in an upstairs room.

Although the fighting continued, it was only sporadic and further negotiations took place: neither the Vienna government nor the Czech leaders wished for a final showdown. However, on June 16 Windischgrätz, who had withdrawn his troops across the river Moldau, decided that further discussion was useless. He ordered a bombardment of the city which continued throughout the night.* On the 17th, with his troops pressing forward on the barricades, an unconditional surrender was received.

June 17th thus saw Windischgrätz firmly back in control, the Slav Congress dispersed, and representative government for Bohemia once more a chimera; the Bohemian Diet was indefinitely postponed and the National Guard disbanded.

Contrary to what the German parliament at Frankfurt believed, Windischgrätz's victory was not a triumph for German nationalism over a Slavic revolt. This fact is demonstrated by those Germans who fought side by side with the Czechs on the barricades, as it is by the Czech moderates—Palacky for one—who, horrified at the radicalism emerging in Prague, sought to make peace with the Habsburg commander. The victory, as Windischgrätz well knew, was one for the Habsburg dynasty, and it was the first the dynasty had gained in four disastrous months.

The revolutions of 1848 were first and foremost urban; despite the recent development of industry, Europe in the 1840s was still predominantly rural. The revolution of 1789 in France had coincided with a period of peasant distress and unrest which had been played upon by political events to produce a peasant revolt. However, though the early stages of the French Revolution had thus involved the countryside, very soon the peasantry had become a conservative force, frightened by disorder and talk of socialism, hostile to military adventure which took sons away from the harvest, and wanting the freedom to enjoy what had been won. It is not, therefore, surprising that universal suffrage in 1848 elected a conservative assembly and a president whose name promised order; and that where the peasantry did participate in events, as in the June Days, it was on the side of the bourgeois and against the working class.

The peasantry in the Habsburg Empire was by no means a

---

* Contrary to popular tradition it seems that care was taken to minimize the damage done by bombardment and very few fires were started in the city.

satisfied class, however, and might have seemed likely to rise in revolt: certainly a great peasant rising in support of the revolution in the capital would have been irresistible and the dynasty would have been forced to surrender. One reason why this never happened was that the social structure of the Habsburg Empire virtually precluded co-operation between town and countryside, peasantry and middle class, because of the differing nations that made up the whole.*
At the same time the peasants, far from seeing them as their oppressors, looked to the Habsburgs as their protectors against the rapacious and tyrannical local landlords. They also had the typical conservative rustic dislike for young and inexperienced students in the city. A traveller of the time reported how in discussing the students with a Styrian peasant he was told that 'no man properly should be allowed to have a voice in public affairs, who is not married and has a household of his own'. But perhaps most important was that the peasants' main grievance was removed by the revolution.

The wish of Maria Theresa and Joseph to enable the peasantry to pay more taxes to the state, allied to genuine shock at its plight, led to attempts to alter the system of forced labour services, the Robot. Although schemes for commutation had been shelved under Francis the dislike for the Robot had persisted and increased among the peasants and their attempts to evade it had made it less profitable to collect. It was certain that the revolution would see an attempt at abolition: one eye-witness remarked that peasants had expressed the belief that a constitution meant the abolition of the Robot. Therefore, after the events in Vienna, the majority of peasants simply refused to render labour services and the landlords were usually in no position to demand them. In fact, soon after the March revolution, the new government issued a rescript which laid down that the Robot should end, leaving negotiations to determine what, and how, compensation should be paid. This did not satisfy the peasants, who were suspicious of the negotiations and refused to take part in them, and it was left to the new parliament, which met in Vienna in July, to carry through the emancipation. A motion was passed which abolished all services and rights that landlords had been able to exact. Some, such as the lord's judicial

* When the Austrian parliament first met, many of the peasant deputies did not understand German, and had no idea what was happening. Consequently they followed the lead of some respected figure as to how they should cast their votes.

rights, were abolished without compensation, others were to be compensated for, the state contributing a share of the payment. With this decision, the peasant problem no longer contributed to the events of 1848 in Austrian lands. It was, in fact, virtually the only productive act of the parliament, which found itself inhibited by national jealousies and differences, spending much of its time in futile wrangling.

Although there was little co-operation between the peasants and the townspeople against the Habsburg government, 1848 had certainly demonstrated a coalition between the liberal nobility, the middle class, the students and the workers. This had broken down by mid-summer, as sectional and class interests came to the fore, but the early part of July did seem to offer new hopes of peaceful reforms being carried out by consent. First, the Archduke John, perhaps the one Archduke who still had the trust of the Viennese, came to Vienna on June 24 as the representative of the Emperor. Although he soon left for Frankfurt to take up his position as Imperial Regent, he was back in Vienna by July 17. On the 18th a new ministry was formed with Doblhoff, a leading figure in the Legal-Political Reading Club, as the dominant minister. This government seemed more in accord with progressive feeling and also contained Bach, another pre-March liberal. Finally, the parliament began to assemble, being declared officially open on July 22. This body had been elected on a very wide franchise and represented all the Imperial lands except those under the Crown of Hungary: it was the single assembly which progressives had wanted. Reconciliation perhaps reached its height with the return of the Emperor to Vienna on August 12.

Nevertheless, the underlying antagonisms remained, notably the grievance of the bourgeois that so many apparently idle workers were being maintained at state expense on supposed public works projects. At the beginning of August the minister in charge of the operations appealed to all workers who possessed other skills to return to their original work; an earnest of the way in which the government's mind was working. Then in the middle of August came the announcement of a reduction in the pay of women and children engaged in these works, which was seen by all as a preliminary to general cuts. After some days of mounting excitement, on August 23 the workers surged into the centre of the city and there staged a major protest which took the form of a mock funeral for the minister responsible for public works. This was treated as a serious threat, and the National Guard was used to suppress the demonstration, sabring and firing on the largely unarmed crowd, killing some and injuring a great many more. This time, the students did not support the cause of the workers; they, too, saw the protest as mistaken. Without the students the poverty of the workers' organization was exposed. The government exploited the defeat of the demonstration to force the Committee of Security to disband, while it despatched more than half those engaged on public works away from Vienna where they were to be used in railway construction. September saw more rioting, again put down with force but this time involving the lower-middle class rather than workers. It was occasioned by the collapse of a bizarre new finance and credit company which the government was, erroneously, supposed to have sponsored. The Court took heart from the turn of events, especially as the end of July had seen Radetzky triumphant in Lombardy. With this military success it seemed that the time was approaching for a confrontation with Hungary.

Negotiations between the Hungarian government and Jellacic had been hanging fire during the summer and Hungarian–Croat relationships had in no way improved. Count Latour, who remained War Minister in the new Dobhloff ministry, had throughout shown pro-Jellacic feelings and with the war against Piedmont won, was now able to reinforce him. Although originally varying in its individual views on Hungary the Dobhloff ministry as a whole was increasingly taking an anti-Hungarian line, largely persuaded by the centralist beliefs of Bach. The Court, whatever Ferdinand had said and thought from time to time, had wholeheartedly opposed dualism inside the Empire and was now clearly persuaded of the necessity to act in order to restore the situation.

On September 4, Jellacic was officially reinstated in all his offices and forthrightly declared to have been no traitor. A Hungarian deputation led by the chief minister Batthyány was greeted by the formal announcement of this in Vienna on the 11th and broke off negotiations with the Court. On the same day Jellacic crossed the Drave and invaded Hungary. The former leader of Hungarian nationalism, Széchenyi, had become mentally unhinged and tried to drown himself; now Batthyány resigned together with the bulk of his government and Archduke Stephen withdrew as Palatine. Finally, seeing Hungary menaced by Jellacic and his

H

army, the Diet appointed a Committee of National Defence to run the country under the leadership of Kossuth.

The break had been made final and the chance of new negotiations being started exploded when Count Lemberg was murdered in Budapest on September 28. A Hungarian and no dyed-in-the-wool reactionary, he had been sent to Budapest by the Emperor as Commissioner Extraordinary with full powers. His assassination, and the extremely brutal and unpleasant manner in which his corpse was dealt with afterwards, served to heighten feeling on both sides. Jellacic was now made commander-in-chief of all Hungarian forces and given power as Ferdinand's representative. However, his advance was suddenly reversed. At the first real opposition he encountered Jellacic took fright and beat a precipitate retreat to the frontier.

It was this situation which persuaded Count Latour to summon reinforcements from Vienna. A grenadier regiment was ordered to entrain for the front on October 6. The soldiers, stationed for some years in Vienna and in close touch with the civilian population, were unenthusiastic but would not have acted without the violent displays of the popular party. Railway lines were torn up, and the bridge over which the troops were then told to march for another station was barricaded. More troops being sent to facilitate the departure led to violence, shooting and loss of life. Passions now exploded and Vienna was in full insurrection, with rival detachments of the National Guard even fighting inside St. Stephen's. This time, the students and the less prosperous section of the National Guard sided with the workers who, led with some confidence, showed themselves much more determined fighters than in August.

Latour, a brave and single-minded man, whether or not his policies are viewed sympathetically, was particularly disliked. He was dragged from the War Ministry and, even though members of the National Guard sought to protect him, was butchered by the infuriated crowd, who then strung up and insulted his mutilated body. This renewal of violence promptly led to the rapid departure from Vienna of more people who felt themselves menaced. 'The hours of that awful night—the alarm-bells pealing from all the steeples in the city; the arsenal at times wrapt in flames; the uninterrupted musket-fire; the thunder of the heavy cannons, and the streets strewn with the dying and the dead,' was how one described the situation that led Ferdinand and the Court again to hasten away from Vienna, this time to Olmütz. Among those members of parliament and of the government who fled was Bach: it was later reported that he first tried to escape from an enraged crowd, dressed as a woman despite his moustache.

It was decided to reduce and recapture Vienna, and Windisch-grätz was given the task of restoring peace 'with full speed, by any means he thinks fit'. He decided to ignore a later Imperial order, kinder in tone, and carry on with his original instructions, demanding on October 20 that the Viennese surrender. At the same time the garrison retreated from the city and joined with the troops outside, there to await Windischgrätz and his army.

In Vienna, a few members of the government had remained but neither they nor a committee of members of parliament, who had also stayed behind, were able to influence events. Power lay in the hands of students and of the Committee of Democratic Clubs. The students in the Academic Legion were considerably reduced in number since the early summer and the National Guard was divided; the more prosperous had either left the city or were lukewarm in its defence.

However, the alliance of workers with the lower-middle class and students, which had broken down in August and September, was resumed and the threat of Windischgrätz gave it a new solidarity. Nevertheless the defection of so many of the bourgeois had made it difficult to find a commander of the National Guard, and it was finally handed over to the tender mercies of the very inexperienced Messenhauser. 'More of a novel-writer than even of a subaltern officer, [he] was totally inadequate to the task,' wrote Engels, a verdict with which Auerbach, who came into contact with him at the time, concurred: 'His whole manner and conduct convinced me that this was not a man destined by Providence to lead a great movement, nor to play any part in the peaceable organization of the State.' A new force, the Mobile Guard, was created and put under a recent Polish arrival, Bem, who was subsequently to earn glory fighting in Hungary.

From October 24 onwards, Vienna was under attack and on the 28th Windischgrätz, having taken the suburbs, intensified operations. At this point the Hungarians again became closely involved with the revolution in Vienna. Having pursued Jellacic to the frontier the Hungarian army remained there. In the light of subsequent events it may seem odd that the Hungarian commanders were so concerned with regard for legality that they would not cross into Austria. But it should be remembered that they were men who had always been in the Emperor's service and it was one thing to chase an invading Croat general, Jellacic, out of their country, quite another to pursue him into Austria and attack the armies of Prince Windischgrätz. However, their hesitancy removed what chance there might have been for the revolution in Vienna.

Unnerved by Windischgrätz's attack, many who had only reluctantly accepted the idea of fighting to defend Vienna, and who had all along counselled negotiation, determined that peace must be made. They were fortified in this by Messenhauser's judgment that Vienna could not be held. Negotiations for surrender to Windischgrätz were therefore begun. At this stage the Hungarians, although they had still not been formerly invited by the Austrian parliament, resumed their advance and crossed the frontier: Kossuth had arrived at the front and overruled the more legalistic generals. Battle was joined with the Imperial troops and, although the Hungarians were defeated and driven back by Windischgrätz, the fighting, seen from Vienna, gave those in the city who were determined on resistance à outrance the justification they needed.

The workers and militants took over the city, believing that they were betrayed by traitors within the gates. Resistance was resumed with the result that Windischgrätz's troops met gunfire rather than the surrender they had been led to expect. This, understandably, infuriated Windischgrätz and his soldiers who saw it as a piece of duplicity and deceit, rather than what it was, the product of disunity and uncertain command. The results were a redoubled ferocity in the bombardment and an excuse for severity and brutality in dealing with the defeated city. For defeated it was, by the end of October 31, in spite of the renewed attempt at defence and the courage displayed.

Somewhere in the region of a thousand were killed in the fighting but no records exist of those slaughtered in the aftermath by the occupying armies and immediately disposed of. Probably some two thousand were arrested, of whom many were conscripted into the army. Among those shot were Messenhauser and, much more surprisingly, Robert Blum. Blum had come to Vienna as one of the delegates from the Left at Frankfurt and had decided that his place was there, in the defence of democracy against reaction. His shooting, a deliberate act by the Austrians, was partly meant as a judgment on the Frankfurt Assembly and the immunity which Blum claimed as a member.

To the accompaniment of looting and rapine, the revolution which had started off with such high hopes in Vienna in March was now defeated. On November 1, the city was put under a state of siege by Windischgrätz with the military responsible for local administration. All those who possessed arms were given sixty hours to hand them over or be liable to trial by Court Martial, no public gatherings of more than ten people were permitted and the press was again made subject to censorship.

'Because of a lack of grapeshot they lost their absolute, untouchable position in March, and they won it back in October, not on account of their understanding and not for convincing reasons, but because of the power of their cannon.' So wrote Küdlich on the Viennese revolution.

The collapse of the revolution in Berlin did not involve desperate fighting; in fact the Prussian army marched back into the city to the sound of music. The occasion for the troops' return had been democratic agitation, culminating in a disorderly meeting of the Second Democratic Congress. A soldier, Count Brandenburg (the natural son of Frederick William's grandfather, Frederick William II), was called upon to form a ministry on November 2, and within a week the Prussian Assembly was exiled to a provincial town where it was instructed to meet after a fortnight to hear the details of the king's new constitution.

Radical members attempted to remain in session, disobeying the order of the king, until the military intervened with Count Wrangel delivering an ultimatum due to expire after fifteen minutes. This was complied with, although not before an injunction had been passed by acclamation, calling upon the Prussian people to refuse to pay taxes (an injunction that was to have singularly little effect).

Martial law followed in Berlin, the Clubs were closed, the Civic Militia were disbanded and disarmed, and strict regulations were issued to control the publishing of papers and posters.

Of course, the revolution in Prussia did not simply and suddenly collapse without warning. The army, never defeated by the revolution but rather called off by the king, had always wanted to return and quell the revolt. Fortified by having put down the Polish rising in Posen and with the king away from Berlin in Potsdam, the army was confident that it could soon be in control of Berlin. The war over Schleswig-Holstein and its outcome had merely increased military scorn for elected bodies and strengthened suspicions that Prussia was being exploited by others in the name of Germany.

The Prussian National Assembly had realized that the military constituted a threat to its position and had sought to alter its composition, or at least secure an oath of loyalty from the soldiers. However, the army had reacted with contempt.

The German parliament at Frankfurt did nothing to assist the Prussian Assembly; it was jealous, it distrusted the Prussian body's decisions, for instance on Posen, and anyhow it had come round to the idea that Germany's best hope of unity now lay in Frederick William. It therefore wished to demonstrate its support for the king, not take sides with his recalcitrant assembly against him.

Again, the relationship of the Prussian Assembly with the Prussian government had never been clearly stated. The succession of more or less 'constitutional' ministries, starting with Camphausen's, had quarrelled with the assembly without knowing where final responsibility lay. Meanwhile the king, in Potsdam, had little to do with his government or his parliament and was becoming increasingly convinced that the Berliners had totally failed to appreciate his generous gestures of the spring.

In this situation it was not surprising that mounting class antagonism in Berlin should have led a sizeable part of the middle class to seek the return of the troops, nor that the king should have decided that it was time to give the army its opportunity.

To discuss the experiences of England in 1848 as the 'revolution in disarray' may be to overstate what was never really a revolutionary situation. The Chartist movement, which, in so far as it can fairly be seen as a single movement, sought the creation of a truly democratic House of Commons chosen by universal manhood suffrage as the way to alleviate the condition of the working class, made its last real effort in 1848. This took the form of a great meeting on Kennington Common on April 10, after which an attempt was made to march to Westminster and there present a petition. However, the procession, under O'Connor, was not allowed across the Thames; only the leaders were permitted to carry the petition further. No real disturbance took place and the movement was to collapse without seriously troubling English society.

Nevertheless the government was ready to use force if necessary, and unlike so many of its continental counterparts, it had made effective plans for the deployment of this force. To meet the possible threat of the Chartist demonstration special constables were enrolled in large numbers (among them Louis Napoleon who was still in England at the time), the police were at the ready and troops were in position under the command of the seventy-nine-year-old Duke of Wellington, discreetly out of sight so as not to provoke trouble. Just as in 1832, when the Reform Bill was passed, the British government was prepared to be ruthless if circumstances demanded it. This last factor is the one similarity between Britain and Russia, where also there was no revolution in 1848. Was it just a more confident and determined government, more skilled at dealing with possible unrest, that distinguished Britain from so much of Europe in 1848, or were there other reasons why she experienced no revolution?

In the short term, the government's behaviour was crucial but there were important differences in the English situation. First, the industrial revolution had progressed much further than anywhere else. This meant that, however deplorable conditions might be, there was work in the expanding towns and cities. A temporary slump brought unemployment and distress but not the same hopelessness where no industrial revolution had occurred, where there was no employment and no prospect of employment.

Secondly, the position of the middle class in Britain was very different. Even if the majority of the middle class did not have the vote, 1832 held out the hope that it might in the future. Also, the reforms which had followed 1832, however slow in coming and unsystematic they might be, demonstrated that parliament was responsive to the wishes of a larger number than merely those who had the vote. The repeal of the Corn Laws showed most clearly the working of a middle-class pressure group on the one hand and the government's reaction on the other. The Trevelyan–Northcote Report of 1853, on the reform of the civil service, was perhaps not the result of a desire to enlarge employment opportunities for the sons of the middle class, but it did have this effect. If, in common with other reforms, the genesis of civil service reform was a desire for greater efficiency this was certainly in accord with middle-class wishes. Above all, the notorious 'socially divisive' public schools and the universities provided a bridge which allowed sons of the middle class to cross over the social and cultural chasm that separated them from the traditional ruling class. Thus the middle classes in Britain never found themselves inciting revolution in their attempts to secure what they felt to be their rightful deserts.

Finally, the situation of the ruling class in England was very different from elsewhere in Europe. The greater social mobility between classes meant that, however decadent were certain individuals, as a whole the aristocracy was never effete and lacking in vitality. It had a basic confidence in its actions. At the same time the ruling class did not only make concessions as part of a cynical bid to retain power, it undoubtedly was partly animated by a feeling of the moral need to respond to the country's wish. The extraordinary situation of the Duke of Wellington, who, although a staunch conservative, was prepared to try to carry through a bill of moderate constitutional reform in 1832 not as an act of abdication or weakness but out of loyalty to his king and a belief that the country needed it, illustrates this attitude; as does Robert Peel's determination to go against the wishes of the landed interest and repeal the Corn Laws.

The poorer classes not seeing their situation as totally hopeless, the middle class not feeling completely shut out from power and position, the upper class confident and yet prepared to respond, albeit slowly, to the country's interest—in all respects nearly the exact opposite of their continental counterparts: this was the situation which goes some way towards explaining the comparative calm of Britain in 1848.

Chapter XIV

REACTION TRIUMPHANT

AFTER THE victory for conservatism in the June Days the future of France was to lie with the new constitution which the assembly was preparing. This sought to separate the executive and the legislature, with the former under a president and the latter to consist of a unicameral assembly, both elected by universal manhood suffrage. Obviously the choice of president would be critical. The candidates, besides the Orleanist General Changarnier, represented the various aspects of the revolution. General Cavaignac personified the right wing of the revolution, those who stood for order and abhorred socialism but were still republican. Lamartine was more to the centre. Then on the left there was Ledru-Rollin and, more extreme, Raspail, who was still in prison for his part in the demonstration of May 15.

The victor, though, was none of these. Instead, he was someone who had taken no part in the revolution nor in the previous regime, the nephew of Napoleon Bonaparte, Louis Napoleon. The results, declared on December 20, 1848, were as follows:

Louis Napoleon . . .	5,434,226
General Cavaignac . . .	1,448,107
Ledru-Rollin . . .	370,119
Raspail . . .	36,900
Lamartine . . .	17,910
General Changarnier . . .	4,790

Obviously the victory of a Bonaparte, particularly such a Bonaparte, the son of ex-King Louis of Holland and Hortense de Beauharnais daughter of Josephine, cannot simply be labelled 'reaction'.

Born in 1808 and in exile since 1815, Louis Napoleon had become the leader of the Bonaparte cause with the death of the Duke of Reichstadt in 1832. The Napoleonic legend which he adopted was that propounded from St. Helena: Napoleon the victim of aggression by other European powers, Napoleon the supporter of nationalist aspirations in Europe, and Napoleon the Emperor of 1815 who intended to work with representative institutions. Louis himself, implicated in a suspected rising in Rome in 1830, had fled northwards and there became involved in anti-Austrian operations. This subversive action, combined with his two attempted coups against Louis Philippe, at Strasbourg in 1836 and Boulogne in 1840, followed by six years' captivity in the French fortress of Ham until his escape in 1840, indicates that his election meant more than merely a triumph for the reactionary forces.

'The Napoleonic idea consists in a rebuilding of French society broken down by fifty years of revolution, and in a reconciliation of Order and Liberty, the rights of the people and the principles of authority,' Louis Napoleon had written in 1839. Clearly, he possessed something which appealed to most Frenchmen. Although his name indicated order, strong government and national self-respect to millions of frightened Frenchmen, both monarchist and republican, it also signified reassurance to the workers who had suffered in June from Cavaignac. Above all, his name meant something to the politically uninterested and illiterate. Nevertheless, bearing in mind his choice of government and, still more, the elections to the new assembly in May 1849, when the great majority of the deputies emerged as monarchists, it is perfectly fair to see 'reaction triumphant' in France.

Although destroying the old centre republicans such as Lamartine, the elections had returned a fortified Left under Ledru-Rollin. Horrified at the direction of events, however, he sought salvation at the barricades. The total failure of the insurrection of June 1849, the apathy of the Paris workers, the confidence of the army, the widespread arrests and the crushing sentences all illustrated just how great were the changes since February 1848.*

While Windischgrätz was restoring order in Vienna his brother-in-law Schwarzenberg was in the process of forming a new ministry. Although his formal appointment did not come until November 23, Prince Felix zu Schwarzenberg, the nephew of Napoleon's conqueror at Leipzig, had already taken up office as Minister-President and Foreign Minister. After joining the cavalry Schwarzenberg's somewhat tempestuous career involved more diplomatic postings

* Ledru-Rollin himself managed to escape to England.

than military commands and was highlighted by his central place in a notorious divorce case while he was in England. He was the Austrian Minister in Naples on the outbreak of revolution in 1848, when he promptly returned to his military duties in the north Italian campaign, being wounded in the battle of Goito. On his recovery he was sent by Radetzky to Innsbruck to convince the Imperial Court that, far from there being any need to sacrifice Italian territory in a bid for peace, if further reinforcements could be scraped together the Italian provinces would be re-conquered. After a short spell as Governor of Milan, Schwarzenberg was back with the Court when he was recommended by Windischgrätz to head a new ministry.

Schwarzenberg was much stronger, more ruthless and more determined than any of the other men who had held office since the March revolution in Vienna. He was also, partly because he came from one of the great Imperial families, utterly without awe of anyone. This self-assurance and arrogance had made for very difficult relations with his brother-in-law when as a young subaltern he had been under the command of Windischgrätz, who, seeking to discipline him, had sought to play the father. The same self-confidence, allied to an utter disregard for private sentiment in public action, is demonstrated by his refusal to work for the sort of Empire which Windischgrätz wished, to the point of open breach. Windischgrätz wanted to re-establish the Habsburg Monarchy on the basis of the old landed class. Schwarzenberg felt that this was impracticable because of the condition of the nobility, as he explained in a letter to his brother-in-law: 'It would be a simple matter to give the new constitution an aristocratic colouring, but I consider it impossible to instill into our aristocracy true life and much-needed resiliency.'

In keeping with this attitude was the cabinet which Schwarzenberg chose and which was based on the search for efficiency and ability rather than the desire to reward loyalty. Count Stadion, a liberal aristocrat, was Minister of the Interior, Bach, the pre-March radical, Minister of Justice, and Bruck, a former industrialist, Minister of Commerce. From the outset, Schwarzenberg had made it clear that he would not take office unless Ferdinand were to abdicate. This idea was not new; it had been discussed by the Empress and Metternich at a time when the insuperable obstacle had been that the desirable heir, Francis Joseph, had not been of age. With the events of 1848, an abdication became more necessary: first, because the strain on Ferdinand had been great—something which much concerned his wife; and secondly the promises made by Ferdinand would embarrass him if he remained Emperor while his government pursued reaction.

With Schwarzenberg in power, abdication could not long be delayed and on December 2, 1848 at Olmütz the ceremony took place. Ferdinand and Charles Louis both had some hesitation in the event but their wives managed to persuade them, Francis Joseph at the age of eighteen becoming Emperor, a crown he was to wear until 1916.

One important piece of unfinished business from 1848 was the Austrian parliament. Summoned to provincial Kremsier on the defeat of revolution in Vienna, this body was left to draw up a constitution. However, just as it was on the point of publishing its results in the spring of 1849, it was dissolved and the astounded deputies, some of whom were arrested, were confronted with the government's own constitution, prepared by Count Stadion. This, besides retaining more power for the Crown, differed from the Kremsier draft in seeking to unify all the Habsburg lands, Hungary included, and in this way appeared as the spiritual child of Joseph II.

Whatever his views on parliaments, Schwarzenberg had always wanted a centralized state.

With Schwarzenberg's government in power, Francis Joseph installed as the new Emperor, parliament dissolved and the government's own new constitution not to come into operation until the state of emergency had ended, it can fairly be claimed that in Austria too reaction was triumphant.

The consolidation of authority in the Austrian Monarchy had immediate repercussions in Frankfurt, particularly when taken in conjunction with the victory of reaction in the constitutional crisis in Berlin. If the Habsburg Empire had collapsed, the German sections of it could have been incorporated into the new German state without more ado; once, with the crushing of the October revolution in Vienna, the Habsburg state seemed assured of a future, the problems of its relations with Germany became acute. This was especially so because, since the events of September in Frankfurt, the parliament had had to accept that when faced with Danish troops or a hostile crowd, moral authority and patriotic invocations were not enough. The assembly's authority might rest on the Sovereignty of the People but its power lay in Austrian and Prussian bayonets. After September therefore, the majority in the Frankfurt parliament, by seeking the alliance of the major states, had abandoned the cause of revolution and was more or less dependent upon the agreement of the existing states for the success of its plans.

Thus, once Schwarzenberg was in power in Austria and had made clear his determination to create a unified Habsburg Empire, there was no chance of a federal German state being able to include the Austrian territories. The Grossdeutsch road to unity blocked and the Prussian state still very much in being, there was only one logical path forward: a German state with the King of Prussia as the executive power. However, many fought against this: those who believed that the Austrian lands must be included because they were Austrian themselves, Catholics who feared a Protestant-dominated state without Austria, and those who wanted no truck with any king and the King of Prussia in particular.

Heinrich von Gagern, now the Minister-President, sought the possibility of some special relationship with Austria but increasingly placed his hopes in Prussia. So it was that on March 28, 1849, Frederick William IV was elected hereditary Emperor of the new German Reich and a deputation left Frankfurt to offer him the Crown. Frederick William refused the offer; at first he demanded that it should be repeated by the princes of Germany, but increasingly he came to display distaste for the scheme itself. Partly, his romantic belief in kingship was offended at the offer coming from a self-constituted assembly; partly, his loyalty to the Habsburg position in Germany was offended, but Prussian self-interest also disliked the possibilities that acceptance might entail with regard to Austrian feelings.

The refusal struck at the roots of the Frankfurt constitution. A recasting of the constitution would have been undignified and absurd but without revolution there seemed no other chance of progress. The moderates and the liberals in the assembly had little choice but to try and persuade the Prussian king to change his mind and to enlist the support of the existing German state governments to this end. Disillusioned and crestfallen they began to drift away from Frankfurt, leaving only the more radical behind. The Left, having always disliked working for union with the governments, was not in such a hopeless position. It soon found itself a majority in the dwindling assembly, and even without the Emperor there still remained the rest of the constitution. This rump parliament could have gone ahead and secured the election of the People's House provided for, and meanwhile demanded that all state governments back the constitution, espousing the cause of revolution against any state government which would not support it. The Imperial Regent, hostile to this policy, could have been deposed at once, a vigorous executive chosen in his place and help summoned to Frankfurt to defend the new Germany from reaction. Or, 'if insurgent troops could not be brought to Frankfurt, then the Assembly could have adjourned at once to the very centre of the insurgent district', as Engels believed. For insurrection had already broken out in various parts of Germany by the middle of May 1849.

However, no determined lead was given and the revolts remained separate and unrelated. Finally the parliament did decide to move but only to Stuttgart in neutral Württemberg. On June 6, von Gagern having resigned sometime previously, the Imperial Regent Archduke John was deposed and a Regency Council of five chosen in his place. But this was too little, too late, and the Württemberg government had the parliament's meeting place closed by troops on June 18. The institution from which so much had been hoped the year before was now dead.

Revolts elsewhere continued. In Saxony the king, accepting the Prussian offer of help from the army, decided to dissolve his Diet and refuse to accept the constitution. He was forced to flee and a provisional government was set up in Dresden. Stephen Born had come from Berlin to Saxony and was there organizing the working class, but it was the Russian anarchist, Bakunin, fresh from Bohemia, with his flamboyant and larger-than-life-sized personality who took the lead in the fighting. Nevertheless, the Prussian army was able to crush the revolt, and Bakunin was captured and delivered up to the Russian government. More fortunate was the composer Richard Wagner, also involved in the revolt, who managed to escape to Switzerland.

Revolutionary outbreaks were widespread in the Rhineland, in Cologne where Marx and Engels were active, in the Palatinate, but most important in Baden, where uniquely, the army sided with the insurrection. With the Grand Duke now a refugee, a republic was declared and the apparatus of state taken over. Revolutionaries flowed into Baden from all parts, and the command of the army was

given to the Pole Mieroslawski, already well known for his subversive activities. For nearly six weeks the revolt was successful,
but the Prussian army was too strong and recaptured Baden for its
ruler. Many of the insurgents fled to the Imperial fortress of
Rastatt, from which Struve had been freed at the start of the revolt.
This was the last home of revolt in Germany. Under the command
of Otto von Corvin, survivor of Herwegh's expedition to assist
Hecker's first Baden revolt, it held out until the end of July.
Corvin escaped the death sentence but many were executed and
long prison sentences were the order of the day. The revolution in
Germany was over.

The revolt in Germany might be over, in the Habsburg Empire
Prince Schwarzenberg might promulgate a constitution in the name
of the Emperor, but revolt and war continued, and in Habsburg
lands at that. When the Hungarians had finally crossed into Austria
and been defeated before Vienna at the end of October 1848, it
might have seemed that Hungary had finally abandoned her
allegiance to the Habsburgs, but this was not the case.

The change of Emperor in Austria was not recognized in Hungary,
where Ferdinand was still considered king; until the time when
Francis Joseph went through the ceremony of becoming King of
Hungary he might be Emperor of Austria but he had no right to the
Crown of St. Stephen. Nevertheless, the claims of the Habsburg
dynasty were still upheld in Hungary. The situation for the Hungarians seemed bleak as Windischgrätz, fortified by his victories
elsewhere, advanced with his army. At first he found little real
opposition and took Budapest on January 5. At the same time the
Serb cause prospered in the south and Transylvania was fast
escaping Hungarian control.

However, Windischgrätz no more shared Schwarzenberg's
schemes for Hungary than he did those for Austria itself. Again he
wished for an alliance with the great nobility, this time against
Kossuth and much of the Hungarian revolution. So he was not
eager to commit himself to too forceful a prosecution of the war
and instead negotiated with the peace party. At the same time
Hungarian fortunes revived. Arthur Görgey, an officer who had
counselled attack upon Austria in October 1848, had been discovered by Kossuth and given command. He now built up a real
army in Hungary, a first-class fighting force. Two Polish soldiers,
Dembinski (a veteran of the Polish rebellion of 1831) and Bem

(fresh from the defence of Vienna) were also given commands and Bem began the reconquest of Transylvania.

Windischgrätz proved an inefficient commander and was replaced in April by General Welden, who proved to be little more successful. Following a brilliant campaign by Görgey, Budapest itself was retaken before the end of May. Meanwhile, however, the political situation was changing. Angered by Schwarzenberg's new constitution and worried by the continuation of the peace party despite military successes and his super-human efforts in improvising supplies for the army, Kossuth decided to force the issue by pushing the deposition of the Habsburg dynasty through the Diet on April 14. He himself became President-Regent.

In fact, the deposition made it more difficult for many of the Hungarian officers to reconcile their position with their previous loyalties to the Habsburg monarch. Görgey himself was far from convinced that Kossuth was right and disagreements between the two grew.

At the same time Schwarzenberg had become convinced that the Austrians could not by themselves subdue the Hungarians. He decided to choke back his pride and ask Tsar Nicholas for aid from Russia. Some Russian troops had already taken part in the fighting in Transylvania and large numbers were near the Hungarian border, so as to protect Russia from infection by the revolutionary virus and also because Nicholas feared that a successful Hungary might launch its armies into Poland. Loyal to his agreement at Münchengrätz more than fifteen years earlier, he was ready to help the Habsburgs if asked.

On Schwarzenberg's request a huge Russian force entered Hungary. At the same time that notorious but very efficient soldier, General Haynau, was sent by Radetzky from Italy to lead the Austrian troops. Now, despite heroic attempts to resist, the Hungarians were defeated. Finally Görgey convinced Kossuth that any further resistance was profitless, and having taken over supreme power, he surrendered to the Russians at Vilagos on August 13, hoping for better terms from them than from the Austrians. This surrender did not, however, completely terminate the fighting; it was not until October 4 that the last fortress capitulated.

Kossuth, in the company of many Hungarians, fled to Turkey where he was offered protection by the Sultan. Görgey himself was saved at the personal request of the Tsar but desperate severity was shown in the punishment of Hungary. Execution, imprisonment, drafting into the army, whole-scale floggings and all manner of humiliations were meted out by General Haynau. Batthyáni and thirteen generals who had been officers in the Imperial army were liquidated among many others, before, on October 28, Haynau was told that the executions must cease. In among the ruin and the grief, clearly the Hungarian revolt had been defeated.

The Sicilian revolt which had been the first to break out in Europe in 1848 was not the last to be crushed but it lasted until mid-way through 1849. Initiatives such as assistance for the revolt on the mainland, and the offer of the Sicilian crown to the son of the King of Sardinia, demanded some action by the King of Naples. Operations were set in hand in August 1848 and, after a fierce bombardment in which much of the city was destroyed, Messina was captured. However, intervention on the part of England and France brought about an armistice on September 11, just as the whole island seemed about to surrender. It was not for a further six months that the fighting was resumed; Palermo fell on May 15, and Ferdinand regained control of Sicily.

The autumn of 1848 saw the government of Piedmont, in common with those of Tuscany and Rome, moving further to the left; this in response to popular pressure. Gioberti, previously the advocate of a federal Italy under Papal presidency, led the government but found himself out of tune with a radical assembly in his policies concerning other Italian states. The cabinet which followed was more radical and stood for a renewal of war. Charles Albert, knowing that his army was in no fit state for fighting, still preferred to accept war rather than a humiliating dictated peace from the Austrians. One of the ubiquitous Polish officers of 1848, Chrzanowsky, was given command and the declaration for a resumption of war was dispatched to the eager Radetzky on March 20.

Brescia alone of the Lombard towns rose against the Austrians and the campaign was soon over, the Piedmontese forces being crushed at Novara. Charles Albert abdicated in favour of his son Victor Emanuel, and escaped through the Austrian lines to Portugal where he died later in the year. 'Since today I have failed to find my death on the battlefield, I make my last sacrifice for my country, I lay down my crown and abdicate in favour of my son, the Duke of Savoy.' This last campaign hardly restored confidence in the competence of the Piedmontese leadership; the most crass behaviour was that of the hero of the radicals, General Ramarino, who had led Mazzini's futile expedition into Piedmont in 1834. He crossed the Po, and the Austrians, by destroying the bridge he had used, effectively removed his forces from the battle. The peace that Radetzky granted Victor Emanuel was lenient, far more so than any he would have granted Charles Albert. Piedmont retained its constitution and D'Azeglio was appointed Prime Minister. However, the war between Piedmont and Austria was now over.

The flight of Grand Duke Leopold did nothing to resolve the problems of Tuscany's future, swaying as she was between a republican union with Rome and attempts to secure the return of the Grand Duke. The constitutionalists finally seized power on April 12 and Guerrazzi was arrested. Leopold agreed to return but broke faith by bringing in the Austrian army. The end of May 1849 saw Austrian soldiers in control of all the central Italian duchies.

The sole part of the Austrian Empire in Italy which remained unsubdued was Venice. In fact, the city was to be the last home of the revolutions in Europe, save for scattered fortresses in Hungary: it only capitulated at the end of August 1849. Venice had briefly merged herself into the kingdom of Sardinia-Piedmont along with Lombardy, but almost immediately Charles Albert was defeated and in flight back to Turin. The union was of necessity dissolved and Manin emerged as the leader of a republic once more.

An important factor in the decision for union with Piedmont had been the inability of the Venetians to defend by themselves the mainland of Venetia from the professional Austrian troops. It was not surprising therefore that the mainland was soon reconquered by the Austrians, save for the fortress of Malghera. Austrian blockade of the city was only half-hearted until the spring of 1849 but, after defeating Charles Albert, Radetzky turned his full attention to Venice. Following heavy bombardment Malghera was taken and the blockade tightened.

What distinguished the Venetian revolution from most of the uprisings of the time was the amazing calm and consideration the Venetians showed in their dealings with one another while prosecuting the war with ruthless determination. Much of this must be attributed to Manin, whose selfless enthusiasm and wisdom was magnificent, substantiating Trevelyan's claim that 'no man raised to power by revolution has left a purer record'. However, Manin was not a great military leader; the fleet whose role should have been crucial was not employed with any imagination and in fact the bulk of the Austrian navy, crewed by Venetians, had been allowed to slip out of Venice's control at the very start of the revolt in 1848. Besieged, starved, bombarded and finally attacked by cholera, the overcrowded city finally sued for peace. On August 24 Manin and a handful whom Radetzky had proscribed sailed from Venice and the Austrians returned in their stead.

On November 24, 1848, when Pius IX left Rome in disguise for Gaeta in the coach of the Bavarian ambassador, it was clear that he was abandoning Rome to the democrats and extremists. It was also clear that the Catholic Powers would not lightly accept the Pope's exile, particularly if Rome declared itself a republic. It was decided to summon a Constituent Assembly to serve for all Italy, and although the Pope attacked it as 'abominable alike for the absurdity of its origin not less than the illegality of its form and the impiety of its aims', the assembly met and on February 9 declared the Roman Republic.

Homeless revolutionaries and exiles, from Manara and his band of fellow-Lombard patricians to Garibaldi himself, flocked to Rome. Most famous of all the newcomers was Mazzini, elected to the assembly before his arrival. Although nominally only one of the triumvirs, it was he who was to hold power in Rome during the early summer.

By the end of April Rome found herself faced by a French attack, with Austrian, Spanish and Neapolitan troops elsewhere in the Papal States. Despite the assistance of those who came from outside to fight for Rome and despite the heroism of its defence, Rome was doomed from the outset. Any hope that there might have been collapsed with the failure of Ledru-Rollin's coup in Paris. It was, however, not until the beginning of July that further resistance was seen to be hopeless. Garibaldi who had been in command of the city's defence made a fighting retreat, Mazzini resigned, and the French entered the city. The Pope's rule was now restored though he himself did not return until April 12, 1850.

The intervention of Republican France to crush the Roman Republic may at first sight seem inexplicable; especially when one remembers that the French president was Louis Napoleon who had himself taken part in an anti-Papal insurrection when a young man. However, on a closer look it becomes more reasonable. After the Romans had declared their republic the Pope appealed for help, and already the Spanish had suggested a congress to determine the means of intervention. With Austria increasingly victorious by 1849 it was important for France that Austrian troops should not also gain all the prestige of restoring the Pope to Rome; particularly was this so when the President of France had the name Bonaparte. Besides, republican sentiment still existed in France and would have been outraged if the French government had meekly aquiesced in Austrian-backed restoration of reaction in Rome. At the same time Louis Napoleon could never have contemplated using force to prevent the Pope's restoration by Austria; his Catholic support in France was too important. Louis's plan therefore—like most of his plans in the field of foreign affairs too complicated and conjectural—was to take the initiative and persuade the Romans to accept Pius's return, while winning republican approval or anyhow acceptance by insisting on a reformed Papal administration. He was sure that a majority of Romans wanted this and were only prevented by extremists from obtaining it; thus a show of force would be enough.

However, Louis Napoleon's hopes for a peaceful restoration of the Pope were to be dashed. Despite the existence of strong anti-Papal feeling in the city and the wish in others to create from Rome the power-house of a new Italian republic, moderation might have prevailed had it not been for the arrival of certain men, in particular Mazzini, during the spring of 1849, determined that it should not. This was so much the case that one liberal Catholic in Rome during this period could write, 'it [the Roman Revolution] became incarnate in Mazzini.'

It is not given to many political philosophers to enjoy political power even for so short a time as three months; but such was to be Mazzini's fate. The episode, from the end of March until the end of June, was the triumph of his life and was bound to be followed by bitter frustration, however much it might serve as the source of a sublime legend.

What in reality can be said of Mazzini's Roman Republic and his work as leader? First, he did not betray his principles. He lived with almost ostentatious frugality and simplicity and never sought to preserve his position with the methods of a Robespierre. Certainly he tried to sustain resistance by the circulation of false stories of impending aid from Britain or the recall of the French troops, but this was the Mazzini of self-deception and illusory optimism, manifested in his earliest conspiracies. Secondly, he was able to inspire the city in its resistance. Admittedly his tolerant authority all too often meant no authority, vandalism and disorder—priests were butchered, churches attacked, private grudges pursued with impunity in the guise of patriotism. Nevertheless, Rome's resistance under his leadership probably did more to fire the imaginations of Italians than all the other actions and writings of Mazzini's life: after this, it would be hard to build an Italy without Rome as its capital.

However, military operations in Rome were under the control of Garibaldi, and no account of the Roman Republic or, in fact, of the revolutions of 1848-9 would be complete without mention of him. One of the most romantic of figures in a period in which such figures abounded, it is almost impossible to disentangle Garibaldi from the legend. But certain qualities do stand out. Above all, he was a man of enormous courage and physical toughness; his whole career, from the youthful conspirator of 'Young Italy' to the veteran fighter against the Prussians in eastern France in 1871, testifies to this characteristic. Secondly, he was a man capable of inspiration, the possessor of charisma, important for all leaders, and vital in the leaders of volunteers and irregulars. Even in his craziest ventures he was able to persuade men to follow him willingly and gladly. Closely allied to this magnetism—part cause, part symptom and part effect—was his flamboyance. One of the difficulties inherent in any estimation of Garibaldi is that he was something of a charlatan; recognition of this fact has led men to underestimate him just as failure to recognize it led to crushing disappointment. His actions, particularly his gesture of self-renunciation and withdrawal into the political shadows, along with his appearance, seem redolent of the poseur but clearly had something genuine to them as well. The mixture perhaps helps to account for the hostility and jealousy felt for him by professional commanders throughout his career.

Was he a great soldier? His defence of Rome demonstrates failings understandable in one with little experience of pitched battles against regular troops where isolated acts of heroism and panache are not usually as decisive as co-ordination and planning. However, some of the battles he fought in 1860 show that he could learn these additional skills. And he had one further priceless asset for a man who aspired to lead guerillas and volunteer armies: his ability to live as a common soldier. However hard Mazzini and many of the other leaders of nationalist uprisings might try, they were unable to metamorphose into men of the people. As townsmen and members of the middle class they could never live close to the earth. Garibaldi, perhaps because of his early life at sea, had a peasant's rather than a poet's understanding of nature.

After a short but successful Alpine campaign in the summer of 1848 he had come to Bologna in his efforts to further the Italian cause. It was here that he and his legion received their summons to defend Rome, where they arrived at the end of April 1849. His heroic but unavailing command of the Roman defences at an end, Garibaldi refused to surrender and, outwitting French, Spanish, Austrian and Neapolitan troops, led over 3,000 of his men into the mountains; they were bound for Venice where the revolution was still holding out. After a long and arduous march he finally disbanded his legion, but pressed on with a small group of followers, including his pregnant wife Anita. After more adventures, calamity struck and Anita died. An outlaw with a price on his head, Garibaldi made his way back to the west coast before embarking for exile. With such a man as Garibaldi still alive, albeit in exile, it is perhaps in the final analysis inaccurate to talk of reaction as triumphant.

PART SIX

AFTERMATH

AFTERMATH

THE FLIGHT of the Metternichs from Vienna after the collapse of March 13 had been far from easy, despite the calm account the Prince gave of it later. 'Not without great difficulties' is how Baron Carl von Hügel, who accompanied them, epitomizes the escape from the capital in the course of a description which testifies to the hasty, improvised nature of the journey. It was undertaken without any clear destination in mind, it was circuitous in order to avoid hostile territory and full of frustrations and frights, 'being night and day in the expectation of some terrible catastrophe'.

The initial plan does not seem to have gone beyond reaching Prince Liechtenstein's castle at Felsberg. However, once they had arrived there it soon became apparent that this would not suffice as a place of refuge, and the journey continued by rail and coach to Holland. After a delay caused by a breakdown in the Prince's health, late in April they crossed to England where they were to live for a year and a half, at first in Eaton Square, later at Richmond and, during the winter of 1848-9, at Brighton.

In England they were received with interest and warmth. They were called upon and lavished with invitations from a variety of the famous, the rising young, and old friends, not to mention fellow exiles. The Prince, despite financial uncertainties over his future, enjoyed England and was in no hurry to depart. However, his wife persuaded him that Brussels might be cheaper and would offer more opportunity of contact with Vienna. For, now that the revolutions had been defeated and the Habsburgs resumed control, reports were coming in that the Prince might be allowed to return. Finally in 1851, after spending the summer months on their Rhineland estates and with all their property restored, the Metternichs moved back to Austria and to their Rennweg Villa.

The Prince never returned to the Imperial service—his age would have made such a move most unlikely—but he was welcomed back into the confidence of the Court. The young Emperor was his frequent visitor and he corresponded once more with members of the government. Although seldom acted upon, his advice was apparently gratefully received; it was certainly freely offered. He watched the Crimean War with disquiet and the beginning of war against France and Piedmont in 1859 with horror. He died mid-way through the hostilities, with Austria's defeat still not certain. The symbol of conservatism in Europe after 1815, thrown down in 1848, was back in most honourable retirement by 1851. Was the fate of the revolutions so very different?

At first sight, it appeared not: the tide of reaction continued to rise. In France a coup on December 2, 1851, saw Louis Napoleon seize power and dissolve the National Assembly. After an attempted insurrection in protest, all opposition was crushed and nearly 27,000 people throughout France were arrested. A huge plebiscite victory (seven and a half million for, to just over half a million against) supported Napoleon's assumption of supreme power and a new, much more authoritarian, constitution was prepared: the National Guard was dissolved, a new press law instituted and all officials ordered to take an oath of allegiance. December 1852 saw the logical development in the creation of the Second Empire, Louis Napoleon taking the title of Napoleon III.

Reaction triumphed in Prussia as elsewhere in Germany; a new constitution was imposed from above with the franchise so arranged that, with voters divided into three groups according to wealth, the rich exerted a disproportionate influence. Nevertheless all attempts to force a closer German unity had not ended with Frederick William's refusal of the Frankfurt assembly's offer. He remained interested and had appointed the influential Frankfurt conservative, von Radowitz, to be responsible for Prussia's German policies. Von Radowitz devised a scheme for a federation excluding Austria but preserving a strong link with her. Prussia would not merge into the federation but would maintain her integrity and would obviously dominate.

He hoped to achieve this result with the support of the princes, backed in addition by popular feeling; thus the proposed constitution allowed more power for the princes than had been the case at Frankfurt and adopted the Prussian electoral system for the lower house of its legislature. At first the plan, which led to the Erfurt Union, promised well but it was wrecked by Austrian intransigence as represented by Schwarzenberg. Austrian-Prussian rivalry finally came to a head in 1850 and in November Prussia deferred to Austrian hostility at Olmütz: Frederick William and many of his advisers were not prepared to risk a war and the Russian Tsar made no secret of his dislike for Prussian provocation of Austria. However an alternative, Austrian scheme for Germany's future met with no support and the structure of the Confederation of 1815–48 was restored.

In the Habsburg Monarchy the Stadion constitution which Schwarzenberg had promulgated was never put into effect and the proposed parliament never met. Meanwhile the centralization of the Empire was carried forward save in Lombardy and Venetia which continued to be treated separately. Although they had gained little in return for their support of the dynasty, the subject peoples such as the Czechs and the Croats remained loyal. The Czech leaders were to continue to work for a future inside the Habsburg Empire into the twentieth century. Their fears for the future of the Czech people at the hands of the Germans and the Russians, if the Habsburg state collapsed, have hardly been shown to be groundless over the past fifty years.

Yet despite the apparent total collapse and failure of the revolts of 1848–9 and the complete success of reaction, the situation twenty-five years later demonstrated that the aspirations of 1848 had not vanished without trace. By the 1870s Germany was unified as the Second Reich, with a German parliament and the King of Prussia as Emperor; the Kleindeutschland of Frankfurt. Denmark had been defeated and Schleswig-Holstein seized. Austria, excluded from Germany, had also been driven out of Italy and had been forced to accept the right of Hungary to virtual autonomy in the lands of the Crown of St. Stephen. Italy was united, with the son of Charles Albert as king. France was once again a republic with power residing in the assembly rather than the president. Why then was the revolution not after all a failure; the new order not a total victory for reaction?

After 1815, whatever the hopes and policies of individual politicians, whatever the aspirations of the leaders of a variety of small states, the heads of the major states had accepted the Europe which the Peace of Vienna had left. Crises could build up over the existence of an independent Greece, the regime of Spain and Portugal and the fate of the Spanish Empire in the New World. Nevertheless there existed a community of interest between the major powers that precluded revisionism on any large scale. With Louis Napoleon in power in France all this changed.

'My impression is that . . . he has invariably been guided by his belief that he is fulfilling a destiny which God has imposed upon him,' was Queen Victoria's verdict in 1855 on Louis Napoleon. The French Emperor, because of his sense of mission and dynasty, in terms of 1815, was a revisionist; for 1815 had signified a defeat for France, a defeat for revolutionary France, but above all, the defeat of Napoleonic France.

In his wish to fulfil the dreams of his uncle, Louis Napoleon was confronted with many difficulties. First, because of the legend of himself which Napoleon had created in exile it was almost impossible to separate reality from wishful thinking. Indeed, it is doubtful whether the aim of a federal Europe of free states really ever was Napoleon's aim. It is equally likely that it was merely part of the self-justifying myth of one eager to blame his preoccupation with war on the enemies who would never accept him. Secondly, Louis Napoleon had a very different character from that of his uncle, being less decisive but more humanitarian and altruistic; this set of values naturally led him to behave differently. Then, his own background and experiences, not least his early Italian involvement which made him favour the cause of Italy thereafter, were unlike those of Napoleon. Above all, leaders are imprisoned in the situation in which they find themselves and are not able to obliterate events and circumstances which have preceded their assumption of power. At best, therefore, Louis Napoleon could only seek to follow his uncle's principles in a different context. The result was that very often he would distort one aspect of the legend so as to justify acting in the way he wanted. Napoleon's foreign policy can only be said to be the key to Louis Napoleon's in the sense that the Bible can be said to be the key to the contradictory actions of different Christians in the sixteenth and seventeenth centuries.

Louis Napoleon's influence was decisive in bringing about two wars in the 1850s which in their consequences totally changed the shape of Europe: the Crimean War in which Britain and France fought Russia, and the Franco-Austrian War of 1859 in north Italy. It is not to argue that Louis Napoleon planned the Crimean War to say that it would not have occurred in the way it did without him; nor is it to underrate Cavour to see Louis Napoleon's initiative as the prime cause of the war of 1859.

Critical to the maintenance of peace after 1815, and restated at Münchengrätz, was the alliance of the three eastern states, Austria, Prussia and Russia. So long as this held firm it was unlikely that any major change could take place in the situation of either Germany or Italy, since any French initiative, as in the past still the most probable source of such a change, would meet the combined resistance of the three powers. Also, so long as the memory of the French Revolutionary and Napoleonic Wars remained with European statesmen, Britain was likely to take sides against France. For any really drastic alteration to the European status quo to occur, either the alliance of the three eastern Courts must break down, or Britain and France must come together prepared to fight it. In fact, both alternatives were to be realized when Britain and France allied with Turkey to fight Russia in the Crimean War, while Prussia remained neutral and Austria mediated on the side of Britain and France.

Austria, as Metternich had always known, would be in a desperate situation if France fought Russia. Whichever side she chose to join, her territories were likely to provide the battle-ground and the source of concessions in future peace negotiations. Prussia had very much the same fear. Again, with regard to Turkey, Austria had radically different aims from those of Russia; she had no wish to see Russian expansion in the Turkish Empire since this would mean Russian power south of the Danube and in an area where Austria was extremely sensitive. Prussia, on the other hand, had no worries about Russia's policy in south-east Europe except in so far as it might break up the alliance of the eastern Courts which she wished to preserve. It was this fear which had led Prussia to take the initiative in the partition of Poland in the eighteenth century so as to preserve Austro-Russian accord which had been jeopardized over Turkey. Now that Poland was partitioned, there was nowhere else where the three powers could come together in the same manner: partition of Turkey would have concerned Britain and France a great deal more than Prussia. Consequently, the relationship between Russia and Turkey had always been the most likely source of friction among the eastern Courts, and had in fact nearly destroyed their alliance at the time of the Greek revolt.

The events of 1848-9 made such a break-down more likely. Metternich was gone, with all his experience and skill. Then, because of the rift between Prussia and Austria over the German question, and the personality of the Prussian representative at Frankfurt, Count Bismarck, Prussia was quite prepared to enjoy Austrian embarrassment. In addition because Russia had helped Austria to suppress the Hungarian rising in 1849, she felt, understandably, that she could count on Austrian co-operation when she was in difficulties, and bitterly resented Austrian unwillingness. Finally, after 1848–9, Austria was extremely sensitive about her Italian possessions and most reluctant to give France the opportunity of assisting Piedmont in a war of liberation in Italy. Thus, neutrality was not really practical politics for Austria, even if it was for Prussia.

1848–9 had also made British participation in a war with Russia more likely because, whatever the attitude of the British government, British public opinion had been profoundly shocked by the Russian suppression of the Hungarian revolt, which gave rise to considerable anti-Russian sentiment.

The resulting defeat of Russia in the Crimean War, leaving her enraged because of Austria's ingratitude and humbled at the Peace of Paris, meant that she would now neither be prepared nor able to assist Austria against France, nor to intervene in order to check an alteration of the status quo in Germany. Thus France was able to defeat Austria in Italy and open up the Italian situation after 1859. Also Prussia and Austria could move into a state of war in 1866 without Russia seeking to act as a balance to preserve peace. There was, therefore, a period of time in Europe after the middle of the century when a mobility existed which there had not been for the previous thirty years, and which 1848 had had a large share in creating.

It is this mobility which does more than anything to explain the unification of Germany and Italy. The desire for the unification of Germany was no stronger among Germans at the end of the 1850s than it was at the end of the 1950s. An international situation, which on the one hand permitted unification and on the other did not, must be seen as fundamental to what occurred in the two periods, however successful Bismarck was in exploiting and even shaping the international situation which confronted him.

Otto von Bismarck, arch-conservative in the Prussian United Diet of 1847–8, became Prussian representative at the reconstituted Frankfurt Diet in 1851. He was not converted to the idea of German unity by the events of 1848–9, although they showed him to what extent German liberals might be prepared to put unity before their liberalism. During 1848–9 Bismarck had in fact been a fierce opponent of the idea of German unification, and he had remained a determined Prussian patriot. It was his time at Frankfurt that taught him to dislike Austrian pretensions in Germany. In 1848–9 he had loathed the idea of Prussia being subordinated to what were supposed to be 'German' interests; now he detested the prospect of Prussia being subordinated to Habsburg interests. He came consequently to work for freedom of action for Prussia, which in the end signified the hegemony of Prussia in Germany and the exclusion of Austria: in fact, German unity for essentially Prussian reasons.

Although a favourable international situation was vital to the successful unification of Italy, the parts played by individual Italians were almost equally important. Cavour, Garibaldi and Pius IX, together with most of the other figures who were to act out their roles in the drama of the creation of Italy, were of course greatly influenced by what had happened in 1848–9. Cavour became quite certain of the folly of ever again exposing Piedmont in a war with Austria without the help of a major ally, most particularly France. He also, while remaining a liberal, was confirmed in his distrust for the extremes of popular feeling. 'We are no longer in 1848. . . . Take no notice of the qualms of those who surround you. The least act of weakness will ruin the government,' he instructed the Governor of Milan in 1859.

Cavour's motives were not as simple as at one time they were considered. He did not want Italian unity at any cost; certainly he did not want it at the cost of Piedmont being submerged in a democratic republic whose policy would depend on the votes of central and southern Italian peasants. A repetition of 1849, with the Mazzinian republic in Rome and Garibaldi's part in its defence, remained a real fear to Cavour in the future when, after 1859, he saw himself threatened by Garibaldi's exploits. Garibaldi for his part became, if it was possible, even more committed to Italian unification after 1848–9 and, unlike Cavour, he was prepared for unification on almost any terms; certainly he was prepared to sacrifice his republicanism.

Above all, however, the events of 1848–9 were decisive with regard to Pius IX and the Papacy. The illusion of the Pope being able to lead a united Italy, of becoming a liberal and even a democrat, was shattered. Pius IX did not become the cruel reactionary, or the cipher of sinister ultra-conservative forces, which some polemicists have claimed, but he did realize the falsity of his position between 1846 and 1848 and determined to avoid its repetition. It was this resolve that led him to condemn communism, socialism and liberalism, and to his categorizing as an error, in the Syllabus of Errors of 1864, the proposition that 'the Roman Pontiff can and should reconcile and harmonize himself with progress, with liberalism, and with recent civilization'.

It was not only the theories of a liberal Papacy which were put to the acid test in 1848–9. The Communist Manifesto may not have had much impact on the events of 1848 but these events went some way to justify the Communist Manifesto. Marx's insistence that the proletariat must fight for themselves, produce their own party and not rely upon the philanthropic members of the upper and middle classes to bring about socialism from above, seemed vindicated. Much of what happened in 1848–9, notably the September riots in Frankfurt, the October revolt in Vienna and, above all, the June Days in Paris, demonstrated the reality of class antagonism and the illusion of the brotherhood of all men.

In a sense, of course, socialism was weakened by the crushing of the revolution with the ensuing imprisonment and exile of so many of the leaders; especially was this so in France. Marx himself believed that the chances of an immediate revolution were gone. When he and Engels made their way back to England they found their view being challenged in the Communist League. So strongly did Marx feel about his opinion that in 1850 he deliberately secured the transfer of the League to Cologne, where it duly died, rather than allow it to fall to those who pressed for immediate revolution. 'We tell the workers; you have to go through fifteen, twenty, fifty years . . . [to] change yourselves, and to make yourselves fit for political power.'

Believing that there was little chance of immediate action, Marx turned to composing the history of the revolution of 1848 in France and the assumption of power by Louis Napoleon; and Engels wrote, under Marx's name, a series of articles for the New York *Tribune* entitled 'Germany: Revolution and Counter-Revolution'. These works, with their penetrating analysis, examined recent events in order to justify Marx's teachings.

However, not all socialists became rigid followers of Marx. To begin with, the belief existed, particularly among German socialists, that their ends could be served by using as means the parliamentary process. Lassalle, before his death in 1864, had for instance founded the General Union of German Workers and tried to bargain with the Prussian government.* But the anarchist strand of socialism, in which Proudhon was perhaps most influential, angered Marx more. In rejecting the state, anarchists repudiated the notion, there in both the Jacobin dictatorship of 1792–4 and Marx's party of the proletariat, of a minority seizing power in the name of, and for, the people. Instead of political action, the anarchists were to rely exclusively on economic activities; looking to a society consisting of independent autonomous communes. When it seemed that Bakunin, the Russian anarchist and revolutionary of 1848–9, might gain control of the International for anarchism, Marx engineered the removal of its headquarters to America where it was dissolved in 1876.†

Nevertheless, although the working class became, after 1848–9, more conscious of the need to organize effectively if they were to help themselves, the same sort of spontaneity and disorganization is revealed in the Paris Commune of 1871 as in the great insurrections of the past. Followers of Proudhon and members of the International were prominent—Marx was even to claim that the Commune was the child of the International—but this was still not a considered socialist uprising. Class bitterness may have been, as a legacy of 1848, more self-conscious than at the start of previous revolutions, but the Commune owed most to Jacobin leaders such as Delescluze, a prominent figure in 1848 but no socialist.

It was in fact an outburst of the poorer citizens, smarting under the humiliation they were called upon to suffer, the aftermath of the siege of Paris and the bitterness which that had aroused, all in front of a back-drop of poverty and social distress. The reason given by Rossel for joining the Commune (he had been a regular officer and was for a time to become Minister of War for the Commune) was: 'I do not hesitate to join the side which has not concluded peace, and which does not include in its ranks generals guilty of

* After 1891 the S.P.D. was to become increasingly involved in the German parliamentary process, emerging as the evolutionary rather than the revolutionary force of the present.

† The International Federation of Working Men was founded in London by workers from various countries, and Marx had become the dominating intellect and personality on the Committee.

I

capitulation.' This declaration smacks more of Danton than of Marx and owes more to 1792 than to 1848.*

Yet, despite the growth of socialism, especially in Germany, and the triumph of the Bolsheviks in 1917 in Russia, the class struggle was not to be the most bitter divisive force in Europe during the century which followed 1848. Instead, that other passion which 1848–9 had demonstrated so amply, nationalism, was to assume the greatest importance as a force for construction with the creation of Germany and Italy, and as a force for destruction with the conflicts which littered the next century, and above all the two world wars.

It was in this way perhaps that the thoughts of Hegel, who had died in 1831, were to prove more prophetic than those of Marx. Marx of course used Hegel as a basis for his own philosophy, notably with his employment of the dialectic (although in the dialectic of Marx the material is primary, whereas with Hegel the material is the interpretation and the impress of man's mind, expressing the Divine Idea or Weltgeist—'History is mind clothing itself with the form of events,' he wrote). But Hegel saw the relationship of man with the state, and not class, as fundamental: 'The state is the Godly idea as it exists upon earth', and, 'the state is the march of God through the world'. It was the role of the state to synthesize the personal, selfish drive of man with the Godly wish of the spirit in him. The state becomes the sole standard of morality: its laws are always just. It was a feeling of this nature, although of course not refined and without the theoretical and philosophic background, that persuaded so many liberals in Germany to accept and work with the Reich which Bismarck fashioned: in a sense, its very success and existence were the justification.

What Marx in common with other observers of the economic situation totally failed to foresee, and what perhaps did most to invalidate his prognosis, was the amazing economic growth of Europe after 1850. Whatever the achievement of the previous century, it was dwarfed into insignificance by comparison with that of the century which followed.

It is of course possible to portray the spread of industrialization across Europe as an unmitigated disaster to the quality of human life; the suffering it caused was certainly intense. However, it is

* However Thiers, faced with Paris in insurrection, did revert to 1848. He employed the tactics he had pressed without success on Louis Philippe: complete withdrawal from Paris followed by its systematic conquest.

difficult to see how else the growing population could have been fed; certainly not by the methods of 'back to the land' which some continued to advocate, for there just was not enough land.* Large-scale industrialism and capitalism have much to answer for but it can be argued that the standard of living of the British working class was to be improved more by Sainsbury's and Marks & Spencer's than by Feargus O'Connor and Marx and Engels.

The population maintained its extraordinary rise throughout Europe—except in France where the increase was more modest—Industrial growth broke records everywhere but above all in Germany. Here coal production went up by over five times from 1850 to 1870, and the steel and textile industries followed a similar pattern. The railway network was completed, thus transforming communications, firms grew in size (Krupp's works at Essen employed seventy-one people in 1848, by 1868 nearly eight thousand), and, as well as becoming larger, enterprises extended their activities back to gain control of raw materials, in this way exhibiting economic maturity.

The economic transformation of Europe extended considerably beyond economic and social matters in its results. In Germany the spread of railways, the growth of a common coinage (the Prussian Thaler became the standard coin in 1857), the industrial supremacy of Prussia, the increasing solidarity of the Zollverein which Schwarzenberg failed to transform or take over, all this guided Germany towards unity. At the same time the different speeds of economic advance from country to country altered the political balance in Europe, as the Franco-Prussian War was to demonstrate.

It is certainly true that the revolutions did something to quicken the process of economic change. The emancipation of the peasantry in the Habsburg Empire did allow the larger and more enterprising landowners to become capitalists and promoted more modern agriculture. Also, although subject to great regional differences, the peasants began to separate into the more energetic and fortunate, who became prosperous farmers, and those who left the land to act as the labour force for the new industries.†

* Even the palliative of emigration to the New World which increased enormously in this period was only possible because of the revolution in communications.

† The movement of peasants away from the country also had the effect of decisively altering the character of the towns in many areas. The new arrivals

The governments which successfully emerged were usually more energetic than their predecessors, and economic activity gained from state action, such as the Habsburg government's creation of a single tariff state in the Empire, the pushing ahead of peasant emancipation in Prussia or Louis Napoleon's attempts to foster economic growth in France. Nevertheless, this economic transformation of Europe was clearly not the result of 1848-9, as a glance at the previous fifty years will show. Its roots lie deep in the Industrial Revolution.

It was not only the economy of Europe after 1850 which stemmed from the eighteenth century. As well as the Commune seeming to have strong links with the French Revolution, developments elsewhere suggested that Europe in the 1870s was still digesting the principles of 1789. At the same time, the growth of the state continued the tradition of the rulers of the previous century; even Louis Napoleon had something of the 'Enlightened Despot' about him.

The revolutions occurred at a time of unprecedented change, economically, socially, intellectually, artistically and politically. The Europe of the late nineteenth century was clearly the outcome of this period of change, and on such a scale it was certain also to be a period of turmoil and muddle. Ideas had been seized upon without any recognition of their logical implications or often their mutual incompatibility; the scale was at best only dimly grasped and by many was resented. So long as all change was regarded with suspicion and fear by authority—as it was after 1815—and governments were successful in opposing it, the chances of the muddles and contradictions being recognized were slight. The collapse of government in Europe as typified by the fall of Metternich freed the process from the distortions which confinement had imposed. 1848-9 did not mean the resolution of the problems implicit in this process; it meant their recognition.

Youth believes itself capable of anything and everything; growing up may destroy the former belief, it is bound to destroy the latter. The revolutions of 1848-9 precluded everything for all and anything for some.

The Europe of the second half of the nineteenth century appears

came in such large numbers that there was no question of their being assimilated by urban culture. Henceforward, those German towns in Slavic lands became Slavic towns with German minorities.

to be the child of Europe of the second half of the eighteenth. Nevertheless, the eighteenth century could have been the parent of several different children. It was Louis Blanc who wrote: 'Conceivably, if there is to be progress, all evil possibilities must first be exhausted. . . . Every revolution then is useful in this sense at least, that it absorbs one disastrous policy.' The revolutions of 1848–9 absorbed not one, but several, disastrous policies. It is in this fashion that the Year of Revolution was a turning point in European history.

SELECT BIBLIOGRAPHY

(A) *General Secondary Works*

This is a list of works which are helpful to understanding the whole or a major part of the period. It is divided into three parts. First into general histories, secondly histories of individual countries and areas, and thirdly works dealing with particular topics running through the period, e.g. international relations.

I. *General Histories*

New Cambridge Modern History. Cambridge, 1959– :
    Vol. VIII: The American and French Revolutions, 1763–93.
    Vol. IX: War and Peace in an age of Upheaval, 1793–1830.
    Vol. X: The Zenith of European Power, 1830–70.
The Rise of Modern Europe. (LANGER, W. L., Ed.):
    BRINTON, C. *A Decade of Revolution, 1789–1799*.
    BRUUN, G. *Europe and the French Imperium, 1799–1814*.
    ARTZ, F. B. *Reaction and Revolution, 1814–32*.
DROZ, J. *L'époque contemporaine, I, Restaurations et révolutions, 1815–1871*. Paris, 1953.
—— *Europe Between Revolutions, 1815–48*. London, 1967.
HOBSBAWM, E. J. *The Age of Revolution: Europe 1789–1848*. London, 1963.
THOMAS, D. *Europe since Napoleon*. London, 1966.

II. *Histories of Individual Countries and Areas*

1. Austrian Empire

CRANKSHAW, E. *The Fall of the House of Habsburg*. London, 1963.
DENIS, E. *La Bohème depuis la Montagne Blanche*. 2 vols. Paris, 1930.
JÁSZI, O. *The Dissolution of the Habsburg Monarchy*. Chigago ed. 1961
KANN, A. *The Habsburg Empire*. London, 1957.

MACARTNEY, C. A. *The Habsburg Empire, 1790–1918*. London, 1969.
——*Hungary, A short History*. Edinburgh, 1966.
SETON-WATSON, R. W. *A History of the Czechs and Slovaks*. London, 1943.
SPRINGER, A. *Geschichte Oesterreichs seit dem Wiener Frieden 1809*. 2 vols. Leipzig, 1863.
TAYLOR, A. J. P. *The Habsburg Monarchy*. London, 1964.

2. Italy
ACTON, H. *The Bourbons of Naples*. London, 1956.
—— *The Last Bourbons of Naples*. London, 1961.
BERKELEY, G. F. H. and J. *Italy in the Making*. (3 vols. Cambridge, 1932–40.) Volume 1: 1815–1846.
BOLTON KING, H. *A History of Italian Unity, 1814–1871*. 2 vols. London, 1899.
WHYTE, A. J. *The Evolution of Modern Italy*. Oxford, 1959.

3. Germany
CARR, W. *A History of Germany, 1815–1945*. London, 1968.
DROZ, J. *Histoire d'Allemagne*. Paris, 1958.
HAMEROW, T. S. *Restoration, Revolution, Reaction. Economics and Politics in Germany, 1815–1871*. Princeton, 1958.
MANN, G. *The History of Germany since 1789*. London, 1968.
RAMM, A. *Germany 1789–1919*. London, 1967.
TREITSCHEKE, H. VON. *History of Germany in the Nineteenth Century*. 7 vols. London and New York, 1915–19 ed.

4. France
BASTID, P. *Les Institutions politiques de la monarchie parlementaire française, 1814–48*. Paris, 1954.
BROGAN, D. W. *The French Nation*. London, 1961.
BURY, J. P. T. *France 1814–1940*. London, 1961.

III. *Particular Topics*
1. International Relations
ALBRECHT-CARRIÉ, R. *A Diplomatic History of Europe since 1815*. New York, 1958.
ANDERSON, M. S. *The Eastern Question*. London, 1966.
SOREL, A. *L'Europe et la révolution française*. 9 vols. Paris, 1885–1911 (1 vol. trans. London, 1969).

2. Religion

VIDLER, A. R. *The Church in an Age of Revolution: 1789 to the present day.* Harmondsworth, 1961.

3. Economic History

These works are dealt with, along with more detailed works and sources, under the bibliography for Part I.

(B) *Works in Connection with Part I*

I. *The Economic Revolution*

1. Primary

POLLARD, S. and HOLMES, C. *Documents of European Economic History: Vol. I. The Process of Industrialization 1750–1870.* London, 1968.
A useful collection.

2. Secondary

ASHTON, T. S. *An Economic History of England: the Eighteenth Century.* London, 1955.

BERRILL, K. E. International Trade and the Rate of Economic Growth. *Economic History Review*, second series, number 12, 1960 (hereafter abbreviated as *Ec.H.R.* II, 12).

BLUM, J. Transportation and Industry in Austria 1815–48. *Journal of Modern History*, XV, 1943.
——*Noble Landowners and Agriculture in Austria, 1815–48: a study in the origins of the peasant emancipation of 1848.* Baltimore, 1948.

CAIRNCROSS, A. K. The Stages of Economic Growth. *Ec.H.R.* II, 13, 1961.

CAMERON, R. E. *France and the Economic Development of Europe, 1800–1914.* Princeton, 1961.

CLAPHAM, J. H. *An Economic History of Modern Britain.* 3 vols. London, 1926–38.
—— *The Economic Development of France and Germany, 1815–1914.* London, 1936 ed.

CROUZET, F., CHALONER, W. H. and STERN W. (Eds.). *Essays in European Economic History, 1789–1914.* London, 1969.

DUNHAM, L. *The Industrial Revolution in France.* New York, 1955.

GREENFIELD, K. R. *Economics and Liberalism in the Risorgimento: a study of Nationalism in Lombardy, 1814–48.* Baltimore, 1934.

HABAKKUK, H. J. English Population in the Eighteenth Century. *Ec.H.R.* II, 6, 1953.
—— and DEANE, P. The take-off in Britain. In ROSTOW, W. W., Ed., *The Economics of take-off into sustained growth.* London, 1963.
HENDERSON, W. O. *Britain and Industrial Europe 1750–1870.* Liverpool, 1954.
—— *The Industrial Revolution on the Continent: Germany, France, Russia, 1800–1914.* London, 1961.
—— *The Zollverein.* Manchester, 1939.
KRAUSE, J. T. Some neglected factors in the English Industrial Revolution. *Journal of Economic History,* 19, 1959.
MANTOUX, P. *The Industrial Revolution in the Eighteenth Century.* London, 1928.
MINGAY, G. E. *English Landed Society in the Eighteenth Century.* London, 1963.
MUSSON A. E. and ROBINSON, E. Science and Industry in the late Eighteenth Century. *Ec.H.R.* II, 13, 1960.
POLLARD, S. Investment, consumption and the Industrial Revolution. *Ec.H.R.* II, 11, 1958.
—— Fixed capital in the Industrial Revolution in Britain. *Journal of Economic History,* 24, 1964.
PURS, J. *The Industrial Revolution in the Czech lands.* Prague, 1960.
ROSTOW, W. W. *The Stages of Economic Growth.* London, 1960.
TUCKER, G. S. L. English pre-industrial population trends. *Ec.H.R.* 16, 1963.

II. *The Political Revolution*

1. Primary

MORSE STEPHENS, H. *The principal speeches of the statesmen and orators of the French Revolution.* 2 vols. London, 1892.
ROUSSEAU, J. J. *The Social Contract.* Everyman ed. London, 1932.
STEWART, J. H. *A Documentary Survey of the French Revolution.* New York, 1951.
THOMPSON, J. M. *English Witnesses of the French Revolution.* Oxford, 1938.
—— *French Revolution Documents, 1789–94.* Oxford, 1933.
YOUNG, A. *Travels in France during the Years 1787, 1788 and 1789.* Cambridge, 1929 ed.

2. Secondary

BRINTON, C. *The Jacobins*. New York, 1961.

COBB, R. *Les armées révolutionnaires, instrument de la Terreur dans les départements, Avril, 1793–Floréal An II*. 2 vols. The Hague, 1961–3.

COBBAN, A. *The Social Interpretation of the French Revolution*. London, 1964.

FORSTER, G. The Nobility during the French Revolution. *Past and Present*, no. 37, 1967.

GREER, D. M. *The Incidence of the Terror during the French Revolution*. New York, 1935.

HALES, E. E. Y. *The Revolution and the Papacy*. London, 1960.

HAMPSON, N. *A Social History of the French Revolution*. London, 1963.

LEFEBVRE, G. *La révolution française*. Paris ed., 1957. (Trans. London 1962 and 1964, 2 vols.).

—— *The Coming of the French Revolution*. Princeton ed., 1947.

PALMER, R. R. *Twelve who ruled*. Princeton, 1941.

—— *The Age of Democratic Revolution*. 2 vols. Oxford, 1959–64.

RUDÉ, G. *The Crowd in the French Revolution*. Oxford, 1959.

SOBOUL, A. *Les Sans-culottes parisiens en l'An II: mouvement populaire et gouvernement révolutionnaire 2 juin 1793–9 thermidor An. II*. Paris, 1958.

SYDENHAM, M. J. *The Girondins*. London, 1960.

—— *The French Revolution*. London, 1965.

TALMON, J. L. *The Origins of Totalitarian Democracy*. London, 1952.

THOMSON, D. *The Babeuf Plot*. London, 1947.

THOMPSON, J. M. *The French Revolution*. Oxford, 1959.

—— *Leaders of the French Revolution*. Oxford, 1929.

—— *Robespierre*. 2 vols. Oxford, 1935.

TOCQUEVILLE, A. DE. *L'Ancien Régime et la Révolution*. 2 vols. Paris, 1952–3.

III. *Revolutionary Heritage—Forces for Change*

1. Primary

BYRON, LORD. *Selected Poetry and Letters*. New York, 1961.

CHATEAUBRIAND, VICOMTE DE. *Mémoires d'outre-tombe*. Paris, 1849–50.

CONSTANT, B. *Œuvres politiques*. Paris, 1874.

FICHTE, J. G. *Addresses to the German Nation*. Chicago and London ed., 1921.

FOURIER, C. *Selections from the Works of Fourier*. London, 1901.

MARX, K. and ENGELS, F. *Selected Works*. 2 vols. London, 1950.

MAZZINI, G. *Life and Writings*. 6 vols. London, 1864–70.

MICHELET, J. *Le peuple*. Paris, 1846.

SPENCER, H. *Social Statics*. London, 1851.

2. Secondary

(*a*) Socialism

CAREW HUNT, R. N. *Theory and Practice of Communism*. London, 1950.

CARR, E. H. *Karl Marx: A Study in Fanaticism*. London, 1934.
—— *Michael Bakunin*. London, 1937.
Both these books and the second in particular are of real importance for the revolutions of 1848.

HOOK, S. *From Hegel to Marx*. London, 1936.

MANUEL, F. E. *The New World of Henri Saint-Simon*. Cambridge, Mass., 1956.

MARCUSE, H. *Reason and Revolution, Hegel and the rise of Social Theory*. London, 1941.

SPITZER, A. B. *The Revolutionary Theories of Louis Auguste Blanqui*. New York, 1957.

WILSON, E. *To the Finland Station*. New York, 1940.

(*b*) Liberalism

HOBHOUSE, L. T. *Liberalism*. London, 1911.

LASKI, H. J. *The Rise of European Liberalism*. London, 1936.

NICOLSON, H. *Benjamin Constant*. London, 1949.

RUGGIERO, G. DE. *History of European Liberalism*. Oxford ed., 1927.

SCHAPIRO, J. S. *Liberalism and the Challenge of Fascism*. New York, 1949.

THOMAS, R. H. *Liberalism, Nationalism and German Intellectuals, 1822–47*. New York, 1951.

(*c*) Romanticism

BRINTON, C. C. *The Political Ideas of the English Romanticists*. Oxford, 1926.

BRION, M. *Romantic Art*. London, 1960.

CARR, E. H. *The Romantic Exiles*. London ed., 1968.

DUFNER, M. and HUBBS, V. C. *Romanticism: Kleist, Novalis, Tieck, Schlegel.* New York, 1964.

NEWTON, E. *The Romantic Rebellion.* London, 1962.

PRAZ, M. *The Romantic Agony.* London, 1960. ed.

TALMON, J. L. *Political Messianism, the Romantic Phase.* London, 1960.

(*d*) Nationalism

BOLTON KING, H. *Mazzini.* London, 1899.

HALES, E. E. Y. *Mazzini and the Societies.* London, 1956.

HAYNES, C. J. *The Historical Evolution of Modern Nationalism.* New York, 1951.

KERDOURIE, E. *Nationalism.* London, 1961.

KOHN, H. *The Ideal of Nationalism, A Study in its Origins and Background.* New York, 1951.

MINOGUE, K. R. *Nationalism.* London, 1967.

SALVEMINI, G. *Mazzini.* Florence, 1925.

(C) *Works in Connection with Part II*

As well as material peculiar to this section, the bibliography for Metternich is listed here.

I. *Metternich*

1. Primary

Metternich, Memoires, documents et écrits. 8 vols. Paris, 1880–84.

Lettres du Prince du Metternich à la Comtesse de Lieven, 1818–19. ed. HANOTEAU, J., Paris, 1909.

GENTZ, F. *Tagebücher.* 4 vols. Leipzig, 1873.

KÜBECK, F. VON. *Tagebücher.* 5 vols. Vienna, 1909–10.

MACK WALKER, *Metternich's Europe, 1813–48.* London, 1969.

TICKNOR, G. *Life, Letters and Journals.* 2 vols. Boston, 1876.

2. Biography

Several of these contain sources very difficult to obtain elsewhere.

BIBL, V. *Metternich, der Dämon Oesterreichs.* Leipzig, 1937.

CECIL, A. *Metternich.* London, 1933.

COUDRAY, H. DU. *Metternich.* London, 1935.

GRUNWALD, C. DE. *Metternich.* London, 1953.

SRBIK, H. VON. *Metternich der Staatsmann und der Mensch.* 2 vols. Munich, 1925.

3. Studies of aspects of Metternich and his policies

HAAS, A. G. *Metternich, reorganization and nationality, 1813–18.* Wiesbaden, 1963.

KRAEHE, E. E. *Metternich's German policy.* Vol. I. Princeton, 1963.

SAUVIGNY, G. DE B. DE. *Metternich and his times.* London ed., 1962.

SCHROEDER, P. W. *Metternich's diplomacy at its zenith. 1820–23.* Austin, Texas, 1962.

II. *Conservatism and the Restoration*

1. Primary

BURKE, E. *The Works of Edmund Burke.* 9 vols. London, 1891–1911.

MAISTRE, J. DE. *Considérations sur la France.* ed. Paris, 1936.

2. Secondary

VIERECK, P. *Conservatism revisited.* New York, 1949.

III. *Metternich and Austria* (Chapter 5)

BIBL, V. *Kaiser Joseph II.* Vienna, 1944.

PADOVER, S. K. *The Revolutionary Emperor.* London, 1934.

WANGERMANN, E. *From Joseph II to the Jacobin Trials.* Oxford, 1959.

IV. *Metternich and Foreign Affairs*

COOPER, D. H. *Talleyrand.* London, 1932.

CRAWLEY, C. W. *The question of Greek independence.* Cambridge, 1930.

FERRERO, G. *The Reconstruction of Europe.* New York ed., 1941.

GULICK, E. V. *Europe's classical balance of power.* Ithaca, 1955.

KISSINGER, H. *A World restored.* London, 1947.

NICOLSON, H. G. *The Congress of Vienna.* London, 1919.

SCHENK, H. G. *The aftermath of the Napoleonic Wars: the Concert of Europe—an experiment.* London, 1947.

TEMPERLEY, H. M. V. *The foreign policy of Canning.* London, 1925.

WEBSTER, C. K. *The Congress of Vienna, 1814–15.* London, 1919.

—— *The foreign policy of Castlereagh.* 2 vols. London, 1925 and 1931.

—— *The foreign policy of Palmerston.* 2 vols. London, 1969.

Many of the works used in connection with Part III are also concerned with the revolution of 1848–9 as well and therefore really belong under Parts IV and V. Therefore the books included in this section are restricted to those principally or entirely concerned with the pre-1848 period. The bibliography then goes on to deal with the revolutions; arranged by geographical areas rather than by the order subjects are dealt with in the book. Finally, a few books found particularly helpful for Part VI are included.

(D) *Pre-1848*

1. Primary

BLANC, L. *Histoire de dix ans*. Philadelphia, 1848.
—— *Organisation du travail*. Oxford ed., 1913.
D'AZEGLIO, M. *Things I remember*. Oxford ed., 1966.
GUIZOT, F. P. G. *Mémoires pour servir à l'histoire de mon temps*. 8 vols. Paris, 1856–64.
MACK SMITH, D. *The Making of Italy, 1796–1866*. London, 1969.
PAGET, J. H. *Hungary and Transylvania*. London, 1837.
PELLICO, S. *My ten years imprisonment*. London ed., 1886.

2. Secondary

ARTZ, F. B. *France under the Bourbon Restoration*. Harvard, 1931.
BERKELEY, G. F. H. and J. *Italy in the Making. Vol. II: 1846–48*. Cambridge, 193.
HOWARTH, T. E. B. *Citizen King*. London, 1961.
JOHNSON, D. *Guizot*. London, 1963.
SAUVIGNY, B. DE. G. DE. *La Restauration*. Paris, 1956.
SIMPSON, F. A. *The rise of Louis Napoleon*. London, 1951.
WHYTE, A. J. *Early life and letters of Cavour*. Oxford, 1925.

(E) *The Revolutions*

I. *General*

FEJTÖ, F. *The Opening of an Era*. London, 1949.
NAMIER, L. B. *1848: the Revolution of the Intellectuals*. Oxford 1945.
—— *Vanished Supremacies*. London ed., 1962.
Two useful essays.
PONTEIL, F. *1848*. Paris, 1947.
POSTGATE, R. W. *Story of a Year: 1848*. London, 1948.
ROBERTSON, P. *Revolutions of 1848*. Princeton, 1952.
WHITRIDGE, A. *Men in Crisis: The Revolution of 1848*. New York, 1949.
There are some useful documents in:
POSTGATE, R. W. *Revolution from 1789–1906*. London, 1920.

II. *The Habsburg Empire* (excluding Italy)

1. Primary

AUERBACH, B. *A narrative of events in Vienna from Latour to Windischgrätz.* London ed., 1848.

FÜSTER, A. *Memorien vom März 1848 bis Juli 1849.* 2 vols. Frankfurt, 1850.

GÖRGEI, A. *My life and acts in Hungary in the Years 1848–1849.* 2 vols. London, 1852.

HARTIG, COUNT F. DE P. VON. *Genesis.* Trans. and bound with: COXE, A. *History of the House of Austria.* London, 1872.

HÜBNER, COUNT J. A. VON. *Une année de ma vie.* Paris, 1891.

HÜGEL, BARON C. VON. The Story of the escape of Prince Metternich. *National Review*, Vol. I. London, 1883.

PALACKY, F. Letter sent by Frantisek Palacky to Frankfurt, 1848. See *Slavonic and East European Review*, vol. 26, 1948.

PILLERSDORF, BARON FRANZ VON. *Austria in 1848 and 1849.* London, 1850.

SONIS, COMTE F. DE. *Lettres du Comte et de la Comtesse de Ficquelmont à la Comtesse Tiesenhausen.* Paris, 1911.

STILES, W. H. *Austria in 1848–49.* 2 vols. New York, 1852.

2. Secondary

GOLDMARK, J. *Pilgrims of 1848: One man's part in the Austrian Revolution of 1848.* New Haven, 1930.

KISZLING, R. *Die Revolution in Kaisertum Oesterreich 1848–9.* 2 vols. Vienna, 1949.

MÜLLER, P. *Furst Windischgrätz.* Vienna, 1934.

PRESLAND, J. *Vae Victis. The Life of Ludwig von Benedek.* London, 1934.

REDLICH, J. *Emperor Francis Joseph of Austria.* London, 1930.

SCHWARZENBERG, A. *Prince Felix zu Schwarzenberg.* New York, 1948.

II. *Italy*

1. Primary

CATTANEO, C. *L'Insurrection de Milan en 1848.* Paris, 1848.

CLOUGH, A. *Prose Remains.* London, 1888.

Correspondence respecting the Affairs of Italy, 1848–49. British Parliamentary papers.

DANDALO, E. *The Italian Volunteers and the Lombard Rifle Brigade.* London, 1851.

DELLA ROCCA, M. *The Autobiography of a Veteran 1807–93.* London ed., 1893.

FARINI, L. C. *The Roman State from 1815–1850.* London, 1851–4.

FLAGG, E. *Venice, the City of the Sea from the Invasion of Napoleon in 1797 to the Capitulation of Radetzky in 1849.* 2 vols. New York, 1853.

GARIBALDI, G. *Memoirs.* Ed. DUMAS, A. London, 1860.

LESSEPS, F. DE. *Ma Mission à Rome.* Paris, 1849.

MARTINENGO-CESARESCO, E. *Italian characters in the Age of Unification.* London, 1901.

ORSINI, F. *Memoirs.* Edinburgh ed., 1857.

OSSOLI, M. F. *Memoirs.* Boston, 1852.

OTT, W. MEYER. *Military Events in Italy 1848–9.* Ed. EGERTON, LORD F. ELLESMERE. London, 1851.

PASOLINI, COUNT G. *Memoirs.* London ed., 1885.

RADETZKY, J. W. *Briefe an seine Tochter Friederike, 1847–57.* Vienna, 1892.

2. Secondary

BERKELEY, G. F. H. and J. *Italy in the Making.* Vol. III. Cambridge, 1940.

HALES, E. E. Y. *Pio Nono.* London, 1956.

HANCOCK, W. K. *Ricasoli and the Risorgimento in Tuscany.* London, 1926.

JOHNSTON, R. M. *The Roman Theocracy and the Republic, 1846–1849.* London, 1901.

MACK SMITH, D. *Garibaldi.* London, 1957.

MARSHALL, R. *Massimo D'Azeglio: an artist in politics.* Oxford, 1965.

TREVELYAN, G. M. *Garibaldi's Defence of the Roman Republic.* London, 1907.

—— *Manin and the Venetian Revolution of 1848.* London, 1923.

WHYTE, A. J. *Political life and letters of Cavour.* Oxford, 1930.

III. *Germany*

1. Primary

BUNSEN, F. *A memoir of Baron Bunsen.* 2 vols. London, 1886.

CIRCOURT, A. DE. *Souvenirs d'une mission à Berlin en 1848.* Paris, 1908.

CORVIN, O. VON. *A life of adventure.* 3 vols. London, 1871.

KLEIN, T. *1848, der Vorkampf deutscher Einheit*. Leipzig, 1914.

LEGGE, J. G. *Rhyme and Revolution in Germany*. London, 1918.

SCHURZ, C. *Reminiscences*. New York, 1907.

SCHUSTER, G. and BAILLEU, P. *Correspondence of Empress Augusta*. Berlin, 1912.

WAGNER, R. *My life*. 2 vols. New York, 1911.

2. Secondary

BLACK, C. E. Poznan and Europe in 1848. *Journal of Central European Affairs*, vol. VIII, no. 2, 1948.

DROZ, J. *Les Révolutions allemandes de 1848*. Paris, 1957.

ENGELS, F. *Germany: Revolution and Counter-revolution*. Chicago ed., 1967. Originally written as newspaper articles under Marx's name, some of this ranks as a primary source.

EYCK, F. *The Frankfurt Parliament*. London, 1968.

NOYES, P. H. *Organization and Revolution: Working-class Associations in the German Revolutions of 1848–9*. Princeton, 1966.

O'BOYLE, L. The Democratic Left in Germany, 1848. *Journal of Modern History*, 1961.

VALENTIN, V. *Geschicthe der deutschen Revolution von 1848–49*. Berlin, 1930–1.

—— *1848. Chapters of German History*. London, 1940 (is a shorter edition of the above).

IV. *France*

1. Primary

CREMIEUX, A. *La Révolution de février*. Paris, 1912.

HEINE, H. *French affairs. Letters from Paris*. 2 vols. London ed., 1893.

HERZEN, A. *My past and thoughts*. London ed.

—— *Letters de France et d'Italie, 1847–52*. Geneva ed., 1871.

HUGO, V. *Choses Vues*. Paris, 1913.

LAMARTINE, A. DE. *Histoire de la revolution de 1848*. 2 vols. Paris, 1849.

NORMANBY, C. H. P. Marquis of. *A Year of Revolution*. London, 1857.

SENIOR, N. W. *Journals kept in France and Italy from 1848 to 1852*. London, 1871.

TOCQUEVILLE, A. DE. *The Recollections of*. London ed., 1948.

2. Secondary

DAUTRY, J. *1848 et la seconde république*. Paris, 1957.

DICKINSON, G. L. *Revolution and reaction in modern France*. London, 1952.

DUVEAU, G. *1848: The making of a revolution*. London ed., 1967.

ELTON, G. *The revolutionary idea in France, 1789–1871*. London, 1931.

MCKAY, D. C. *The National Workshops*. Cambridge, Mass., 1933.

MARX, K. *The Class Struggles in France, 1848–1850* (again really a primary source). New York ed., 1924.

—— *The 18th Brumaire of Louis Bonaparte*. Chicago ed., 1914.

STEWART, N. *Blanqui*. London, 1939.

(F) *Part VI. Aftermath*

Bismarck, the Man and the Statesman: Being the reflections and the reminiscences of Otto Prince von Bismarck. 2 vols. London ed., 1896.

HOWARD, M. *The Franco-Prussian War*. London, 1961.

MACK SMITH, D. *Cavour and Garibaldi in 1860*. Cambridge, 1954.

MOSSE, W. E. *The European Powers and the German Question, 1848–71*. Cambridge, 1958.

SIMON, W. M. *Germany in the age of Bismarck*. London, 1968.

SIMPSON, F. A. *Louis Napolean and the Recovery of France*. London, 1951.

TAYLOR, A. J. P. *Bismarck*. London, 1961.

—— *The Struggle for Mastery in Europe*. Oxford, 1954.

—— *The Italian Problem in European Diplomacy, 1847–9*. Manchester, 1934.

THOMPSON, J. M. *Louis Napoleon and the Second Empire*. Oxford, 1965.

WOODCOCK, G. *A hundred years of revolution: 1848 and after*. London, 1948.

ZELDIN, T. *The political system of Napoleon III*. London, 1958.

Dates of editions given refer to the ones actually used, likewise whether a translated edition is mentioned or not depends upon the one used; the bibliography does not set out to give the first or even (e.g. Garibaldi's Memoirs) the most faithful edition.

INDEX